VOLUME 465 JANUARY 1983

THE ANNALS

of The American Academy *of* Political *and* Social Science

ISSN 0002-7162

RICHARD D. LAMBERT, *Editor*
ALAN W. HESTON, *Associate Editor*
THOMAS FOGARTY *and* DAVID LUDDEN,
Acting Associate Editors

HOUSING AMERICA

Special Editor of this Volume
WALLACE F. SMITH
Professor
Department of Business Administration
University of California
Berkeley

SAGE PUBLICATIONS *BEVERLY HILLS LONDON NEW DELHI*

THE ANNALS

© 1983 *by* The American Academy *of* Political *and* Social Science

MARY V. YATES, *Assistant Editor*

Editorial Office: 3937 Chestnut Street, Philadelphia, Pennsylvania 19104.

For information about membership (individuals only) and subscriptions (institutions), address:*

SAGE PUBLICATIONS, INC.
275 South Beverly Drive
Beverly Hills, Calif. 90212 USA

From India and South Asia, write to:
SAGE PUBLICATIONS INDIA Pvt. Ltd.
P.O. Box 3605
New Delhi 110 024
INDIA

From the UK, Europe, the Middle East and Africa, write to:
SAGE PUBLICATIONS LTD
28 Banner Street
London EC1Y 8QE
ENGLAND

**Please note that members of The Academy receive THE ANNALS with their membership.*

Library of Congress Catalog Card Number 82-042843
International Standard Serial Number ISSN 0002-7162
International Standard Book Number ISBN 0-8039-1947-6 (Vol. 465, 1983, paper)
International Standard Book Number ISBN 0-8039-1948-4 (Vol. 465, 1983, cloth)

Manufactured in the United States of America. First printing, January 1983.

The articles appearing in THE ANNALS are indexed in *Book Review Index; Public Affairs Information Service Bulletin; Social Sciences Index; Monthly Periodical Index; Current Contents: Behavioral, Social, Management Sciences;* and *Combined Retrospective Index Sets.* They are also abstracted and indexed in *ABC Pol Sci, Historical Abstracts, Human Resources Abstracts, Social Sciences Citation Index, United States Political Science Documents, Social Work Research & Abstracts, Peace Research Reviews, Sage Urban Studies Abstracts, International Political Science Abstracts,* and/or *America: History and Life.*

Information about membership rates, institutional subscriptions, and back issue prices may be found on the facing page.

Advertising. Current rates and specifications may be obtained by writing to THE ANNALS Advertising and Promotion Manager at the Beverly Hills office (address above).

Claims. Claims for undelivered copies must be made no later than three months following month of publication. The publisher will supply missing copies when losses have been sustained in transit and when the reserve stock will permit.

Change of Address. Six weeks' advance notice must be given when notifying of change of address. Please send old address label along with the new address to insure proper identification. Please specify name of journal. Send change of address to: THE ANNALS, c/o Sage Publications, Inc., 275 South Beverly Drive, Beverly Hills, CA 90212.

Origin and Purpose. The Academy was organized December 14, 1889, to promote the progress of political and social science, especially through publications and meetings. The Academy does not take sides in controverted questions, but seeks to gather and present reliable information to assist the public in forming an intelligent and accurate judgment.

Meetings. The Academy holds an annual meeting in the spring extending over two days.

Publications. THE ANNALS is the bimonthly publication of The Academy. Each issue contains articles on some prominent social or political problem, written at the invitation of the editors. Also, monographs are published from time to time, numbers of which are distributed to pertinent professional organizations. These volumes constitute important reference works on the topics with which they deal, and they are extensively cited by authorities throughout the United States and abroad. The papers presented at the meetings of The Academy are included in THE ANNALS.

Membership. Each member of The Academy receives THE ANNALS and may attend the meetings of The Academy. Membership is open only to individuals. Annual dues: $26.00 for the regular paperbound edition (clothbound, $39.00). Add $6.00 per year for membership outside the U.S.A. Members may also purchase single issues of THE ANNALS for $6.95 each (clothbound, $10.00).

Subscriptions. THE ANNALS is published six times annually—in January, March, May, July, September, and November. Institutions may subscribe to THE ANNALS at the annual rate: $45.00 (clothbound, $60.00). Add $6.00 per year for subscriptions outside the U.S.A. Institutional rates for single issues: $10.00 each (clothbound, $15.00).

Second class postage paid at Beverly Hills, California.

Single issues of THE ANNALS may be obtained by individuals who are not members of The Academy for $7.95 each (clothbound, $15.00). Single issues of THE ANNALS have proven to be excellent supplementary texts for classroom use. Direct inquiries regarding adoptions to THE ANNALS c/o Sage Publications (address below).

All correspondence concerning membership in The Academy, dues renewals, inquiries about membership status, and/or purchase of single issues of THE ANNALS should be sent to THE ANNALS c/o Sage Publications, Inc., 275 South Beverly Drive, Beverly Hills, CA 90212. *Please note that orders under $20 must be prepaid.* Sage affiliates in London and India will assist institutional subscribers abroad with regard to orders, claims, and inquiries for both subscriptions and single issues.

THE EIGHTY-SIXTH ANNUAL MEETING OF THE AMERICAN ACADEMY OF POLITICAL AND SOCIAL SCIENCE

APRIL 22 AND 23, 1983
THE BELLEVUE STRATFORD HOTEL
PHILADELPHIA, PENNSYLVANIA

The annual meeting of The Academy is attended by hundreds of distinguished scholars, statesmen, authors, and professionals in diverse fields, including representatives of many embassies, academic institutions, and cultural, civic, and scientific organizations.

This 86th Annual Meeting will be addressed at each session by prominent scholars and officials and will be devoted to the topic of

NUCLEAR ARMAMENT AND DISARMAMENT

Members of the Academy are cordially invited to attend and will receive full information. Information on Academy membership can be found in each volume of THE ANNALS.

- Proceedings of the 86th Annual Meeting will be published in the September 1983 volume of THE ANNALS.

• FOR DETAILS WRITE TO: THE AMERICAN ACADEMY OF POLITICAL AND SOCIAL SCIENCE • BUSINESS OFFICE • 3937 CHESTNUT STREET PHILADELPHIA, PENNSYLVANIA 19104

CONTENTS

BOOK DEPARTMENT CONTENTS

INTERNATIONAL RELATIONS AND POLITICS

AFRICA, ASIA, AND LATIN AMERICA

EUROPE

SOCIOLOGY

ECONOMICS

PREFACE

Housing is an artifact. Some families in Calhoun County, West Virginia, inhabit very rough homes with dirt floors and tar paper where window panes ought to be, according to a mid-1982 *Wall Street Journal* report. Most of the residential inventory in the United States is much better than that, but it is physically diverse.

Housing is also a matter of location. Industrial and office employment in San Francisco is moving perceptibly to the suburbs, away from city residents who can afford neither suburban homes nor the cost of the longer commute.

And housing is a capital good. For the past 30 years, most American households were able to attain the security and opportunity of homeownership by virtue of tax subsidies and artificially improved access to credit markets. The capital market begrudges housing's large share of savings because housebuilding is so-called nonproductive investment. It does not increase the nation's productive capacity.

These three basic characteristics of housing evoke different types of public response, and the pattern of response varies considerably among nations. The United States does little with housing as an artifact except to condemn seriously deficient dwellings—that is, to prevent buildings from being used. We have compounded the problems of location, perhaps inadvertently, and only recently have put some modest programs in motion to address this issue.

As to the third attribute, the terms on which housing may be acquired, this nation assembled an extraordinary mesh of infrastructure and effectively manipulated the marketplace for over 30 years. Indirectly, the physical inventory was dramatically improved, but problems of location were exacerbated. This financial infrastructure began to crumble at the beginning of the current decade. The housing sector of the economy, in the role of a nearly innocent bystander to the nation's inflation-interest debacle, saw its horizons shrink as economists and policymakers argued that it should be cut adrift in the marketplace.

Why have any form of public intervention? Some hard-nosed economists regard this as an almost rhetorical question, but there are many answers in the long literature of housing. Seriously deficient housing—in the physical or dirt floor sense—has been held responsible for disease, crime, and social-political malaise; it is hazardous to the rest of the community, the logic runs. Another argument likens a physically unsuitable dwelling to a bad apple: if left alone, it will infect others. Then there is simple egalitarianism, or revulsion at squalor.

Low-density, owner-occupied houses discourage crime, the local police will tell you. Homeowners are more conscientious than are renters about civic responsibilities. Housebuilding creates jobs, and communities must have housing inventories in order to attract and keep other kinds of employment. From the macroeconomist comes the view that housing construction provides a nearly spontaneous balance wheel for an inherently cyclical pattern of business. A nice list of pluses. It adds up to a political constituency, and even in a staunchly market-oriented national economy, a political constituency has its say.

The location issue—who inhabits which part of the housing inventory—while it attracts little explicit attention from policymakers, may be interpreted as the central element in the way our housing economy is constructed. A perceptive visiting scholar has given us just that view in clear and challenging terms.

Several years ago, in the capacity of director of a university research center, I was requested by our State Department to host a visiting scholar from the Soviet Union whose field of expertise is the American city. Professor Evgeny Mikhailov made diligent use of the center's library, conferred with American scholars, and traveled within the United States. Some time after returning to the Soviet Union, he contributed to an English-language publication of the USSR Academy of Sciences an article summarizing his perceptions of housing and related urban issues in the United States.[1] The publication is not readily available in the United States; it seems safe to assume that not many social scientists in this country have seen what Professor Mikhailov wrote about us. In the interest of perspective, then, the following is a review of the article's main points as I understood them.

In truth, virtually all of the points have been made by urbanists in the United States, and acknowledgment is given. The article organizes these points to support a thesis. The reader may smile or sigh at learning that the thesis attributes the whole panoply of American urban ills to self-destructive capitalism, but let us hear Professor Mikhailov out. His story is at least challenging, and it may be useful.

At an earlier stage the American city, like the European city, was industrial, making its living primarily by manufacture. It was also self-contained, an integral political unit. While there were rich and poor, workers and employers, and identifiable neighborhoods of different classes, they all lived and worked within a small space and under the same civic administration. They shared the infrastructure.

The very density of a successful industrial city, and resulting high prices for land, made it difficult for manufacturing firms to expand. Employers began to consider moving to outlying sites. The wealthier population became conscious of the deterioration of the industrial city as a place to live—deteriorating environment, obsolete infrastructure, and social unrest or the likelihood of unrest.

The automobile opened up suburban areas for both industry and middle and upper classes of residents. Its proliferation, Mikhailov asserts, was encouraged by the political power of the automobile, oil, and road-building industries. As private entities, these industries were free to ignore the environmental damage and the harm to the social and fiscal integrity of the central city suburbanization would bring in its wake. Indeed, when the automobile and outward expansion of the community made privately owned mass transit operations unprofitable, these private firms used political influence to sell their assets to subservient government agencies, the

1. Evgeny Mikhailov, "Urbanisation in the U.S.A.," *Soviet Geographical Studies*, 39:247-68 (1976).

deficits thus becoming a charge to taxpayers rather than to stockholders.

Movement of both industrial employment and upper-income residence to the suburbs was far more than just deconcentration. Lowering of densities, desirable as that might be per se, produced "socioterritorial polarization," since suburban communities enjoy political autonomy, and the "law of the market"—the housing market in particular—determines that the lower-income population will live in the older, deteriorated housing inventory in the central city. The poor are also left with obsolete infrastructure, now deficit-ridden and tax-supported. The central city, where the poor now predominate, cannot level taxes on suburban real estate. Outlying communities, however, with tax bases enriched by new industrial properties and expensive dwellings of the affluent, can afford first-rate public schools, fine roads, parks, and other services which, though nominally public, are available only to the well-to-do.

Suburbanization, then, Mikhailov says, is a "class process," making a geographic, political fact out of the economic hierarchy that inheres in capitalist production. We do not just have a high-income class, we have high-income cities, separate and privileged, which are de facto inaccessible to lower-income households for either residence or employment.

Suburban residents, however, are free to make use of whatever attractions the central city possesses. And though significant forms of employment have left the old city, the metropolitan center retains its retail and service sector primacy, by virtue of location at the transportation hub and because of agglomeration. The old city still has facilities that cannot be replicated in the suburbs—museums, opera houses, specialized medical facilities, and so on—that appeal mainly to suburbanites but are now supported by low-income central-city residents.

The greatest attraction to suburban dwellers is the intensifying concentration of office-type employment in the central city, well-paid, clean work involving communication rather than manual skills. It is pulled to the center mainly because the agglomeration economies in communication are great. It thrives there despite the impoverished infrastructure and the distance its workers must travel. Because of inequality in education and class or racial prejudice, the population living closest to this desirable new employment is excluded from it.

So the poor and their needs are confined within the old city, which has diminishing power to help the poor or to find them work. Suburbia benefits from what the central city provides but avoids the costs the city bears. A process whose roots are in market determination of housing supply, industrial location, and intraurban transportation modes is reinforced by a class-specific system of government. There are pretty new houses in the suburbs precisely because there is decay and poverty in the central city, and vice versa.

This litany of troubles and unhappy logic about which Professor Mikhailov has written can be found in the oratory of any U.S. conference of mayors. It is not the invention of a remote ideologue. Indeed, it is probable that to this point the whole sequence of observations and ideas was discovered in our own urban literature by Mikhailov. Nor should we be anxious to disown it; candor in public affairs is the rarest of treasures.

Mikhailov's startling theorem claims that this process—unfettered market-determination of land uses and urban interaction—is "non-optimal" in the highly specific sense Western welfare economists assign to that word. These are the points he offers in support:

1. Infrastructure which becomes redundant in the central city must be duplicated elsewhere. He cites housing abandonment, for example.
2. Labor is wasted when central-city residents cannot find or obtain industrial employment in factories that have moved to the suburbs, work for which they are otherwise qualified.
3. Abandoned housing serves as a breeding ground for crime.
4. The fiscal bind of central cities results in curtailing police, fire, educational, and other services, thus making problems of antisocial behavior—robbery, arson, and so on—and unemployability even worse.
5. Decay and social disorder in the central city lower the value of mortgage holdings there by financial institutions.
6. Crimes against property, which helped cause businesses and the well-to-do to flee to the suburbs, spread to those same suburbs, since attractive property is now concentrated there.
7. Reliance on private transportation and increasing separation of places of work and residence are wasteful of resources and cause air pollution.

These are items for a benefit-cost analysis of the system we have for deciding what goes where in urban communities. That system, to reprise Mikhailov, is private ownership of land and business, market-determined transportation modes, and substantial control of public decision making by the upper classes. His bottom line is that "The capitalist system is becoming . . . an obstacle to solving the problems that arise in the city."

Is that hyperbole—political rhetoric? Is the idea behind it usefully provocative? Most urbanists in the United States would probably be inclined to respond as follows:

1. The costs of suburbanization previously enumerated are real and significant.
2. Though Mikhailov does not discuss the benefits that might tend to offset these costs—such as upgrading the housing inventory and infrastructure—the balance is indeed likely to be negative. The evidence is that we have rather recently undertaken public programs or announced strategies, such as urban infill, intended to check suburbanization.
3. Metropolitan government could internalize many of the costs. Mikhailov decided that given our sociopolitical character, the perennial proposals for regional government are "not realistic."
4. The assessment that the system—in particular the land market—is responsible for socioterritorial polarization is essentially correct.
5. It does not follow, however, that ending market control over land use and transport modes and reconcentrating local government's authority would in themselves ensure better allocation of resources. While we have a fairly explicit conception of how the decision-making process functions in a market economy, we have no such model of nonmarket decision making. Starving oneself is not a reasonable remedy for indigestion. We admit we have indigestion but we believe—perhaps foolishly—that it is not going to kill us.

6. Still, we would like to mitigate the kinds of social costs Professor Mikhailov saw and read about and about which he heard us talking among ourselves.

7. What we want is a way to internalize external costs without going all the way. This is almost an endorsement of ad hoc and experimental responses to situations giving rise to social costs.

8. What we do not want is a head-in-the-sand approach that claims that an unfettered, private decision-making, market approach to land use allocation and related phenomena can do no wrong.

Most of the contributions to this volume raise the subject of government's role, explicitly or implicitly. Housing is a matter of social concern precisely because, in the minds of people and their governments just about everywhere, it entails externalities—costs and benefits affecting many members of the community who are not directly involved in a particular transaction or decision.

In any case, we have had several decades of governmental intervention to make homeownership generally possible and to encourage upgrading of the inventory. It was not all push; neither consumers nor the business sector held back from the lures that were provided. In response to the constituency or to the arguments for government intervention, we erected a system of housing taxation and finance that flourished but then broke down. Economists—some of them, anyway—are telling us that we erred not in the design of the system so much as in the intention, and that we should now disengage government from housing. Let consumers pay the full price of what they buy, whether houses or crates of melons, and if the quality of our housing inventory shrinks as a result, so be it.

Before accepting that advice, we should reflect carefully on the complex nature of housing and on the external costs which uninhibited private market decision making may produce.

That the general standard of housing is good in this country is not in serious dispute. Is our fortunate situation due to reliance on market decision making, or does it exist because we have—until recently at any rate—employed public policy to good effect in harnessing market forces? Are we—mostly—well housed because of the marketplace or in spite of it? Like it or not, we are engaged in a nationwide experiment to shed light on that question by terminating major elements of public involvement; by the end of the decade we will probably have a better understanding of whether past governmental involvement has been beneficial or harmful.

WALLACE F. SMITH

ANNALS, *AAPSS*, **465**, January 1983

Where Will the Money Come From?

By MARK J. RIEDY

ABSTRACT: A host of extremely critical challenges is facing the housing industry. Inflation and volatile interest rates have seriously disrupted the nation's mortgage finance and delivery system. Sources of funds to the traditional suppliers of mortgage credit have become scarce. The ability of consumers to afford housing has been reduced by escalating prices and declining real incomes. As a result, the mortgage finance industry is in a period of transition to new types of mortgage instruments and new sources of money for mortgages. Among these new sources are the nation's pension funds. Pension funds had been effectively excluded from extensive residential mortgage investments, but new changes in Labor Department Employee Retirement and Income Security Act (ERISA) regulations could open the way for billions of dollars in private pension fund investment in mortgages. Much of this investment will come through an expanded national secondary market with a conventional mortgage-backed security. Mortgage bankers will be in the forefront of these developments.

Mark J. Riedy is executive vice president of the Mortgage Bankers Association of America (MBA) and is responsible for the overall management of the association, including research, education, and extensive government liaison activities. Headquartered in Washington, D.C., the MBA represents nearly 2000 member firms involved in the mortgage banking business. Dr. Riedy has a wide background in the fields of housing and mortgage finance. He obtained his B.A. in economics in 1964 from Loras College in Dubuque, Iowa; his M.B.A. from Washington University, St. Louis; and his Ph.D. in business economics from the University of Michigan in 1971.

IN discussing some of the more critical short- and long-term challenges facing the housing finance industry today, I plan to sort out the major crosscurrents now buffeting residential mortgage markets, and to share my personal views on prospects for the sources of housing credit in the long-term context. My intention is not to debate whether housing has enjoyed too great or too small a share of this nation's real and financial resources over time. You are free to reach your own conclusions on that matter. For the sake of discussion, however, I assume that the federal government is more likely to decrease than to increase its direct and indirect support for housing finance in the future.

THE CURRENT CRISIS

The American economy is currently undergoing a policy-induced recession that has brought the nation's housing, automobile, and related industries to their knees. In effect, these major industries are on the verge of execution, living sacrifices on the altar of supply-side economics, restrictive monetary policy, and rapid inflation.

The excessive and unprecedented inflation rate and volatility of interest rates in recent years severely disrupted this nation's mortgage finance delivery system and created serious housing affordability problems. Sources of funds to thrift institutions—savings and loan associations and mutual savings banks—the traditional suppliers of the bulk of residential mortgage credit, simultaneously became prohibitively expensive and scarce. The historically popular long-term, fixed-rate mortgage instrument became an albatross around the necks of investors in home mortgages, from thrifts to the government-sponsored credit agencies, the Federal National Mortgage Association (FNMA) and the Federal Home Loan Mortgage Corporation (FHLMC), as well as to commercial banks, life insurance companies, and other institutions holding mortgages as investments.

Intense competition from money market funds and the rapid deregulation of depository institution liability structures exacerbated these problems to be sure, but it was nonetheless a response to the inflation and interest rate volatility plaguing the economy. Similarly, the inflationary climate fostered and accommodated a rapid increase in housing demand and prices that now has come crashing down on housing consumers, especially first-time homebuyers. Mortgage rates peaking above 18 percent for long-term, fixed-rate debt were not a surprising result of these phenomena and probably mark the end of an era of housing as a prime investment vehicle for future purchasers of new and existing homes.

Supply-side economic policy and restrictive monetary policy are now in place in an attempt to dampen inflation permanently and to restore greater incentives to productive capital investments that bring stable economic growth in their wake. We are in only the first quarter of this game, but head coaches Reagan and Volcker are already under a great deal of pressure to discard their game plans in order to react to the mounting deficits on the scoreboard.

The massive $750 billion, three-year tax cut legislated in 1981 and the 1981-82 recession now have combined to produce the large and growing federal government deficits forecast for the next few years. The administration has revised its deficit estimate for fiscal year 1983 to $160 billion, a long way from the balanced budget promised earlier for 1984. Congress and the administration now are working toward a budget compromise to shave the deficits for fiscal year 1983 and beyond without reversing the fundamental program. Only a favorable outcome of the current negotiations can calm the financial markets and lead to reduced interest rates and a sustained economic recovery.

As a representative of a broad range of mortgage lenders and investors feeling some of the worst effects of the onslaught, I am tempted to encourage these coaches to abandon the original game plan because conditions have deteriorated so badly. But that would be bad advice, in my judgment. The nation's mortgage delivery system is in the midst of a fundamental adjustment process that would have been difficult in any event, although its problems are being compounded by current events. We should stick to the basic economic game plan, therefore, while we do a better job of managing the transition in mortgage finance.

THE TRANSITION PROCESS

Let me attempt to describe this transition process and offer some ideas on its direction in the years ahead. The residential mortgage market grew rapidly during the postwar years in an environment characterized by an upward-sloping yield curve and relatively plentiful sources of mortgage credit. Inflation was not particularly a problem for housing, and government policies clearly favored housing as a social objective of high national priority. Tax policies encouraged homeownership, as did the availability of Federal Housing Administration (FHA) and Veterans' Administration (VA) financing and the growing support over time of the federal home loan bank system, the FNMA, the FHLMC, and the mortgage-backed security program of the Government National Mortgage Association (GNMA). In addition, tax policies encouraged thrift institutions to be primary investors in home mortgage debt.

The cornerstone of this support system without doubt was the long-term, fixed-rate mortgage instrument that made everyone a winner—homebuyers and sellers, builders and developers, mortgage originators and mortgage investors. The unprecedented inflation and interest rate volatility that has worsened in each cycle for the past decade or more unfortunately has caused this system to come unglued.

There have been many attempts to replace the long-term, fixed-rate mortgage with newer, more flexible loan types that would provide the investor with protection from the forces of inflation and interest-rate escalation. This has resulted in the creation of mortgage instruments such as the adjustable-rate mortgage (ARM), the shared-appreciation mortgage (SAM), the renegotiable-rate mortgage (RRM), and the price-level adjustable mortgage (PLAM), to name a few. This alphabet soup of mortgage types, along with their relatively more complicated loan terms, has created confusion and resistance among prospective mortgagors. To a lesser degree, this is also true of mortgage lenders and investors. These entities were successful in originating, selling, and investing in traditional fixed-rate mortgage loans, a success that has not yet been translated into the alternative market.

Until these newer instruments are sorted out by standardization and subsequent securitization, both sides of the mortgage market will continue to struggle. This friction is the major reason that the fixed-rate mortgage, along with variations such as the wraparound mortgage, the graduated-payment mortgage, and the buydown mortgage continue to enjoy such widespread acceptance.

TRADITIONAL MORTGAGE CREDIT

It is not necessary for the purposes of this discussion to determine the macroeconomic causes of that inflation and interest rate volatility. Let us take them as given. Their effects, however, are another matter.

As a result of many changes that have occurred in the last decade, the supply of consumer savings has diminished as a share of disposable income. Moreover, because of increased financial sophistication on the part of consumers and the growing inability of thrifts, in particular, to compete effectively for those savings, mortgage credit has become less readily available and increasingly expensive over time.

To the extent that there exists today a sizable pool of consumer savings potentially available for residential mortgage finance, I believe it resides in this nation's vast public and private pension funds—a topic to which I will return shortly. But the point is that the old traditional sources of mortgage credit may not be available in the 1980s. One hopes that the old faithful lenders will reemerge as mortgage investors in the future, but they will look and behave much differently. And rather than being captives of the mortgage credit markets with nowhere else to invest their funds, these department-store-like financial institutions will rent their money to the highest mortgage or nonmortgage bidders on the most suitable terms consistent with future inflation and financial prospects.

The old faithful lenders, especially thrift institutions, historically operated primarily in local markets with their costs of funds artificially constrained by deposit rate regulation. The born-again thrift, whatever its generic name, will operate nationwide, both seeking and investing its funds at highly competitive capital market rates. Indeed, it is this transition from localized, protected savings and mortgage markets to nationwide, fully competitive markets that lies at the heart of the transition problems in the real estate finance industry.

And, while the traditional mortgage finance institutions are still in the throes of this difficult transition, I submit that the mortgage marketplace has run ahead and virtually completed the transition. It is a nationwide, highly competitive marketplace. It sorely lacks money to meet potential demand, however, for several reasons. The mentality and management philosophy of mortgage originators, as well as investors, have not yet adjusted to the capital market realities of the 1980s. And the regulatory and legislative structure, at both the state and federal level, is only slowly and reluctantly being brought up to date to accommodate the new nationwide, impersonal, highly competitive character of the residential mortgage market.

FILLING THE GAP

It is interesting to think about the lenders who have moved into this temporary vacuum and filled the real estate financing gap. Consumers have already made this move. Sellers of homes have become direct mortgage lenders. The euphemism for this cottage industry is "creative financing," and the realtors tell us that the majority of existing home sales today, which far outnumber sales of new homes, are being structured through loan assumptions with the added direct financial assistance of the sellers of those homes. But let us return to the longer-term transition process. Evidence of the transition of the mortgage marketplace to a nationwide capital market is most clearly presented by activity in the secondary mortgage markets, through which loans originating in one place are funded by being sold to investors who may be located anywhere in the country. This is where mortgage bankers come into the picture.

SECONDARY MARKET ACTIVITY

The mortgage banking industry, and mortgage bankers or mortgage companies specifically, have always operated in a nationwide market, largely unfettered by regulatory or legislative barriers to interstate operations. Mortgage bankers historically have sold virtually all of the loans they originated, rather than acting as portfolio lenders. Further, mortgage bankers historically provided the great majority of FHA and VA financing, and relied heavily on the GNMA-guaranteed mortgage-backed security. Roughly $120 billion of these GNMA guarantees have been issued during the past decade. In truth, the mortgage banking industry pioneered the secondary mortgage markets of this country and, through their success and profitability, served as a role model for the old faithful portfolio lenders, especially thrifts, when the squeeze began during the last decade.

Thus it was not until 1977 that the savings and loan industry, in the aggregate, sold more mortgage loans than it purchased. More recently, mutual savings banks and commercial banks too have taken more active selling roles in the mortgage markets. One statistic can shorten this part of my discussion dramatically. In 1981, all mortgage originators combined—savings and loans, commercial and mutual savings banks, and mortgage bankers—sold $54 billion of one- to four-family home loans, a volume for the first time exceeding half of their total mortgage originations, 55 percent.

Now, since the traditional portfolio lenders plus mortgage bankers sold more than half of their total loan production in 1981, we have to ask the question, Where did the money come from? Some loan originators, especially savings and loans in more mature markets, continued to purchase loans in 1981. But the bulk of the purchasers were capital market-oriented institutions, such as FNMA, the FHLMC, and institutional investors in GNMA pools. A small volume of conventional mortgage-backed securities was also sold, primarily on a private placement basis.

NEW SOURCES OF CREDIT

Looking ahead over the entire decade of the 1980s, a period of unprecedented potential housing demand for first-time homebuyers in particular, we can expect to see three major prospective sources of residential mortgage credit: pension funds, both public and private; born-again thrift institutions and commercial banks; and consumers investing not in creative financing stopgaps but in retail certificates backed by residential mortgage credit.

State retirement or pension funds are already showing great interest in residential mortgage investments. Private pension funds to date have been effectively excluded from mortgage investments, but in December 1981, President Reagan announced an initial relaxation of some offending regulations, largely under Labor Department Employee Retirement and Income Security Act (ERISA) restrictions, that could open the hundreds of billions of dollars in private pension funds to residential mortgage investment.

If and when investment in mortgages again becomes attractive, depository institutions, including banks and thrift institutions, could again become mortgage investors, not just originators that engage in mortgage banking. This result can follow only after the instruments and legislative and regulatory parameters catch up with the realities and demands of the marketplace. Only when the mortgage instrument is revised to become fully competitive in the capital markets—when the secondary markets accommodate conventional mortgage-backed securities (CMBS) on a large scale and the current plethora of adjustable-rate mortgage instruments sort themselves down to a smaller number of highly marketable, rate-sensitive designs—only then will depository institutions be willing and able to originate or purchase mortgages for their own portfolios.

By the same token, FNMA over time has taken on the characteristics of a gigantic thrift institution, with a mortgage portfolio in excess of $58 billion. Like the thrifts, FNMA will be reborn as a major accumulator of mortgages only when future developments occur that make mortgages once again attractive to thrift institutions. In the interim, however, FNMA will enlarge on its new-found capacity and determination to be a capital market mortgage conduit and guarantor of conventional mortgage-backed securities. The FHLMC, by the way, is performing a similar, equally important role in the capital markets.

The success of FNMA and the FHLMC in developing viable, conventional mortgage-backed securities on a volume basis will be important determinants of the pace of the overall rejuvenation of residential mortgage markets. In addition, mortgage rates need to decline substantially in order to stimulate effective demand for mortgage credit. This in turn will speed the process of winnowing the variety of adjustable rate loans and hasten the market acceptance of new conventional mortgage-backed securities. Until then, the GNMA mortgage-backed security will remain the only significant acceptable mortgage-backed securities vehicle for tapping capital markets to attract residential mortgage credit.

Finally, we should not be surprised to find consumers investing someday in home mortgages, perhaps via the over-the-counter sale by depository institutions of small denomination—say $10,000 minimum—participations in larger mortgage-backed securities.

One thing is clear. Whether a pension fund manager, a depository institution, consumer, or other investor, all will demand inflation protection for the purchasing power of their investment dollars. In the end, the cost and availability of residential mortgage credit will be a function of the investment quality of the mortgage instruments and mortgage-backed securities that are still in the midst of a rapid metamorphosis. They will depend, too, on the ability of regulators and legislators at the state and federal level to remove market impediments and to catch up with the many changes that have already occurred in the marketplace for mortgages. Because of the fragmented, disjointed, uncoordinated approach we have taken with regulatory and legislative initiatives affecting the mortgage markets in this country—at the state and federal level—progress has been slow, and indeed, actions have been counterproductive at times.

For those who intend to participate in the residential mortgage markets of tomorrow, whether as borrowers, originators, or investors, it will truly be a challenge of the survival of the fittest.

ANNALS, *AAPSS*, **465**, January 1983

Inflation: A Blessing or a Curse?

By LEO GREBLER

ABSTRACT: Inflation has generated large wealth shifts among the various population groups involved in housing. The most significant shift is a gain of mortgage borrowers at the expense of lenders and savers. Homeowners, however, have not profited as uniformly as is widely believed, and landlords have generally suffered a sharp decline of net operating income. The severe cycles in residential building since the early 1970s reveal the destabilizing impact of inflation. The housing sector as a whole obtained a disproportionate share of total credit, but its growth and quality improvement did not accelerate apace. Credit expansion without equivalent expansion of real capital illustrates one of the striking maladjustments during inflation. Under a new regime of sustained price stability, housing will still be exposed to prolonged aftereffects of the inflation, notably the reconstruction of a shattered mortgage finance system. The recent trend toward larger and more luxurious dwellings will give way to leaner products. Whether the viability of the rental sector can be restored remains questionable. Under continued or renewed inflation, however, the prospects for housing are far worse.

Leo Grebler is emeritus professor of urban land economics at the University of California, Los Angeles. Born and raised in Germany, he witnessed there the devastating effects of hyperinflation after World War I. He held positions at the Federal Home Loan Bank Board (1938-44) and the National Housing Agency (1944-48) and was a senior staff member of the President's Council of Economic Advisers (1955-57). Between 1948 and 1955 he served as a professor at Columbia University. A Guggenheim fellow, Grebler is the author of numerous books and journal articles.

AMONG the forces affecting American housing in the past 10 years, without question inflation ranks at the very top. To illustrate, inflation has enriched homeowners —or so it seems. It has impoverished mortgage lenders and the savers who supplied the funds for loans. It has changed the public's perception of the benefits of homeownership. Once bought mainly for its consumption services, the owner-occupied dwelling was increasingly viewed as an investment that offered protection against inflation. Landlords' operating profits have deteriorated, yet inflation has brought rent control in a growing number of areas—for the first time in the absence of a war emergency. Nominal mortgage interest rates reached unprecedented levels, raising lenders' income from new loans. Nevertheless, inflation has come to threaten the very survival of savings and loan associations, the residential financiers par excellence.

These and other distributional impacts of inflation on the various groups involved in housing as homeowners, renters, landlords, builders, and lenders call for some detailed analysis. In addition, the influence of inflation on the housing sector as as whole warrants review. In what ways has inflation changed the sector's performance? Equally important, what would be the long-term consequences of inflation if its abatement in mid-1982 should open up a new era of prolonged price stability?[1] Would the housing and mortgage markets return to preinflation normalcy?

This article is written from a nationwide perspective, with housing treated as an agglomeration of local markets which always show diverse trends. Some readers may therefore encounter facts at variance with their experience.

BORROWERS VERSUS LENDERS

One of the most drastic effects of inflation is a huge wealth shift from lenders to borrowers, especially pronounced for long-term debt. Borrowers gain and lenders lose from loan payments in cheaper dollars. Housing is a prime case of such shifts because it is the most heavily indebted major sector of the economy. In the past few decades, the amount of residential mortgages outstanding has exceeded the total credit-market liabilities of the U.S. Treasury, the long-term corporate debt, and, by a wide margin, the obligations of state and local governments.

The size of wealth transfers in the housing sector can only be illustrated. Every $100 of residential debt at the beginning of 1973, the first year of inflation, and still outstanding at the beginning of 1982 was worth only $39 when the Consumer Price Index (CPI) is used to adjust nominal dollars for the intervening price increase. Since average income gains of homeowners more than matched the price rise, the real debt burden on household budgets was greatly reduced. To take an individual case, the typical purchaser of a new home in 1975 priced at $44,600 and financed with a conventional mortgage on the then prevailing terms committed himself to monthly payments of about $280

1. Successful stabilization is compatible with moderate increases of the price level. According to U.S. experience, a price rise averaging about 2-3 percent per year does not generate the inflationary expectations caused by protracted higher rates of price advances.

for interest and amortization. The real value of the payments had shrunk to $163 by early 1982.

Borrowers have also been favored by low mortgage interest rates on loans made during the inflation period—a seeming paradox in light of the steeply climbing nominal rates. According to a widely accepted rationale, nominal interest should comprise a real rate of 3 percent[2] plus a premium for inflation, disregarding allowance for risk. The rates on home loans made by the major types of financial institutions, reported by the Federal Home Loan Bank Board, fail this test in seven of the nine years from 1972 to 1980, with the result of negative real rates. Lenders' expectations of general price increases were below the actual increases, or the competition for mortgages in a period of prevailing abundance of funds kept nominal rates below the level required by the formula.

Beneath the surface of inflation-induced wealth losses of lenders are those suffered by savers, the ultimate sources of funds. The decline in the real value of savings deposit balances mirrors the decline for mortgage balances, already illustrated. The drop in real returns on deposits was reinforced by regulatory ceilings on interest rates. Only since 1978 have savers rebelled by shifting huge amounts to the unregulated money market funds, forcing the authorities to allow financial institutions to accept six-month Treasury Bill accounts at competitive yields. As a result, the rewards for saving have somewhat improved. For example, nominal rates paid by savings and loan associations in the last half of 1977 averaged 6.4 percent; with an annual inflation rate of 6.8 percent, the real return was negative. The corresponding figure for the second half of 1981, the latest reporting period, was 11.3 percent versus the annual CPI increase of 8.9 percent, yielding a moderate return in constant dollars.

But the increased payments to savers, essential for preventing a massive flight of funds from financial institutions, aggravated the earnings problem of mortgage lenders. The spread between their cost of money and the average return on their mortgage portfolios which include large amounts of older low-yield loans was rapidly diminishing and turned negative in a growing number of cases. In the last half of 1981, the average yield on mortgages held by savings and loan associations was only 10 percent, as against the 11.3 percent paid to depositors. This scissor movement is at the root of the much-publicized difficulties of savings banks and savings and loans, compelling the government deposit insurance agencies to undertake unprecedented rescue operations. Other types of institutions have encountered similar problems, but these are less threatening since their residential mortgages account for a small part of their total investment portfolios.

2. At this writing, some financial analysts perplexed by persistent high interest rates in the face of receding inflation conclude that the real rate has risen above the conventionally assumed 3 percent. Be that as it may, this analysis deals with the period preceding the current debate about nominal versus real interest rates.

HOMEOWNERS AS BENEFICIARIES OF INFLATION

According to a widely held notion, homeowners have been among the leading inflation profiteers. There is an element of truth in this view. First, homeowners account for the bulk of the residential mortgage debt, so they have greatly benefited from the decline of loan payments in real dollars. Second, the value increase of their properties exceeded the general price rise at least through 1979—a sector inflation beyond the overall inflation. Between 1973—again, taken as the start of CPI escalation—and 1979, average transaction prices for existing single-family dwellings rose by 95 percent, or 16 percent per year, the CPI by 63 percent. Third, the income tax deduction of mortgage interest added greatly to the attractiveness of homeownership. After-tax interest rates adjusted for inflation became trivial or even negative in many cases. The value of deductions has been especially great for recent buyers who pay high nominal interest rates on large mortgage loans commensurate with steep house prices. Home purchase provided tax shelter as well as consumption services and prospects for capital gains.

To appraise the inflation benefits of homeowners more fully, however, one must distinguish between different groups.

First, there are those who sold their property during the heyday of the boom without acquiring other property. This group usually realized large capital gains even after allowance for transaction costs. Its size can be conservatively gauged by the 4.8 million owners who became renters in 1976-79, when house prices increased at the fastest rate.[3] If the sellers were over 55, they were exempt from the capital gains tax up to $100,000.

Second are those who sold their property and simultaneously bought other. They did not have to pay tax on capital gains from the sale, but their inflation profits are in many cases uncertain. If the equity proceeds from sale exceeded the downpayment for the next home, owners clearly obtained a cash profit. If not, the outcome depends on the house price and the owner's equity at the time of the next sale. Besides, mortgage payments and other homeownership expenses may have become more burdensome than expected. In the glow of anticipation of never-ending house price increases, some homeowners who traded up committed themselves to larger outlays than they could afford. Inflation in the form of property appreciation or income gains or both would bail them out, they thought. If these anticipations remain unmet, members of this subgroup may be forced to sell at a loss to avoid default and foreclosure. The employment and income effects of the economic recession experienced at this writing undoubtedly contribute to distress sales.

The number of owners in the second group is estimated at 10.3 million for the 1976-79 period, but there is no basis even for guessing how many of them may become

3. See Policy Development and Research Division, Department of Housing and Urban Development, and Census Bureau, Department of Commerce, *Annual Housing Surveys* (Washington, DC: Government Printing Office). The numbers are reported each year in Part D of the *Annual Housing Survey*, which deals with recent movers. The data refer only to households with the same head before and after the move. The total in the text assumes that the 1976-79 sellers bought their property before 1976. It is imprecise to the extent that a mover from an owner-occupied to a rental dwelling unit may have later moved again to an owner-occupied house.

inflation losers rather than reapers of the anticipated benefits.[4] I bypass the speculators in single-family homes; their transactions involved only short-term occupancy or none whatever. Moreover, it is impossible to draw the line between speculators and the homebuyers who engaged in repetitive purchases and sales for expected capital gains.[5]

Third are the so-called sitting homeowners who neither bought nor sold their property during the house price inflation. This group on average has enjoyed a notable gain in the book value of their homes and, other things being equal, in their net worth. Although the gain is not realized, it can have considerable economic significance. It improves the owners' credit standing and borrowing potential. The higher value of their property and especially their equity may cause owners to save less if they become more indifferent to further wealth increases. Mortgage borrowers in this group have, of course, greatly benefited from the decrease of their debt payments in real dollars.

The number of sitting owners, defined as those who moved into their homes before 1973, is roughly estimated at 31 million at the end of 1979.[6] The extent of their unrealized gains from inflation depends, of course, on future house prices. It is highly unlikely, however, that average prices will return to the 1973 level, so this group will probably remain among the beneficiaries of inflation.

On the whole, then, homeowners have not profited uniformly and include some potential losers. The groups described previously omit the buyers and sellers of 1980-82, since the information on house prices has become utterly unreliable. Many transactions in these years were featured by creative financing, a euphemism for sellers financing the buyers in whole or in part at below-market terms. The result is a concealed price reduction not reflected in the reported data.[7]

4. The 10.3 million is derived from the source given in footnote 3 and represents the recent movers from one owner-occupied housing unit to another in each year of the 1976-79 period. The qualifications stated in note 3 apply to this estimate as well. At this writing, home mortgage lenders report a sharp increase in delinquent loans, but there is no information on whether delinquencies are concentrated among borrowers who bought homes during the height of the house price inflation.

5. For the extent and market impact of speculation, see Leo Grebler and Frank G. Mittelbach, *The Inflation of House Prices* (Lexington, MA: D. C. Heath, 1979), pp. 58-66.

6. The *Annual Housing Survey of 1979* (Part I: General Housing Characteristics) reports 51.4 million owner-occupied housing units. Of these, 23.4 million were occupied by households that had moved into their homes before Apr. 1970. To arrive at the larger number of pre-1973 owners, I used the annual average of moves into owner-occupied units for 1970-79 to estimate the number of owners who moved into their units between Apr. 1970 and 1972: 7.9 million. Adding this figure to the 23.4 million yields 31.3 million.

7. Creative financing takes many forms. In one variant, property sellers finance buyers with relatively short-term purchase-money mortgages at below-market interest, which usually provide for only partial amortization or none. If the sellers were to dispose of such loans, sizable discounts from par would cut their proceeds substantially. In another variant, builders facilitate sale through buy downs—that is, they undertake to pay for several years the difference between the market interest rate and a stipulated lower rate. These practices entail considerable risks. The builder, for example, may discontinue contributions to interest payments when in financial difficulty. This would impose the full interest burden on the buyer. In the case of short-term unamortized or partially amortized purchase-money mortgages, the buyer may be unable to refinance the loan

When these indirect price concessions are taken into account, all one can say is that average prices have softened in current dollars and surely declined in real terms. Since 1979, even the reported house prices have risen at a much lower rate than the CPI. The sector inflation has come to an end.

Finally, the house price escalation of the 1970s, combined with higher interest rates, produced a group of inflation victims: the frustrated first-time homebuyers. Their access to the market has narrowed, though not as severely as the public debate over their plight would suggest.[8] In many of these cases, purchase may be merely postponed.

LANDLORDS AND TENANTS

The house price inflation has not been paralleled by rent inflation of any comparable magnitude. Rents increased less than the CPI. Residential landlords on average have been squeezed by operating expenses rising more sharply than gross income. Their net operating return fell in constant dollars.

In 1973-81, the rent index increased by 67 percent, the CPI by nearly 105 percent. By this yardstick renting was a bargain. While the statistics are clear, their explanation is puzzling. One would normally expect rents and house prices to change in tandem, at least in the longer run, since the markets for tenant- and owner-occupied housing units are interrelated. But the inflation years were not normal. The demand for homeownership was stimulated by the public's search for inflation hedges. The demand for rental units was not so favored, and rent increases were kept down by notable changes in the clientele for tenant-occupied housing.

First, there has been a marked shift in the income position of homeowners and renters. Between 1973 and 1979, the median income of owners rose by 59 percent, that of renters by only 40 percent.[9] A similar discrepancy probably continued after 1979. The partly inflation-induced preference for homeownership, including condominiums, seems to have drained the rental market of many of its more prosperous tenants. Rental housing, in turn, has become more of a poor man's good. Hence even the moderate rent increase since 1973 meant a higher housing expense relative to tenants' income. This condition helped generate the pressure for rent control, now in force in at least 200 jurisdictions, including several major cities.

Second, the household composition of renters has greatly changed. Broken families accounted for 30 percent of all tenant households with two or more persons in 1973 but 42 percent in 1979. Single persons represented 31 percent of all renters in 1973 but 36 percent in 1979.[10] The

balance when due and the seller would be forced to take the property back.

8. First-time homebuyers accounted for about 50 percent of all home purchasers in the mid-1970s but less than 40 percent in 1979. The 50 percent is derived from data on previous renters becoming homeowners (*Annual Housing Surveys*, Part D). The 1979 survey reports directly that 39 percent of all movers into owner-occupied dwellings during that year were first-time buyers (after adjustment for unreported cases).

9. The data are from the *Annual Housing Surveys*, Part D, and represent the income of families and primary individuals.

10. Source: *Annual Housing Surveys*, Part D. Broken family is my shorthand designation for the census categories "other male head" and "female head" of households with two or more persons. Complete families in census parlance are "male head, wife present,

slow increase of tenants' median income is partly related to these changes. One surmises that the shifting composition of the tenant population made it difficult for landlords to raise rents to a level commensurate with escalating operating costs.

The experience of landlords is best portrayed in a recent analysis by Lowry for metropolitan areas.[11] Gross rental revenue increased by 63 percent between 1973 and 1980, operating cost by 94 percent, and net operating return by 26 percent. The latter, crucial yardstick declined by 32 percent in constant dollars. By this reckoning, landlords as a group have been notable inflation losers. Lowry's estimates of costs, however, exclude depreciation that makes property holdings attractive to investors seeking income tax shelters. They exclude also landlords' inflation gains from the declining real value of mortgage payments. Whether these advantages offset the poor operating performance remains an open question.

Lowry's findings are supported by the sharp decline of private construction for rent during the inflation, in contrast to the boom in homebuilding.[12] Had the existing stock of rented dwellings yielded profits competitive with those from other investments, entrepreneurs would have been enticed to add to the supply. The dismal record of rental housing investment is also pointed up by the escape routes sought by landlords: the conversion of apartments to condominiums and, in extreme cases, complete abandonment of properties.

As for tenants, their housing consumption improved in the 1970s, as it did for homeowners. Space consumption per capita increased. The median number of persons per renter-occupied dwelling unit decreased from 2.3 in 1970 to 2.0 in 1979, as average household size was shrinking while the average number of rooms per unit remained unchanged. The census criteria for housing quality, such as plumbing, bathrooms, heating, and kitchen facilities, show moderate advances. These improvements occurred despite rents lagging behind the rise of general consumer prices.

THE HOUSING CYCLE DURING INFLATION

Inflation is often said to stimulate economic activity, a correct observation up to a point. Expectations of price increases, usually associated with expected gains in business profits, lead to greater production. But the history of protracted inflations includes many cases of short-lived booms ending in severe recession, if not collapse.

The two housing cycles since the early 1970s provide a conspicuous example of the destabilizing effects of inflation. Fluctuations of private housing starts were far more extreme than those of the five preceding cycles in the post-World

no nonrelatives." The owner-occupied sector shows also increasing proportions of broken families and one-person households, but at a much lower level.

11. Ira S. Lowry, *Rental Housing in the 1970s: Searching for the Crisis* (Santa Monica, CA: Rand Corporation, Jan. 1982). This section of the article owes much to Lowry's analysis.

12. Housing starts of structures with three or more dwelling units accounted for 42 percent of all private starts in 1972-73, only 21 percent in 1975-76, and 31 percent in 1980-81. The increase between the last two periods is deceptive. It includes a portion of the rapidly growing volume of subsidized Section 8 housing under legislation enacted in 1974.

War II period.[13] Sales of existing single-family houses dropped by 21.5 percent per annum in 1978-81, after a nearly uninterrupted 10-year increase of spectacular magnitude. Sales of new homes fell by nearly 60 percent, the largest decline since the beginning of this statistical series in 1963. In view of growing cancellations of sales contracts, the actual decline was still greater.

The enormous cyclical gyrations are largely attributable to inflation and the associated steep rise of interest rates. Expectations of ever-increasing house prices fed the homebuilding boom preceding the recent debacle, with starts and sales of single-family units doubling in 1975-78. As usual, an excessive expansion was followed by sharp contraction. Because of favorable demographic factors, the basic potential demand for housing and homeownership remained high throughout the 1970s and the early 1980s.

The change from boom to bust has been extremely painful for builders, suppliers, and construction workers. Many homebuilders, burdened with growing inventories of unsold houses, went out of business or were forced into bankruptcy. The recession developing in 1981 aggravated their precarious position. The downturn since 1979 has affected builders more severely than did any previous contraction since the end of World War II.

THE HOUSING SECTOR'S PERFORMANCE DURING INFLATION

Did the allocation of resources in the inflation period favor or disfavor housing? The first test, in Table 1, compares the growth of residential construction (RC) with that of gross national product (GNP). RC rose at a substantially faster rate than GNP in both 1971-75 and 1976-80 in current dollars, which reflects disproportionate price increases for new housing as well as changes in real output. In constant dollars, RC growth was still ahead of GNP growth in the early part of the 1970s but fell far behind in 1976-80. Thus the stimulating effect of inflation on new housing was wearing off at the height of inflation. The reduced real growth of RC resulted partly from the sharp decline in multifamily construction for rent, already mentioned. In addition, the 1976-80 period includes the beginning of the general housing slump. It should again be noted that demographic factors continued to favor residential building. Slowing income gains, however, may have contributed to the poor performance of RC in 1976-80. Per capita disposable income in real dollars increased by only 7.5 percent in this period, as against 9.2 percent in 1971-75.

Table 1 makes it possible to derive the share of RC in GNP. New housing claimed a growing part of total output in current dollars. In real terms, RC rose from nearly 4 percent of GNP in 1961-70 to 4.5 percent in 1971-75 but fell back to 4 percent in 1976-80. The larger allocation of resources to residential building was short-lived.

The second test compares changes in the value of the entire housing stock with those for the nonresidential capital stock, mostly

13. On the basis of seasonally adjusted data, the amplitude of fluctuations of housing starts in the last two cycles was in the range of 160 percent (the sum of percentage rise and fall), as against an average of 86 percent for the preceding five cycles. The latest figure used in this calculation is for the last quarter of 1981.

TABLE 1
GROWTH OF RESIDENTIAL CONSTRUCTION EXPENDITURES AND GROSS NATIONAL PRODUCT (GNP) IN DESIGNATED PERIODS
(annual averages for dollar figures)

	1961-70	1971-75	1976-80
	CURRENT DOLLARS		
Residential construction, billions	27.3	53.8	100.6
Residential construction, percentage growth	—	97.1	87.0
GNP, billions	730.4	1289.7	2166.4
GNP, percentage growth	—	76.6	68.0
	CONSTANT (1972) DOLLARS		
Residential construction, billions	36.4	54.0	56.3
Residential construction, percentage growth	—	48.3	4.2
GNP, billions	938.7	1209.0	1414.5
GNP, percentage growth	—	28.8	17.0
Inflation rate per year*	2.98	6.58	8.95

SOURCE: For both residential construction and GNP, National Income and Product Accounts, in Special Supplements to the monthly *Survey of Current Business*, Office of Business Economics, U.S. Department of Commerce, comp. (Washington, DC: Government Printing Office).

*Computed from the Consumer Price Index.

business fixed capital (Table 2). Whether gross or net value is considered, one can detect no favorable influence of inflation on the housing sector; in fact, the growth of its net value declined between the 1960s and the 1970s. Relative gains of nonresidential capital in the two decades exceeded those of housing capital by substantial margins. This evidence, as far as it goes, fails to support the thesis that the home investment boom during inflation diverted resources from business investment. True, nonresidential capital in the 1970s increased at a lower rate than in the 1960s, but this change could be due to forces outside the housing sector.

The third test involves the quality of the occupied housing stock and its utilization. Virtually all yardsticks used by the Bureau of the Census show that quality improvement and lower average density per dwelling unit continued in the 1970s.

Thus it seems that inflation has not materially altered the historical trend toward growth and better quality of the housing inventory. Further, even the much-touted homebuying spree has led to a smaller gain in homeownership than one might expect. According to the Annual Housing Surveys, 65.5 percent of all occupied units were owner-occupied in 1979, as against 64.4 percent in 1973. The small increase is explained not only by the relatively short period of the home purchase boom but also by considerable shifts from owner to tenant status. Between 1973 and 1979, eight million households changed tenure from owner to tenant, offsetting a large part of the 13 million who

TABLE 2
AVERAGE ANNUAL PERCENTAGE INCREASES IN VALUE OF PRIVATE RESIDENTIAL AND NONRESIDENTIAL CAPITAL STOCK
(based on data in 1972 dollars)

	RESIDENTIAL		NONRESIDENTIAL	
PERIOD	GROSS STOCK	NET STOCK*	GROSS STOCK	NET STOCK*
1950-60	3.6	4.7	3.8	4.5
1960-70	3.4	3.8	4.8	5.8
1970-79†	3.4	3.4	4.5	4.1

SOURCE: John C. Musgrave, "Fixed Capital Stock in the United States: Revised Estimates," *Survey of Current Business,* 61 (2): 57-68 (Feb. 1981).

*After depreciation.

†Last reported year.

made the change from rental to ownership.[14]

Inflation has had a far greater effect on housing credit. The growth of the residential mortgage debt accounted for over 33 percent of the total debt increase in 1970-80, as against 25 percent in the 1960s. It equaled nearly 54 percent of the growth of long-term debt in the recent decade, compared to 47 percent in the 1960s.[15] The totals in these calculations exclude U.S. debt; the credit demand of the Treasury Department is insensitive to interest rates and will always crowd out other borrowers when rates are high and rising. Hence the larger share of housing in the aggregate debt increase has pinched the rest of the private sector as well as state and local governments. In this sense, the contention that inflation has favored housing seems valid.

The disproportionate growth of the residential debt reflected, of course, the house price inflation, the associated rise in loan amount per dwelling, and the homebuying binge. Policies of mortgage lending institutions on the whole did not resist inflationary forces. Not until 1979 did the institutions begin to reduce loan-price ratios, and then by only moderate margins.

The increase of financial resources allocated to housing did not induce commensurate increase of the housing stock, as previous tests demonstrated. Credit expansion without equivalent expansion of real capital is one of the notable and ultimately unsustainable maladjustments during inflation.

LONG-TERM IMPACT OF INFLATION

One can write a host of scenarios on the future of housing, but I must limit the discussion to two: a future without inflation, and one with continued or renewed inflation. "Without inflation" in this context means a stable price level maintained long enough to banish inflationary expectations from individual and business

14. This reckoning necessarily ignores multiple changes in tenure during the 1973-79 period.

15. *Flow of Funds Accounts,* Federal Reserve Board. "Long-term debt" is identified in the source as "debt capital instruments," consisting of state and local government obligations, corporate bonds, and mortgages.

decisions, plus policies effective in curbing a resurgence of such expectations.[16] If this condition is met, housing still will not return to normalcy for some time to come. On the contrary, the aftereffects of inflation are likely to be more adverse than the inflation experience itself. No easy restoration of the familiar market structures of the 1950s or the 1960s is in sight.

The residential finance system has suffered a breakdown, not just a temporary lapse of performance. Whether savings banks and savings and loan associations can regain their traditional role as prime mortgage lenders is highly dubious. At best, it will be many years before the thrift institutions recover their viability. The process is complicated by the diversification of authorized savings and loan investments, initiated by the Depository Institutions Deregulation and Monetary Control Act of 1980 and intensified under the Depository Institutions Act of October 1982. Residential mortgage lending stands to suffer from such a change. If the legislation is implemented in savings and loan investment practice, the United States will be an advanced country with no major private-sector intermediary specializing in housing finance.

An altered structure of housing finance, comprising elements of the old and some new suppliers of funds, will no doubt develop when inflation stops and mortgage investment can again be expected to yield profits. Such an evolution takes considerable time, however. Meanwhile, there is a real threat of a supply-demand gap. The regular demand for residential mortgages will be augmented by the need to refinance the recent short-term loans made by property sellers during the episode of creative financing. The condition is aggravated by reduced market support of the federal mortgage-purchase agencies. Their curtailed activity under the present administration is rooted in an earlier policy decision to restrain the growth of U.S. credit agencies. The prospect of large federal deficits in the next few years will reinforce this policy shift.

The crucial long-run issue is the efficiency of a new structure of mortgage lenders. Under the influence of inflation and the pervasive policy of deregulation, the whole financial system is changing from functionally defined though overlapping units to more homogeneous entities or supermarkets for financial services. The question is not only how much of their resources the emerging institutions will allocate to housing, but whether they can handle the rather complex mortgage lending operation as efficiently as did the system of bygone days.

Long-term interest rates will be high by the standards of the 1960s, even if they no longer include a premium for inflation. The financial markets face huge federal demands for funds along with large pent-up corporate demands to convert excessive short-term borrowings into

16. See footnote 1.

long-term debt. The saver will be in the saddle because his product is so badly needed. High returns on savings spell costly credit, a special handicap for housing. As a policy response to the problem, income tax benefits for savings are unlikely after the ill-conceived tax-free certificates of 1981 are allowed to lapse. The already precarious federal deficits, moreover, will limit the size of any program that reduces tax revenue or, through stepped-up housing subsidies, increases government spending. Altogether, the financial prospects for housing confirm an old observation: much of the price a nation pays for inflation is exacted in the postinflation period.

Another legacy of inflation is a greater variety of mortgage payment plans. The long-term, level-payment, fully amortized loan at a fixed interest rate, standard since the 1930s, will be supplemented by some of the alternatives developed in recent years. Many lenders, stung by losses from the standard mortgage, will seek to limit their interest rate commitment even in the absence of inflation. The variable-rate loan shifts much of the burden of rate increases—and the benefits of rate decreases—to the borrower. So does the rollover mortgage with rates set for, say, five years. The borrower additionally bears the risk of loan renewal under possibly adverse financial conditions—a severe problem in the 1930s. The graduated payment plan, which requires small outlays in the first few years offset by larger later outlays, favors borrowers but does not appeal to lenders who abhor the hazards of negative loan amortization in the initial period. On the whole, alternative mortgage instruments are unobjectionable in principle, but those most likely to survive the inflation period expose borrowers to greater risks.

Proceeding from finance to the real side, one of the most crucial issues is the postinflation prospect for the rental housing sector. Will rents increase to a level that makes the ownership of property once more a profitable proposition in comparison to other investments? Will the trend toward rent control persist even in the absence of inflation and stifle landlords' attempts to raise rents? To what extent will the previously described changes in the tenant clientele impede higher rents? Will entrepreneurs return to the building of new apartments?

At this juncture, skepticism seems to be the proper response to these questions, but it is somewhat modified by the tax incentives for rental housing, and especially low-income housing, that are offered in 1981 legislation. The law increases depreciation allowances and shortens capital recovery periods. Also, federal subsidies will probably be channeled into housing allowances for tenants in qualified existing dwellings instead of the past concentration on new construction for the poor. How effective these measures will be in reviving the rental sector remains to be seen.

As for homeownership, the mix of consumption and investment motives for house purchase, tilted in favor of the latter during inflation, should return to normal. Buyers' concern over future asset value will once more focus on the potential resale price of a particular property. This shift will have an important consequence. During inflation, purchasers tended to acquire homes too large for their household needs. The higher the price, the greater the amount of the inevitable value appreciation, they believed. In the absence of this illusion, consumers acting under the usual income and house price constraints will again opt for dwellings of a size and quality geared to their housing requirements. This means a new production mix for builders and the conversion of some existing houses to two-family or larger units. The demand for more modest dwellings should be strengthened when lower house prices and interest rates open the market to larger numbers of first-time homebuyers. The overcommitment of some recent purchasers will lead to a shake-out that depresses house prices at least for a while.

The severity of the aftereffects of inflation on housing and mortgage markets depends, of course, on the level of overall business activity under a stable currency regime. But this article is not designed as an economic forecast. Rather, I turn to the alternative scenario of continued or renewed inflation, a distasteful but not implausible projection that can only be sketched here.

To judge from the experience of countries with chronic inflation, such a condition would mean pervasive rent control and the demise of private rental housing. Even if new units were excluded from control, most entrepreneurs and lenders would be unwilling to gamble on the permanence of the exemption. Governments would become the main supporters of rental construction, but their fiscal troubles under inflation would restrict the subsidies they could offer. Hence there would be perpetual shortage reinforcing the pressure for continuing rent regulation. The conversion of apartments into condominiums would accelerate unless it was restrained or prohibited by government action. The remaining stock of rental housing would deteriorate, as landlords have little incentive to maintain and improve their properties. Access to units becoming vacant would be increasingly reserved to consumers willing to make under-the-table lump sum payments—an illegal practice openly tolerated in countries with prolonged rent control.

New and old homes for owner-occupancy would be in great demand as hedges against inflation and as an alternative to the restricted supply of rental housing. Long-term mortgage loans, however, would be more difficult to obtain, command high interest rates reflecting inflationary expectations, and cover a smaller portion of the purchase price. Mortgages of only 30-50 percent of acquisition cost are not at all unusual in inflation-ridden countries. In extreme cases, the supply of long-term loans from non-government sources has dried up. Thus the potential demand increase for homes would be curbed by severe problems of borrowing, and government would be called on to supply funds. Housing would clearly become a semipublic sector of the economy.

These trends have been observed not only in underdeveloped countries but also in some of the advanced nations of Europe which suffered from rampant inflation after each of the world wars. The only difference is the greater capacity of rich countries to overcome postwar inflations and cope with the aftereffects on housing and mortgage finance. Yet some of these effects are even now evident in prolonged rent control and a large government role in residential construction.

In a few cases, the indexing of prices, wages, rents, debt claims, and interest rates, or of savings and mortgage obligations alone, has helped to keep the housing market from collapse. Nearly all countries resorting to this palliative, however, have also adopted subsidy programs for borrowers unable to meet the indexed payments. On the whole, such automatic adjustments for inflation have had disappointing results.[17]

CONCLUSION

To venture a short answer to the question posed in the title, inflation has certainly not been a blessing for housing. It has been a curse in the sense that imbalances created by inflation, especially the breakdown of the mortgage market structure, will require costly and time-consuming correction when price stability is reestablished. If the postinflation cost of inflation appears high, the damage to housing from continued or renewed inflation would be far greater and the ultimate cure of distortions still more painful. Thus the best general housing policy on the current agenda is a policy to restore and sustain a stable price level.

17. See Harold Robinson, "Readjustable Mortgages in an Inflation Economy—A Study of the Israeli Experience," *Journal of International Law and Economics*, 5(2):169-84 (Jan. 1971).

ANNALS, *AAPSS*, **465**, January 1983

Homebuilding in the 1980s: Crisis or Transition?

By NED EICHLER

ABSTRACT: At the end of World War II, pent-up demand and favorable government action—notably, better financing and highway building—combined to create the setting for a boom in house construction. This bred a new type of company, merchant builders, who brought together every aspect of homebuilding, from land acquisition to consumer finance and marketing. After receding somewhere in the late 1950s and most of the 1960s, housing starts reached all-time highs in the 1970s. Throughout all of the postwar period, merchant builders with annual volume of 100 units or more came to dominate the industry. Dozens of firms sought far greater scale, and some even dreamed of creating truly national firms. The rampant inflation of the 1970s, particularly the last half of the decade, and the coming of age of the postwar baby boom generated enormous volume in starts, resale transactions, and merchant-builder profits. But events since 1979 may well mark that year as the end of a golden era. For the past two years, transactional velocity and profits have been severely constrained, a situation that will continue for several more years. Dreams of glory are being shattered. However, by the middle of the decade this harsh transition will have ended, and the industry will return to conditions much like those of the early 1960s.

Ned Eichler has two careers simultaneously. As a businessman, he has spent many years in homebuilding and real estate, most recently as manager of major properties of the Penn Central, and as president of Levitt and Sons (1975-79). As an academician, he has taught at the Graduate Schools of Business of both the University of California, Berkeley, and Stanford University. He has also lectured extensively and has written two books, the most recent of which, The Merchant Builders, *published in 1982 by MIT Press, is a history of the homebuilding business since 1945.*

FOR 15 years before 1945, there was little residential construction in the United States. Annual housing starts were about 200,000 in the 1930s and, except for units built specifically at military bases or for munitions workers, were almost nonexistent during the war. In the 1920s, construction was higher, reaching a peak of over 900,000 in 1925. However, not only did starts decline thereafter, but most activity was in building apartments. Housing for ownership was not significant. Furthermore, the vast majority of building for owner-occupants was conducted by small contractors or speculators.

After the war, a special set of conditions converged to provide a setting for a boom in the production and sale of homes: (1) the war had accomplished what the New Deal could not—it had induced prosperity; (2) the dearth of homebuilding, combined with the demobilization of some nine million people, created enormous potential demand; (3) a massive highway program was bringing vast areas of inexpensive land within acceptable commuting ranges; and (4) local and state governments for the most part were anxious to cooperate with developers. For this demand to be made effective, two more ingredients were needed. One was a ready supply of long-term low-interest mortgages requiring little or no down payment. This was provided by federal governmental guarantees or insurance—Federal Housing Administration (FHA) and Veterans' Administration (VA)—and by governmentally sheltered lenders, such as savings and loan associations.

It also required a special breed of men to initiate and coordinate the complex and often chaotic process of acquiring raw land, getting local government approval, arranging financing—both for working capital and for consumers—installing site improvements, constructing houses, and marketing them. In no other industry did businessmen cover such a broad spectrum of activities, starting from raw material and ending with a sale, a closing, and even customer service. Yet the opportunity was enormous, and, as has always been true, men rose to grab it. As individuals or in partnerships, most of them young, inexperienced, and without capital, thousands virtually overnight became what I call merchant builders.[1]

THE RISE OF THE MERCHANT BUILDERS

Before the war, only about 10 percent of houses were started by merchant builders with annual volume of over 100 units per year. By 1959, with annual production having risen more than five times the rate in the 1930s, this percentage was over two-thirds. The instrument for bringing housing to most Americans in the last 35 years has been merchant builders. Certainly one aspect of their business was the favorable conditions previously cited. The other is the peculiar nature of management and decision making that is inherent in merchant building. Not even the largest firm has any of the advantages of dominant companies in other fields. Little or no capital is required for plant and equipment. Money to buy land, install improvements, build houses, and pay overhead has been increas-

1. "Merchant builder" is the term commonly, but not exclusively, used to designate a person or a company that purchases a parcel of raw land and turns it into a group of houses for sale.

ingly available to small operations at a cost at most marginally higher than that for larger firms. What little technology exists is available to all. No large firm has a dealer network, supplier arrangements, a national reputation, or any other characteristics that gives it a meaningful edge over smaller ones.

Merchant builders vie with each other by trying to make better judgments about site selection and product choice and by maintaining better control over all activities, principally construction and marketing. Observers and practitioners of merchant buildings have often been misled by the magnitude of money that flows through even a modest-sized company. A 100-house-per-year operation may generate annual dollar volume in excess of $10 million. But despite these large sums, merchant building is, as it always has been, a management-intensive business, in which many important decisions are made daily and little can be routinized.

Merchant builders, material suppliers, subcontractors, and lenders responded vigorously to the favorable postwar conditions. By 1949, U.S. housing starts reached 1.25 million and have exceeded 1 million per year ever since. Credit crunches, business cycles, overbuilding, variations in government funding, inflation, and changes in demographics induced sharp peaks and deep valleys. Lows came in 1960 (1.25 million), 1966 (1.15 million), and 1975 (1.15 million). Highs were in 1950 (1.9 million), 1972 (2.35 million), and 1978 (2.0 million).

For about 15 years, after much of the demand pent up from low production rates during the depression and the war was met in 1955, until postwar babies began to enter the market in 1970, merchant building was a fiercely competitive business. The environment was good enough to allow merchant builders to prosper, and even to grow, if they maintained tight control and reacted well to cyclical changes. Pretax profits of 10 percent of sales were projected and were occasionally achieved or even exceeded. But there were many who not only could not make their 10 percent but who experienced construction cost overruns, selected the wrong locations and product, created too much overhead, and had too much inventory—and therefore debt—in bad times and went bankrupt in the process.

In 1970, as volume began to grow and as merged or public companies were expanding, large-scale merchant building seemed to have triumphed. But by 1971, the giants began to experience problems. Over the next three years, as Boise Cascade, Levitt, Larwin, Lyon, and a number of others faltered, the difficulties of growing and diversification became more apparent. The recession that began in late 1973 seemed to drive the nails into the coffin of large multicity merchant builders. When Kaufman and Broad reported a $19 million loss for 1974, after proclaiming to the financial community its invincibility, the game apparently ended.

But the next five years, 1975 to 1979, constituted a period unlike any in the history of merchant building. Acting as if inflation were but a passing phenomenon and encouraged by the federal government, mortgage lenders—especially savings and loans—showered cheap money on eager buyers of new and used houses. When home purchasers anticipated a general rate of inflation of at least 12 percent by 1980, lenders were offering 30-year fixed-rate loans at 9 percent or less. In effect, they were paying people to borrow. In the peak year, 1978, total housing transactions were 5.5 million—3.9 million used and 1.6 million new. In the peak year of the previous decade, 1968, this total was less than half, 2.5 million.

Not only were buyers being given low-interest mortgages for their own use, but increasingly, by statute and court decisions, they were enabled to sell the loan with the house without rate renegotiation. Certainly part of the increase in home sales was due to purchases by investors, people buying not to live in the house but to rent it and later resell it. Even occupants viewed their newly acquired dwelling more as an investment than as a place to live. Deductibility of interest; property taxes and depreciation for investors; capital gain treatment on sale by investors; complete deferral for occupants who bought another house within 18 months; and exemption of any tax on the first $100,000 of gain for people 55 and older—all this only made buying a house more attractive.

This amazing behavior of government and lenders was part of the special climate of the late 1970s; the other was demographics. Household formation soared as the postwar babies came of age, as more women entered the work force, and as divorce became rampant. It is no wonder that this generated not only high transaction velocity but rapidly rising prices. Even in 1979, when both production and used-home sales declined—from 2 million to 1.7 million, and from 3.9 to 3.7 million, respectively—house prices rose faster than the general inflation rate.

MERCHANT-BUILDER SUCCESS

Clearly, merchant building has served the American consumer well. Two-thirds of all American families now own their own homes, almost double the number at the end of World War II. For the quality of houses purchased, we are the envy of the world. In both absolute and relative terms, Americans have paid less money for more space and more features than people in any other country.

Potential demand, general prosperity, and the facilitating actions of government spawned a mass market. Entrepreneurs, whom I have called merchant builders, capitalized on this setting. With the exceptions of Canada and England and, to a small degree, France, in no other country were private firms the instrument for housing its growing and prospering population. Per capita unit production in the postwar era may have been nearly comparable in several other nations, notably Sweden and the Soviet Union. But the vast majority of dwellings were small apartments built directly by the government.

Although no precise data are available or even possible, there is no doubt that merchant building has been a much more efficient way to bring houses to consumers than the smaller-scale custom building that predominated before World War II. One indicator is that for many larger merchant builders, cost per square foot of house construction from 1950 to 1960 stayed constant despite a doubling of hourly wage rates and increases in quality. Unable to compete with such mass building, smaller operations for the most part abandoned lower- and even middle-priced markets. They concentrated instead on higher-priced homes where individualized design and special locations were crucial.

In the late 1940s and 1950s, as large-scale merchant builders—100 units per year or more—became the dominant suppliers of homes, most of the postwar improvements in production organization and techniques were made. As unit costs began to rise rapidly in the 1960s, because of higher quality, high land and site development costs, and inflation, there was heightened interest in the possibility of another round of increased efficiency from greater scale and technological breakthroughs. Many firms did grow, mostly by geographic expansion. Several broke out of the 100-1000-unit range to annual volumes over 5000. By 1980, U.S. Home brought its unit production to 15,000. However, there were no significant changes in technology or even methodology. Nor is there clear evidence that U.S Home, Ryan, Pulte, or other multicity builders have yet achieved economies of scale.

DEVELOPMENTS IN 1980 AND 1981

In order to assess the possibilities for changes in merchant building in the 1980s, it is necessary to review occurrences in 1980 and 1981. During these two years, there was increasing comment and concern that recent events signaled changes in the climate for U.S. homebuilding that would be fundamental, far-reaching, and, for both merchant builders and consumers, catastrophic. The evidence cited for this contention is a sharp drop in housing starts, from 2 million in 1978 to 1.7 million in 1979 to 1.3 million in 1980 and to under 1.1 million in 1981, as well as in used-home sales, from 3.9 million in 1978 to 3.7 million in 1979 to 2.9 million in 1980 and to 2.4 million in 1981.

However, these reductions in sales and production could be seen as nothing more than normal phases in the cycle after the great boom years of 1976-78. In 1973, 1974, and 1975, following peak production of 2.3 million units in 1972, the declines were even sharper. In other words, 1980-82, like 1973-75, is perhaps simply the inevitable pause before still another boom in sales and starts.

Until recently this was the prevailing view. Most analysts were predicting a strong resurgence of sales in the second half of the year, starts reaching an annual rate of well over 1.6 million by the end of the year, and several consecutive years of production in excess of 2 million. However, this optimism has largely given way to predictions of far lower sales and starts. The reasons for this new perception lie in the apparent economic policies of the Reagan administration and, more specifically, in the plight of savings and loan associations.

The most important factor in the environment for merchant building will be what methods the federal government uses to combat inflation and how effective they will be. From 1965, when inflation began to grow significantly, through 1979, no administration and no Federal Reserve Board made curbing and rolling back inflation a primary goal. It was a matter of concern, occasionally serious concern, as when the Nixon administration imposed wage and price controls; but recession and unemployment were seen as much more dire threats. The twin actions necessary to fight inflation—restricting the growth of the money supply and reducing federal deficits—were perceived as politically feasible only for short periods.

Despite apparent ineptitude and inconsistency in its behavior in 1980, Federal Reserve Board actions signaled a new idea—that inflation might be a more important problem than interim unemployment and stagnation, that a sound economy depended on more stable prices. This was the essential campaign claim of Ronald Reagan. When he won the election overwhelmingly, it seemed to signal a new approach in which less government intervention, lower deficits, and stricter monetary policies would be the policies to fight the twin enemies—rising inflation and declining productivity.

Since the housing market is so dependent on, and affected by, the cost and availability of credit, this change in the government's priorities could affect it dramatically. For several years, in fact, some critics had been contending that the volume of home sales and construction not only was aided by but contributed to the inflation of the 1970s. In 1978, for example, Alan Greenspan, one of President Reagan's principal economic advisers, characterized the situation as follows: "Shoring up the mortgage market clearly contributed to the underlying bias in the economy. While it may have sustained the home building boom, this probably has been accomplished at a significant cost to the economy's overall stability."[2] Budget Director David Stockman has condemned special subsidies and low-interest loans to aid consumers to buy or to rent housing. The president's 1982 budget proposals reflect this view.

Even before the election, the belief that government support of housing should end, or at least be reduced, manifested itself in significant legislation. In 1980, Congress created a special body, the Depository Institutions Deregulations Committee (DIDC), to supervise phasing out those provisions that on the one hand protected savings and loans and on the other hand restricted their lending mainly to housing for sale. DIDC moved quickly, authorizing both banks and savings and loans to offer Now Accounts—interest-bearing checking—eliminating the historic rate differential between banks and savings and loans—the latter could previously pay .25 percent more—and permitting savings and loans to make consumer loans.

Moving much faster than expected, DIDC was well on its way toward putting banks and savings and loans on an equal footing. At the same time, bank and savings and loan regulators, working with secondary market institutions—Fannie Mae, Ginny Mae, and Freddie Mac—began trying to devise a mortgage instrument that would protect lenders from borrowing for short periods, subjecting themselves to wide variations in their cost of money and lending on a long-term basis. The low interest rates of the 1970s were usually fixed for 30 years. As inflation drove up interest rates, mortgage lenders, mainly savings and loans, were badly hurt. Some approached insolvency. The answer for the future was clearly a loan whose interest rate rises and falls with the lender's cost. This mechanism, called a variable-rate mortgage, may be the only way to

2. Alan Greenspan, "The Explosion of Mortgage Credit," *Wall Street Journal*, 21 Nov. 1978.

finance home purchases in the 1980s.

None of this means that there will not be funds available for mortgage loans. What it may signify is a situation quite different from the recent past, not in the availability but in the cost to the homebuyer of mortgage loans. No longer would the federal government provide subsidies, direct or indirect, or allocate credit to give homebuyers any significant edge in borrowing money. If savers can get higher yields from bonds or money market funds, so be it. If home purchasers are thus forced to pay more to compete, so be it. And if Federal Reserve restrictions in money growth keep all interest rates high until inflation recedes, so be it.

Presidential advisers and other advocates realize that this will probably restrict residential construction and make houses less attractive investments. They seem willing to accept such results as part of the price for restructuring our economy. In fact, many analysts think we have invested far too much in housing in recent years and not enough in so-called productive plant and equipment. In a period of declining productivity, when the United States is apparently becoming less competitive with other countries, this is a compelling argument.

CONTINUING TRENDS IN THE 1980s

Some observers believe that the administration and the Federal Reserve will alter course by early 1982. Faced with minimal growth in the Gross National Product (GNP), rising unemployment, fear of bank and savings and loan failures, and a depressed housing market, it is claimed that the Federal Reserve will loosen monetary reins and that elected officials will reinstate housing subsidies. The latter could take many forms—direct loans, subsidies, tax credits, savings used for home purchases, and so on. The result would be lower interest rates in general and reinstitution of at least some of the historical advantage given borrowers who buy houses.

Such policies would create an environment for merchant builders and consumers much like that of 1975 to 1979. As one skeptic puts it, "Lenders and the government will forget all this in a few months. They'll give home buyers and builders one more turn of the wheel." If this happens, there will most likely be rising inflation, high rates of sale and production, rapidly increasing prices, and therefore large profits for merchant builders and homeowners. The structure of the business and the product it offers would change very little.

If, however, as it certainly would have us believe, the government is willing to live with all the problems cited, viewing control and reduction of inflation as of transcendent importance, almost certainly the 1980s will be different from not only the 1970s but the entire period since World War II.

For example, mortgage interest rates would go down, but only as the anticipated inflation rate also declines. Lenders will demand variability to protect themselves against later reversals of the inflation trend. While the rate of inflation is falling, presumably over a period of several years, the real interest rate on mortgages—the coupon rate in relation to anticipated inflation—will be well above 3 percent. The difference between such a scenario and recent history would be dramatic. This can be illustrated by examining the mortgage interest rate at the beginning of the previous recoveries.

Assuming a rate of 13.75 percent in late 1982, as a percentage of the previous rate, the increase was 20 percent in 1967 and 1971, 17 percent in 1975, and 57 percent in 1982. Thus at the start of the upturn in another business cycle, prospective purchasers would find themselves being offered homes at prices and at an interest rate that have risen faster than the general rate of inflation. Nevertheless, the rate will be variable and should decline if inflation does too. But variability will ensure that purchasers cannot, as they did in the 1970s, gain against rising inflation at the expense of lenders.

This set of conditions would eliminate most if not all of the investment component of homebuying, which in the last decade became a housebuying panic. In fact the reverse may occur—many people may conclude that at current prices and interest rates, houses are overpriced. It would not be out of the question for house prices to fall for a period and after that rise less slowly than current or even anticipated inflation rates.

This does not mean that no one will buy a house. It does suggest that if the real mortgage interest rate remains high, and if inflation gradually recedes over the period 1983 to 1985, compared to the last half of the 1970s or even any previous postwar recovery, the financial climate would not encourage homebuying. The velocity of home sales, new and used, and the rate of price increase would be under severe downward pressure. People would purchase houses, but only for traditional reasons—tenure, the right to make changes and improvements, recovery of the increased value of such improvements, and, most of all, to get the house they want. Lower rates of house price increase and lower levels of production would moderate the rising value of land. Where land prices went up sharply, there could even be decline, although sellers with substantial net worth will generally hold out.

Reduced rates of house price increases, below the inflation rate, would put the gross margins of merchant builders under severe downward pressure. Those with substantial land inventories would be incurring severe interest burdens, a problem obscured by a new accounting rule of the Financial Accounting Standards Board, FASB 34, which requires interest to be capitalized, thus adding the cost as an asset and not deducting it from profit as an expense. Gross margins would not go back to 1974 levels, but a rate of 15 to 20 percent would be quite likely—a sharp drop from the level of 20 to 32 percent reached by all except Ryan in the late 1970s.

MERCHANT BUILDERS AND THE CONSUMER

Higher interest rates, lower total production, and reduced margins may well affect the structure of merchant building. One possibility is that these conditions will unmask the relative inefficiency of large multicity firms. The high overhead and debt service of most such firms, except Ryan, may once again become a major problem. As returns on equity shrink, stockholders may press management either to diversify or to liquidate.

On the other hand, the United States may follow the pattern of

England and Canada, where thousands of smaller operators have disappeared and the business has become more concentrated in the larger firms even as total volume declined. This trend may have been determined mainly by who has access to financing, especially working capital.

As described earlier, small and middle-sized builders have constantly been able to raise money to buy land, to install improvements, and to build houses. Increasingly in the 1970s, the principal source for such working capital was savings and loans. These institutions may become so limited in their ability to provide such funding that they may abandon the field to pursue other activities—consumer loans or mortgage banking, for example. This would dramatically restrict smaller firms. The larger ones would continue to be able to raise capital through credit lines, commercial paper, and securities offerings. Despite their relative inefficiency in management, national companies might then greatly increase their share of the market.

Such concentration would not be advantageous to the consumer. It would mean less production at higher prices. But even if smaller merchant builders can get working capital, if interest rates remain high, purchasers of homes will for several years pay a higher share of their incomes and/or get less housing than they have in the past 35 years. Gradually other cost components—land, construction, overhead, and profit—might decline relatively and absorb some of the effect of more expensive financing, but it would be a long time before such adjustments were significant.

CONCLUSION

All the foregoing suggests that if the government tries seriously to control inflation, and even if over the next three or four years it succeeds in stabilizing it at a lower level, merchant builders, homeowners, and homebuyers will bear a considerable part of the burden. Just as their horizons soared in the last half of the 1970s, they may be severely limited in the 1980s. If this occurs, the existing housing stock will be used more intensely—sharing, subdividing existing houses, and so on; new houses will be smaller and more often high density—townhouses and multistory buildings; and more young families will rent. Absent controls, rents will rise dramatically.

Such conditions would represent a painful transition for many people, but they would not be catastrophic, especially if small and medium-sized merchant builders could get adequate working capital. If national production averages about 1.5 million in the next few years, the industry as a whole will be operating at something close to optimum efficiency. As young families defer buying, as their incomes rise faster than house prices, and as interest rates gradually follow the decline of the rate of inflation, the potential for a strong housing market in the late 1980s will develop.

Americans have a penchant for characterizing newly perceived problems as crises. For a long time we ran our economy with very cheap power, principally fueled by oil. In 1973 the Organization of Petroleum Exporting Countries (OPEC) was created, and the energy crisis was declared. We did have a problem, but we have survived and have even prospered. Furthermore, although we will probably never again have the luxury of such low-priced power, through conservation, the development of alternatives, and acceptance of higher costs we seem now well able to handle the situation.

The housing crisis is likely to run the same course. For a few years we will have to make a difficult adjustment to a new reality. Just as we have learned to be more careful in our use of power and to pay more for it, so we will use our existing housing stock more carefully and accept the somewhat higher cost to finance it. As we absorb the shock of these two changes in the American economy, as we build fewer cars and fewer houses, as we consume less oil and gasoline, resources will be released for other uses.

No doubt new problems will arise. One would like to think that we will have learned enough and matured enough not to label every painful transition a crisis. In doing so, we dishonor perhaps the greatest strength of our economy, our political system, and our national character—the ability to adapt to changing conditions, to avoid the rigidity that has weakened and even destroyed so many societies.

ANNALS, *AAPSS*, **465**, January 1983

A Five-Year Housing Forecast

By MICHAEL SUMICHRAST

ABSTRACT: Even to attempt to make a long-term forecast seems like a useless and idiotic exercise. In the climate we live in today, we are not smart enough to see beyond a couple of days, or at most, a few weeks. Still, it has to be done, not just to fill the pages of magazines, but for planning purposes. So we look at possible scenarios under various assumptions. Housing, as we all know, is highly credit sensitive. Thus our assumptions are heavily weighted toward future developments in the financial markets. What we are actually saying is that if interest rates decline, more people will be willing—and able—to buy homes. If interest rates do not decline, people will not buy. There are three ways of looking at things: the optimistic, the pessimistic, and the most likely forecasts. All three will be mentioned in this article.

Michael Sumichrast is chief economist and staff vice-president of the National Association of Home Builders. Dr. Sumichrast studied industrial engineering in Czechoslovakia, continued his studies at Melbourne University in Australia, and received his Ph.D. from Ohio State University. After a career in the construction industry, he became affiliated with the National Association of Home Builders in 1963. His books include Where Will You Live Tomorrow? *(Dow Jones-Irwin, 1981),* The Complete Book of Home Buying *(Dow Jones Books, 1979), and* Housing Markets *(Dow Jones-Irwin, 1977).*

THIS article is divided into three parts. The first shows how well—or badly—we did in the past in forecasting housing activity. The second part presents tables for each of three forecasts—the optimistic, the pessimistic, and the most likely—along with short explanations of each one, including the assumptions on which each forecast is based. The third part has concluding comments as to changes in products, as well as some of the geographical differences.

HOW WELL DID WE DO?

Our short-term forecast did quite well, as shown in Table 1. Our long-term forecasts were never very good, but they were probably within the acceptable limits of the actual data themselves. In the past decade, for example, we were supposed to build 17.6 million new units. The decennial census actually shows that we ended the decade with over 20 million units; the Bureau of the Census is still looking for some 3 million units that are in the ground but not in the statistics.

The last five years of the decade, 1976-80, show the official number of new units started as 8.582 million. Of these, 6.093 million were single-family units and 2.489 million were multifamily units. The three available forecasts for this period are presented in Table 2. The figure for actual starts may be revised after the Bureau of the Census determines what actually happened to the

TABLE 1
ACTUAL HOUSING STARTS VERSUS NATIONAL ASSOCIATION OF HOME BUILDERS ESTIMATES, 1962-81 (units in thousands)

DATE OF NAHB FORECAST	FORECAST YEAR	NAHB ESTIMATE	ACTUAL HOUSING STARTS
2/62	1962	1362	1492
2/63	1963	1492	1635
11/63	1964	1585	1561
12/64	1965	1525	1510
5/66	1966	1310	1196
11/66	1967	1100	1322
8/67	1968	1450	1545
12/68	1969	1514	1500
10/69	1970	1370	1469
12/70	1971	1880	2085
10/71	1972	2150	2379
10/72	1973	2000	2058
10/73	1974	1600	1353
8/74	1975	1100	1171
1/76	1976	1549	1547
12/76	1977	1736	2002
12/77	1978	1869	2036
12/78	1979	1714	1760
1/80	1980	1326	1313
1/81	1981	1366	1100

SOURCE: NAHB *Economic News Notes*; U.S. Bureau of the Census, Series C-20; compilation by NAHB Economics Division.

TABLE 2
HOUSING STARTS, FORECAST AND ACTUAL, 1976-80
(units in thousands)

FORECASTER	SINGLE FAMILY	PERCENT ERROR	MULTI-FAMILY	PERCENT ERROR	TOTAL	PERCENT ERROR
Weicher (HUD)*	6122	0	4023	+62	10,145	+18
Langevin†	3150	–52	6025	+142	9355	+9
NAHB‡	6000	–2	2190	–12	8190	–5
Actual§	6093		2489		8582	

*John C. Weicher, Senate Banking Committee, Estimators of Housing Needs, 75-80, September 1975.

†Donaldson, Lufkin, and Jenrette, *Research Bulletin*, May 1976.

‡NAHB Forecasting Service, October 1976.

§Bureau of the Census.

additional units they discovered in the counting of the decennial census. But for the time being, the official number of about 8.6 million new units will serve.

THE FORECAST THROUGH 1986

The point should be made that in the past a long-term forecast could be made with some degree of accuracy. However, future forecasts probably will not have the same chance of doing well, because we have entered a new era of financial uncertainty, with volatile and record-high interest rates, the near demise of the thrifts, and a restructuring of the financial intermediaries. All of this leaves us with a great deal of uncertainty about the future behavior of consumers, their spending habits, their ability to buy, and so on.

Under normal conditions, one would have to be satisfied with a point forecast. That is, one number or one forecast would be quite sufficient. Now, however, we must get into ranges or, if you will, several types of forecasts, depending on which financial variable one assumes. That is the reason for having three forecasts: optimistic, pessimistic, and in-between or most likely.

Pessimistic forecast

This forecast, shown in Table 3, is based on the assumptions that the economy will be in recession for the next several years, with unemployment reaching over 10 percent, interest rates high, the prime rate reaching over 20 percent, and inflation staying at double-digit levels. Such a scenario will produce fewer than one million starts in 1982; 1.1 million in 1983; 1.1 million in 1984; 982,000 in 1985; and 1.4 million in 1986. The total for the five-year period would be 5.5 million new housing starts.

Optimistic forecast

This forecast, shown in Table 4, assumes a low and declining inflation rate to below 6 percent, a declining unemployment rate to below 5 percent, and interest rates dropping consistently throughout the period, with the prime rate as low as 9 percent. This scenario gives us three

(text continued on page 54)

TABLE 3
PESSIMISTIC FORECAST

	ACTUAL		FORECAST				
ASSUMPTIONS	1980	1981	1982	1983	1984	1985	1986
Economic Indicators							
Personal income per capita (dollars)	9522	10,341	10,984	12,168	13,440	14,803	16,548
Percentage change	10.25	8.60	6.22	10.78	10.45	10.14	11.79
Disposable income per capita (1972 dollars)	4483	4536	4468	4513	4457	4367	4411
Percentage change	−0.47	1.18	−1.50	1.00	−1.25	−2.00	1.00
Consumer price index (end of year)	258.4	281.5	311.1	345.3	393.6	442.8	492.6
Percentage change	12.40	8.94	10.50	11.00	14.00	12.50	11.25
Employment	90,834	91,350	90,863	90,382	90,783	89,826	89,709
Unemployment rate	7.10	7.60	9.40	9.84	9.70	10.27	9.93
Interest Rates (percentages)							
Prime rate	15.27	18.87	19.00	17.50	20.00	21.50	16.00
91-day Treasury bills	11.51	14.08	15.50	16.25	16.00	17.50	15.00
AAA bond loans	11.94	14.17	16.00	15.00	15.50	16.00	15.75
Savings and loans (average funds cost)	8.88	10.81	11.57	11.71	11.67	12.15	11.50
Commercial banks	9.00	10.34	11.05	10.83	11.30	12.05	10.80
Mortgage rates							
Commitments:							
Federal Home Loan Bank Board	14.00	16.70	17.44	16.96	17.10	17.72	17.14
Federal National Mortgage Association	14.43	16.64	18.11	17.76	17.87	18.63	17.77
Federal Home Loan Mortgage Corporation	13.63	16.47	17.36	17.13	17.19	17.93	17.04
Closings:							
Federal Home Loan Bank Board	12.65	14.75	16.33	16.97	17.20	17.82	17.24

TABLE 3 (Continued)

	ACTUAL		FORECAST				
FORECAST	1980	1981	1982	1983	1984	1985	1986
Housing Starts (units in thousands)							
Single family							
Detached	774.00	587.92	470.01	504.87	473.79	475.36	778.44
Attached	78.00	118.18	124.67	137.18	133.28	137.79	184.09
Public	2.30	1.40	1.50	1.50	1.50	1.50	1.50
Total	854.50	707.50	596.17	643.55	608.57	614.66	964.03
Multifamily							
2-4 units	109.50	91.60	82.93	73.91	59.31	54.33	75.61
5+ lowrise	260.90	239.52	235.79	268.92	323.28	256.12	324.07
5+ highrise	69.60	49.38	46.75	69.21	118.41	52.36	70.11
Public	18.17	14.70	10.00	5.00	5.00	5.00	5.00
Total	458.17	395.20	375.47	417.05	506.00	367.81	474.79
Total starts	1312.67	1102.70	971.64	1060.59	1114.57	982.47	1438.82
Mobile home placements	228.60	225.00	199.37	208.71	285.49	254.97	284.44
Sales of existing homes	2881	2347	2097	2291	2368	2463	3159

TABLE 4
OPTIMISTIC FORECAST

ASSUMPTIONS	ACTUAL 1980	ACTUAL 1981	FORECAST 1982	FORECAST 1983	FORECAST 1984	FORECAST 1985	FORECAST 1986
Economic Indicators							
Personal income per capita (dollars)	9522	10,341	11,287	12,338	13,447	14,615	15,856
Percentage change	10.25	8.60	9.15	9.31	8.99	8.69	8.49
Disposable income per capita (1972 dollars)	4483	4536	4684	4834	4983	5133	5287
Percentage change	-0.47	1.18	3.25	3.20	3.10	3.00	3.00
Consumer price index (end of year)	258.4	281.5	301.9	323.0	345.0	367.8	391.3
Percentage change	12.40	8.94	7.25	7.00	6.80	6.60	6.40
Employment	90,834	91,350	92,491	95,477	98,702	102,092	105,710
Unemployment rate	7.10	7.60	8.13	7.04	5.88	4.95	4.14
Interest Rates (percentages)							
Prime rate	15.27	18.87	13.00	11.00	9.20	9.10	9.00
91-day Treasury bills	11.51	14.08	9.70	8.00	7.80	7.60	7.30
AAA bond loans	11.94	14.17	12.00	11.00	9.60	9.50	9.40
Savings and loans (average funds cost)	8.88	10.81	8.85	8.22	8.03	8.05	8.05
Commercial banks	9.00	10.34	8.15	6.70	7.20	7.10	6.95
Mortgage rates							
Commitments:							
Federal Home Loan Bank Board	14.00	16.70	14.50	13.10	12.11	11.79	11.67
Federal National Mortgage Association	14.43	16.64	14.58	13.11	12.17	11.86	11.72
Federal Home Loan Mortgage Corporation	13.63	16.47	14.09	12.72	11.94	11.66	11.51
Closings:							
Federal Home Loan Bank Board	12.65	14.75	14.39	13.20	12.21	11.83	11.57

TABLE 4 (Continued)

	ACTUAL		FORECAST				
FORECAST	1980	1981	1982	1983	1984	1985	1986
Housing Starts (units in thousands)							
Single family							
Detached	774.00	587.92	1052.86	1192.12	1256.43	1291.27	1308.02
Attached	78.00	118.18	184.53	179.84	169.08	165.91	166.18
Public	2.30	1.40	1.50	1.50	1.50	1.50	1.50
Total	854.50	707.50	1238.88	1373.47	1427.01	1458.68	1475.70
Multifamily							
2-4 units	109.50	91.60	125.43	137.79	136.87	138.56	140.29
5+ lowrise	260.90	239.52	240.48	333.74	412.28	350.08	418.11
5+ highrise	69.60	49.38	21.96	67.99	128.70	91.73	148.04
Public	18.17	14.70	10.00	5.00	5.00	5.00	5.00
Total	458.17	395.20	397.87	544.52	682.84	585.36	711.44
Total starts	1312.67	1102.70	1636.75	1917.99	2109.86	2044.04	2187.14
Mobile home placements	228.60	225.00	208.43	258.39	366.21	362.71	408.08

TABLE 5
MOST LIKELY FORECAST

ASSUMPTIONS	ACTUAL 1980	ACTUAL 1981	FORECAST 1982	FORECAST 1983	FORECAST 1984	FORECAST 1985	FORECAST 1986
Economic Indicators							
Gross national product, percentage change (1972 dollars—real)	–0.2	2.0	–1.2	2.6	3.3	3.0	1.9
Real disposable income per capita, percentage change (1972 dollars—real)	–0.5	1.2	1.0	2.8	3.2	3.3	2.1
Consumer price index, percentage change	13.6	10.1	6.0	5.6	7.0	8.4	9.5
Unemployment rate	7.1	7.6	9.2	8.8	8.5	7.8	8.0
Interest Rates (percentages)							
Prime rate	15.3	18.9	14.0	11.0	10.0	12.0	15.0
91-day Treasury bills	11.6	14.0	10.8	9.2	8.0	10.0	12.0
AAA bond loans	11.9	14.1	13.0	11.0	10.4	11.5	13.0

TABLE 5 (Continued)

	ACTUAL		FORECAST				
FORECAST	1980	1981	1982	1983	1984	1985	1986
Housing Starts (units in thousands)							
U.S. total	1292	1084	1182	1496	1787	1767	1515
Single family	852	706	763	990	1131	1145	970
Multifamily	440	378	420	506	656	622	545
Northeast	125	117	137	188	181	177	150
Single family	87	84	98	141	116	118	99
Multifamily	38	33	39	47	65	59	51
North Central	218	166	178	260	289	286	243
Single family	142	110	105	146	191	195	164
Multifamily	76	56	73	114	98	91	79
South	643	562	604	679	858	835	721
Single family	428	363	391	455	551	545	466
Multifamily	215	199	213	225	397	290	255
West	306	240	264	369	459	469	401
Single family	196	148	169	249	273	287	241
Multifamily	110	92	95	120	186	182	160

(text continued on page 54)

years of housing starts at over 2 million units, for a total of 9.9 million units for the five-year period. Further, it suggests a strong recovery for 1982, with 1.6 million housing starts.

Most likely forecast

This forecast, shown in Table 5, assumes a slow economic growth in 1982, with the Gross National Product (GNP) declining about 1.2 percent, but with an improvement in 1983 and beyond. Inflation will moderate to below 6 percent, but unemployment will stay high, getting only just below the 8 percent level. Interest rates will decline, and the prime rate will not fall below 10 percent but will actually increase in 1986, as we face another economic decline in 1986-87. This scenario gives us a peak housing year of 1.8 million units in 1984, and a total of 7.7 million housing starts for the five-year period.

REGIONAL DISTRIBUTION

As Table 6 shows, the most likely scenario suggests a recovery in the West, and in the next five years the West's share of total housing starts should reach 25.3 percent. In the 1980-81 period, starts in the West declined sharply to a 23 percent share. The South will still remain the dominant factor in housing production, with close to 48 percent of all new housing starts. In the past two years, this region accounted for 50.7 percent of all new starts. The North Central region will capture about the same share—16.2 percent—as it has in the past two years. The Northeast region will improve slightly, from 10.1 to 10.7 percent.

Comparison with other five-year periods

Table 7 shows a comparison with all postwar five-year periods by type of unit started. It shows that the most likely scenario is not inconsistent with what has happened in the past. In the eight five-year periods—the production for 1982, 1983, and 1984 is estimated—we started 58.627 million private units, or an average of 7.3 million units per period. The lowest period was 1945-49, when we built only 5.4 million units; the highest period was 1970-74, with 9.3 million units. So forecasting 7.7 million units—or 7.8 million, if we add public housing—for the five-year period 1982-86 does not seem unreasonable in light of past activity.

Of all private production—there is no breakdown available by type of structure for all units including public, only for private starts—single-family units accounted for 73 percent, or 42.762 million new units. This gives us an average of 5.3 million units every five years, and our forecast calls for close to 5 million units in a five-year period. The peak in singles was reached in the 1950-54 period, with 6.9 million starts; the second peak was in the 1975-79 period, with 6.1 million starts.

The multifamily sector has shown a great deal of volatility, starting with only 591,000 units during the five-year period 1945-49 and reaching a peak of nearly 4 million units during the 1970-74 period. A 2.7 million five-year forecast seems reasonable and, of course, depends on the assumption that interest rates will decline. The multifamily sector will be helped by sharply increased rents and a general shortage of rental units.

TABLE 6
REGIONAL DISTRIBUTION OF TOTAL NEW HOUSING STARTS, ACTUAL STARTS FOR 1980-81 AND MOST LIKELY FORECAST FOR 1982-86
(units in thousands)

REGION	ACTUAL 1980-81		FORECAST 1982-86	
	Starts	Percentage	Starts	Percentage
Northeast	242	10.1	833	10.7
North Central	384	16.2	1256	16.2
South	1205	50.7	3697	47.7
West	546	23.0	1962	25.3
Total	2377	100.0	7748	100.0

TABLE 7
U.S. HOUSING STARTS BY FIVE-YEAR INTERVALS, WITH PROJECTIONS TO 1986 (units in thousands)

YEARS	TOTAL, PUBLIC AND PRIVATE	PRIVATE		
		TOTAL	SINGLE FAMILY	MULTIFAMILY
1945-49	5445	5379	4788	591
1950-54	7936	7709	6916	793
1955-59	7155	6957	5951	1006
1960-64	7349	7160	4943	2217
1965-69	7073	6904	4297	2607
1970-74	9344	9226	5293	3933
1975-79	8516	8450	6132	2318
1980-84	6940	6842	4442	2400
Total 1945-84	59,758	58,627	42,762	15,865
1982-86*	7850	7747	4999	2749

SOURCE: Bureau of the Census; NAHB Forecasting Service.
*From most likely scenario, Table 5.

A RATIONALE FOR THE FORECAST

As with any long-term forecast, this one is based on the ability of the economy to recover from the current recession and on the strength of underlying demand. Underlying demand is the result of the increase in population, the need to replace lost housing, desire for second homes, and the need to increase production if we want to keep the vacancy rate at about the same level.

Population

The Population Division of the Bureau of the Census tells us that on the average we will have about 1.6 million new household formations during this decade. The type of household, however, is quite different from those of the past.

First, the size has decreased to 2.7 persons per household for 1982; in 1970, it was 3.1 persons. Second, 27 percent are nonfamily households, not the traditional married couple

TABLE 8
AGE OF HOUSING INVENTORY, 1980 (units in thousands)

	OWNER-OCCUPIED		RENTER-OCCUPIED	
AGE	UNITS	PERCENTAGE	UNITS	PERCENTAGE
10 years or less	12,568	24.0	5646	20.5
10-15 years	5800	11.0	3110	11.3
15-20 years	5427	10.3	2416	8.7
20-30 years	10,158	19.3	3269	11.9
30-40 years	4884	9.3	2546	9.2
40 years or more	13,680	26.1	10,569	38.4
Total	52,517	100.0	27,556	100.0

SOURCE: U.S. Department of Commerce, Bureau of the Census, *Annual Housing Survey: 1980*, Part A, Table A-1 (Washington, DC: Government Printing Office), pp. 1, 2.

households. The Census Bureau also tells us that the peak of the postwar baby boom is yet to come. This means that the 29-32 age group that typically buys homes is at the edge of that demand. Moreover, it is no longer possible for many young women to wait to have children. It is coming to the now-or-never point; and instead of three, four, or more children, it is more likely to be one or two. This group always prefers homeowning to renting. But those who delay marriage and live independently tend to opt for short-term rent-lease arrangements.

We cannot accept the defeatist notion that private industry will not be responsive enough to provide attractive units for this segment of our population. Need can be translated into demand simply by giving the consumer more affordable housing and by making it possible to finance these units—even if interest rates stay higher than they have been since the postwar period.

Housing losses

We lose about 1 percent of the housing inventory each year. With over 88 million year-round housing units, this would suggest a loss of about 880,000 units per year. However, any recession—coupled with the inability of people to move because of high interest rates—causes the net removal rate to drop substantially. Even if we assume a drop of, say, 0.7 percent or even 0.5 percent, that still means that at least 400,000 units are being taken out of the inventory, and these should be replaced. Older cities and older units have much higher losses than new towns or subdivisions.

Table 8 shows the age of the housing inventory as of 1980. Over 38 percent of the rentals are 40 years old or older, and over 26 percent of the owner-occupied units are at least 40 years old, for a total of more than 24 million units. Many of these are demolished each year, particularly in the central cities.

Second homes and vacant units

The demand for second homes has been estimated at somewhere between 80,000 and 120,000 units annually. As long as the economy does not fall apart, this demand will undoubtedly continue.

As for vacant units, we currently have over 6 million. Of these, about 1.5 million are for rent and about 800,000 are for sale. The rest, about 3 million units, are divided equally between "vacant units held for occasional use" and "other vacant." Vacant units are important, as they provide the means for people to move. The rental vacancy rate has been declining steadily for the past 20 years, from a peak of 8.5 percent in 1965 to 5 percent. The vacancy rate for owners also peaked in 1965 at 1.7 percent, but it was as low as 0.9 percent in 1978 and currently is 1.4 percent.

Since the total number of housing units is increasing each year by about 1.8 million units, it takes more vacant units to keep the vacancy rate at the same level. For instance, in the past decade we increased the number of vacant units by 1.7 million, or 170,000 units each year, yet the rental rate dropped sharply from 6.6 percent to 5.1 percent, and the owner vacancy rate increased slightly from 1.2 percent to 1.4 percent.

When you add all this together, the forecast for each year of the 1980s looks like this:

TABLE 9
HOUSING NEEDS FOR THE 1980s (units in thousands)

	HIGH	LOW
New household formations	1600	1200
Net removals	800	400
Vacancies	150	100
Second homes	100	50
Total	2650	1750

ANNALS, *AAPSS*, **465**, January 1983

The Crisis in Rental Housing: A Canadian Perspective

By LAWRENCE B. SMITH

ABSTRACT: Concern has recently been raised in the United States and Canada about a growing crisis in rental housing. Since many of the issues raised in connection with the possibility of a U.S. crisis have surfaced earlier or in magnified form in Canada, this article examines the question of a rental housing crisis from the Canadian perspective. The article begins with a discussion of the background of the rental crisis and an examination of the pre-1972 tax preferences for rental housing. Evolution of the crisis is then analyzed, focusing on the 1972 restructuring of the tax system, expectations of accelerating inflation, government support for competing housing forms, and rent control. The impact of high interest rates on the decline in rental construction and changes in the socioeconomic composition of tenants and in the affordability of rental housing are also discussed. The article concludes with an analysis of the outlook for rental housing.

Lawrence B. Smith is professor of economics, Department of Political Economy, University of Toronto. He has a B.Com. from the University of Toronto and an A.M. and a Ph.D. from Harvard University. He has written widely in the fields of monetary economics, housing and land economics, and public policy. Professor Smith has acted as a consultant for a number of private corporations and government agencies, and recently served as deputy chairman of the Federal Task Force on Canada Mortgage and Housing Corporation.

NOTE: The research for this article was partially funded by the Social Sciences and Humanities Research Council of Canada, Research Award 451-81-2999.

CONCERN has been raised recently in the United States and Canada about a growing crisis in rental housing. This concern has been triggered by a number of factors. During the last decade and a half, the national vacancy ratio declined from 8.25 percent to 5.0 percent in the United States, and from 5.7 percent to 1.2 percent in Canada. Between 1973-74 and 1980-81, private multifamily dwelling starts declined 40 percent in the United States and 77 percent in Canada, and during the 1970s, the rent-to-income ratio of renter households rose from .21 to .25 in the United States[1] and from .18 to .22 in Canada.[2]

Citing the American data, the U.S. General Accounting Office asserted in 1979 that the United States was in a rental housing crisis.[3] On the other hand, at a 1980 conference sponsored by the Office of Policy Development and Research, the U.S. Department of Housing and Urban Development, the majority of participants disputed this assertion. They suggested instead that the rental housing market was simply adjusting to changing economic influences,[4] primarily in taxation and the perception of inflation.

Since many of the issues central to the U.S. debate have surfaced earlier or in magnified form in Canada, this article examines the question of a rental housing crisis in Canada. Because of the similarities in institutional structures, government programs, household aspirations, and economic, demographic, and social trends, Canadian experience is highly relevant for the U.S. debate.[5]

THE RENTAL HOUSING CRISIS IN HISTORICAL CONTEXT

To understand the current state of the rental housing market in Canada, it is necessary to place it in historical perspective. At the end of the 1960s, Canada was extremely well housed. Canada ranked first in the Western world in terms of number of rooms per dwelling, was tied for first with the United States for the

1. Ira S. Lowry, "Rental Housing in the 1970s: Searching for the Crisis," in *Rental Housing: Is There a Crisis?* eds. J.C. Weicher, K.E. Villani, and E.A. Roistacher (Washington, DC: Urban Institute Press, 1981), p. 32. This increase is disputed by Kenneth T. Rosen, "The Affordability of Housing in 1980 and Beyond," Center for Real Estate and Urban Economics Working Paper 80-10, Institute for Business and Economic Research, University of California, Berkeley, p. 11.

2. This is probably overstated. The 1972 figure is from Michael A. Walker, "What Are the Facts?" in *Rent Control a Popular Paradox*, eds. F.A. Hayek et al. (Vancouver: Fraser Institute, 1975), p. 29. The 1980 figure is based on average head of household income in 1979 from the HIFE tape increased by 5 percent and compared to the average of all household rents for Apr. 1980, as supplied by the Canada Mortgage and Housing Corporation. Since households often have income in addition to that of the head, the 1980 ratio and hence the increase is overstated.

3. U.S. General Accounting Office, *Rental Housing: A National Problem that Needs Immediate Action*, Report to the Congress by the Comptroller General, CED-80-11, 8 Nov. 1979.

4. Elizabeth A. Roistacher, "Introduction," in *Rental Housing: Is There a Crisis?* p. 10, and other articles in this volume.

5. Although the conversion of rental apartments to condominiums is a major aspect of the U.S. market, it is of little significance in Canada and thus is not discussed in this article. The lack of such conversions may be explained in large part by federal and some provincial housing programs which heavily subsidized the construction of new low- and moderate-priced condominiums, making private condominium conversions relatively unattractive, and by widespread local by-laws prohibiting such conversions.

lowest occupancy and crowding densities, and was second to the United States in the provision of basic facilities. The percentage of families not maintaining their own households was a relatively low 3.4 percent in 1971, and the percentage of dwellings occupied by nonfamily households was a relatively high 18.4 percent.[6]

These accomplishments were achieved to a large extent through the vigor of the private multiple-dwelling sector, as rental apartment starts accounted for 47 percent of all housing starts between 1963 and 1970, and 85 percent of these were private nongovernment-assisted starts. At the beginning of the 1970s, private apartment vacancies were a relatively high 5.0 percent. Nevertheless, it was clear to some observers that a cost-expense-rent squeeze was looming and that a sharp reduction in private multiple rental starts was likely unless rents were to rise substantially.[7] On the other hand, it was feared that such a rise would generate intensified pressure for rent control and that this would lead to a rental housing crisis.[8]

Although Canadian housing standards continued to improve throughout most of the 1970s, the engine of growth shifted from the private rental sector to the government-supported homeownership sector and the public rental sector.[9] In contrast to the 1960s, private nongovernment rental construction declined steadily throughout the 1970s, and by 1980-81, private rental starts had fallen to 10 percent of total starts. In 1981, private rental completions were less than 20,000 or only 1.5 percent of the existing private rental apartment stock,[10] and the national vacancy rate in private rental dwellings of six or more units was only 1.2 percent. Moreover, a number of major cities, such as Calgary, Halifax, Ottawa, Toronto, and Vancouver, had vacancy rates below 1.0 percent. The severity of the crisis in rental housing is thus clearly indicated by the simultaneous lack of rental vacancies and private rental starts.

This current state of the rental housing sector is in sharp contrast to the extremely vigorous nature of the rental housing sector in the 1960s, when rental housing was supported by a favorable tax structure and increasingly positive demographics.

Pre-1972 tax preferences for investment in rental housing

Prior to the 1972 restructuring of the tax system, the tax structure was relatively favorable for housing, especially for investment in rental housing. Homeownership

6. For an elaboration of this, see Lawrence B. Smith, *Anatomy of a Crisis: Canadian Housing Policy in the Seventies* (Vancouver: Fraser Institute, 1977), p. 14.

7. Lawrence B. Smith, *Housing in Canada: Market Structure and Policy Performance* (Ottawa: Canada Mortgage and Housing Corporation, 1971), p. 16.

8. Ibid., p. 18.

9. For a discussion of this shift, see Lawrence B. Smith, "Canadian Housing Policy in the Seventies," *Land Economics*, 57(3):338-58 (Aug. 1981).

10. The number of rental apartment completions is likely overestimated, since the final tenure form of some units could be changed before occupancy to condominium status.

benefited from the absence of taxes both on capital gains and on imputed net rent—the net rent a homeowner would receive if a home were rented rather than occupied by the owner. The effect of these benefits was relatively modest, however, because capital gains on other assets were not taxed, housing expenses—such as mortgage interest and property tax—were not tax deductible, and inflation was not anticipated to be high.

Rental housing, on the other hand, benefited substantially from tax incentives, because capital cost allowances—depreciation—were in excess of true economic depreciation, rollover provisions enabled the postponement of recaptured depreciation on the sale of an investment property, capital gains were not taxed, book losses were deductible against other income—which enabled a tax sheltering of other income—and special tax treatment was provided on death. These investment incentives increased the equilibrium stock of rental housing and, although they were primarily for rental housing, lowered the user cost of housing in both the rental and homeownership sectors.[11]

When tax concessions are provided for investment in rental housing, they increase the desirability of such investments. This is depicted in Figure 1 by a shift in the supply curve of rental housing from SR-SR to SR′-SR′. This shift in the supply curve lowers rents from R° to R′, since the price of rental housing services is determined by the intersection of the rental supply curve with the demand curve for rental housing DR-DR. Since the relative price of homeownership is an important component in the tenure choice decision, lower rents encourage households to change their demand from homeownership to rental housing, and thus the homeownership demand curve D-D shifts to the left to D′-D′ when rents in the rental sector decline from R° to R′. The slope of the rental demand curve reflects both this shift in homeownership demand and the increase in net new housing demand associated with the lower rent. This shift in demand lowers the nominal price of housing from P° to P′, and thereby lowers the user cost of homeownership, since mortgage costs, property taxes, and the opportunity cost of equity funds fall with the decline in the nominal price of housing.

Tax concessions for investment in rental housing also alter the allocation of resources both between housing and the rest of the economy and within the housing sector itself. Since relative after-tax investment yields are increased for rental housing and after-tax user costs of housing are reduced, the total demand for housing increases, and the equilibrium stock of housing increases. Within the housing sector, the equilibrium rental housing stock increases from HR° to HR′, and the equilibrium homeownership stock declines from H° to H′. Thus a tax structure which provides significant relative tax benefits for investment in rental housing increases the equilibrium stock of rental housing and lowers user costs of both rental and homeownership housing services.

Since the pre-1972 tax preferences for housing had long been an integral part of the Canadian tax

11. Offsets to the decline in user costs would occur if the fall in the price of houses generates expectations of future price declines and/or if the higher equilibrium demand for housing raises the mortgage yield/bond yield spread, reducing the decline in mortgage costs and the opportunity cost of homeowner equity.

FIGURE 1
INTERACTION OF RENTAL AND OWNERSHIP HOUSING MARKETS

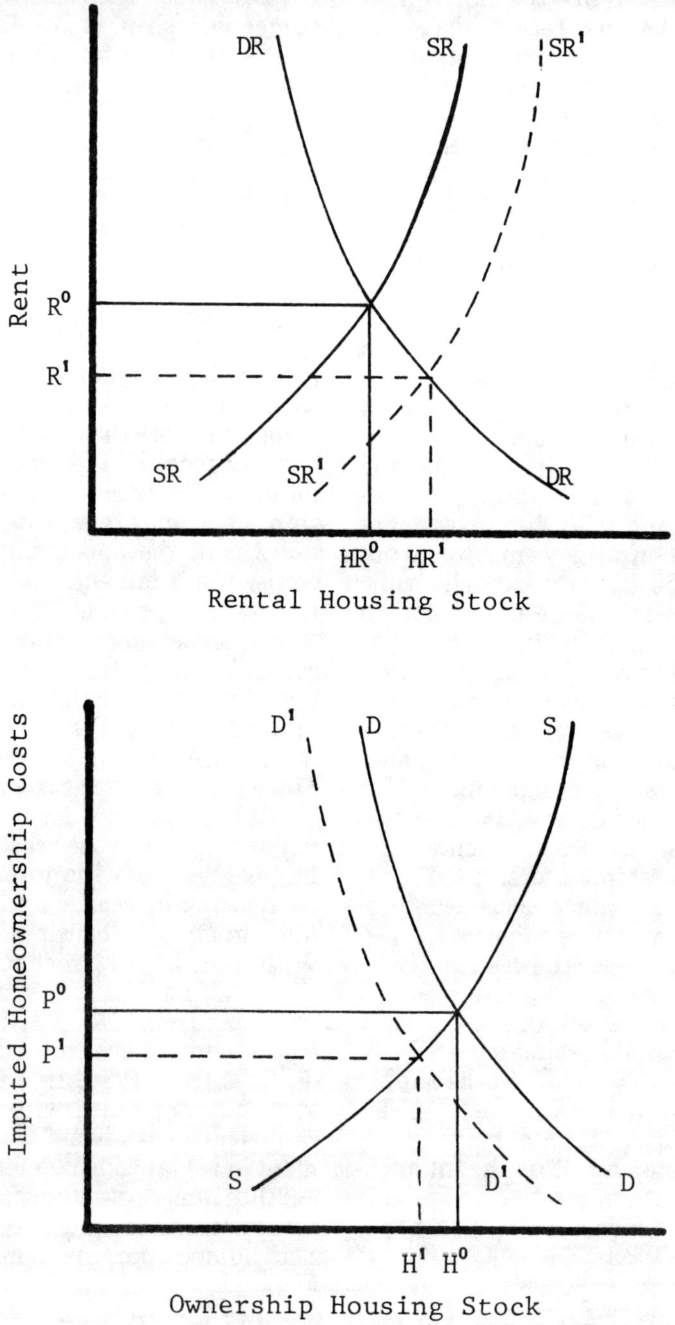

system, housing and financial markets had adjusted to these preferences and were reflected in the housing stock and new residential construction activity in the 1960s.

Demographic changes and the rental construction boom

In the late 1960s, these tax preferences, expectations of rising inflation, and the growing realization that profound, favorable demographic changes were occurring interacted to generate a construction boom in rental housing. Between 1968 and 1971, new construction of rental apartments rose to 103,100 units annually, or 50 percent of total housing starts, up from 67,600 units, or 43 percent in the preceding five years. Moreover, despite the adverse tax changes of 1972, multiple rental starts remained strong in the early 1970s. This strength was partially in response to the continuation of favorable demographics for rental housing,[12] primarily the coming of age of the postwar babies, the sharp rise in the divorce rate, and the steep decline in the birth rate. These forces combined to increase annual net household formation 59 percent between 1961-66 and 1966-76 and annual net nonfamily household formation 84 percent between 1961-66 and 1966-76.

Nevertheless, despite the strength of the underlying demographic forces, the extraordinary boom in rental housing construction increased vacancies and suppressed rents in the early 1970s.[13] This suppression in rents, together with the increasing awareness that the demographic forces favorable to rental housing would soon peak and decline, set the stage in the mid-1970s for a downward adjustment in new rental construction.[14]

EVOLUTION OF THE CRISIS

The downward adjustment in new rental construction was converted from a normal market correlation to a complete collapse by four major structural shifts: the 1972 restructuring of the tax system, the growing perception that inflation would persist and probably accelerate, the shift in public policy away from private rental housing in favor of nonmarket rental housing and homeownership housing, and the imposition of rent control.

Revisions to the tax structure

The Canadian tax structure underwent a major revision in 1972, and a number of changes had a profound impact on housing. From a housing viewpoint, the most important revisions were these:

—the introduction of a capital gains tax on realized gains on all financial and real assets, except for a principal residence;

—the termination of rollover provisions enabling the postpone-

12. Other forces maintaining the high level of multiple rental starts include the long planning and preconstruction lags, rising inflationary expectations, and a low real mortgage rate.

13. For a discussion of the relationship between vacancies and rents, and of the natural vacancy rate, see Lawrence B. Smith, "A Note on the Price Adjustment Mechanism for Rental Housing," *American Economic Review*, 63(3):478-81 (June 1974).

14. For example, the net change in the number of households in the 15-34 age bracket—the primary group for rental housing demand—declined from an annual average of 116,500 in 1971-76 to 90,100 in 1976-81 and is expected to fall to 62,100 in 1981-86.

ment of recaptured depreciation on the disposition of a depreciable asset above depreciated value;

—the elimination of paper losses in real estate as deductions against non-real-estate income for tax purposes—that is, the elimination of investment real estate as a tax shelter; and

—the deemed realization on death of part of the gain on real estate, other than a principal residence.

These changes significantly increased the relative attractiveness of homeownership and reduced the relative attractiveness of rental housing investment, especially in an increasingly inflationary environment.

Homeownership incentives. The introduction of a capital gains tax on all assets except a principal residence conferred a substantial tax benefit on homeowners, since homeownership became the only vehicle by which a nontaxable capital gain could be realized. In 1979, this benefit was estimated to be $2.5 billion in the form of government tax expenditures[15]—that is, lost government revenue as a result of the differential tax treatment of the realized gains on the sale of principal residences from the gains on other capital assets. In addition, as discussed in the following, the benefit of the nontaxation of imputed net rent rose considerably as a result of inflation, and in 1979 this benefit was estimated to be $3.7 billion.[16] As a result, the relative desirability of homeownership as opposed to renting increased considerably.

Disincentive for investment in rental housing. The elimination of the tax loss features of real estate investment, the recapture and treatment as income of accumulated depreciation on the disposition of a property, the deemed realization on death of part of the gain on real estate, and the imposition of the capital gains tax substantially reduced the attractiveness of investment in rental properties by reducing the aftertax yield and the liquidity of real estate investments.

The most significant of these changes were the elimination of the tax shelter and rollover provisions. The capital gains tax, while reducing the desirability of residential rental investment, had a smaller effect than might be imagined, because all major equity investments, other than a principal residence, were similarly treated.[17] On the other hand, the elimination of the tax shelter was considered so important that in December 1974, the government reversed its position and temporarily reallowed losses on new multiunit residential buildings (MURBs) for which construction was started within a specified period to be applied against other income. This MURB provision was extended annually until the end of 1979, when it was terminated for new construction. It reappeared for one year in 1981.

15. Government of Canada, Department of Finance, *Government of Canada Tax Expenditure Accounts* (Ottawa: Queen's Printer, 1979), p. 43.

16. Ibid.

17. However, it discouraged equity investment vis-à-vis debt investment because a higher proportion of the total yield in equities was in the form of capital gain.

The effects of these changes for homeownership and investment in rental housing are demonstrated in Figure 2. The tax concessions for homeownership shift the homeownership demand curve to the right, from D-D to D′-D′, and the rental demand curve to the left, from DR-DR to DR′-DR′, as some renters are induced to switch their tenure form. These shifts raise the imputed before-tax user cost of homeownership from P° to P′ as nominal home prices, and possibly the mortgage rate, are bid up, but lower the imputed after-tax user costs of homeownership from P° to P^2, assuming the tax benefits are $P'P^2$.[18] The reduction in rental demand lowers rents in the rental sector from R° to R′ and reduces the equilibrium stock of rental housing to HR′. The reduction in tax incentives for investment in rental housing shifts the supply curve of rental housing to the left and further reduces the equilibrium stock of rental housing to HR^2. In the longer run this adjustment in the supply will cause rents to move upward to R^2. Nevertheless, by increasing the relative attractiveness of homeownership—the shift in the demand curve to DR′-DR′—and reducing incentives for investment in rental housing—the shift in the supply curve to SR′-SR′—the 1972 tax revisions significantly reduced the desirability of rental investment and reduced the equilibrium stock of rental housing—from HR° to HR^2 in Figure 2.[19]

18. This representation is not strictly correct, since it is relative rather than absolute after-tax costs which fall as a result of the comparative gain in the investment aspect of homeownership arising from the increased tax on alternative assets.

19. Other tax changes in the 1970s reinforced this. These changes included the introduction of Registered Home Ownership Savings Plans to encourage homeownership, and the capitalization for tax purposes of some development and carrying costs associated with real estate development.

Increasing inflationary expectations

During the late 1960s and early 1970s, the perception grew that inflation was becoming institutionalized in the Canadian economy[20] and that it was likely to accelerate. This perception significantly altered household preferences for homeownership and, to a lesser extent, investor preferences for rental housing.[21]

Anticipation of accelerating inflation affects the tenure decision, both by changing the expected relative user cost of housing independent of the tax system, and by interacting with the tax system to increase the relative benefits of tax preferences for homeownership.

Independent of the tax system. The expected user costs of homeowner-

20. This is reflected in the indexation of the income tax in 1974.

21. For a discussion of user costs and inflation in the tenure choice decision, see Douglas B. Diamond, Jr., "A Note on Inflation and Relative Tenure Prices," *Journal of the American Real Estate and Urban Economics Association,* 6(3):438-50 (Winter 1978); Patric H. Hendershott, "Real User Costs and the Demand for Single-Family Housing," in *Brookings Papers on Economic Activity, 1980,* 2, eds. W.C. Brainard and G.L. Perry (Washington, DC: Brookings Institution, 1981), pp. 401-44; Patric H. Hendershott and Sheng-Cheng Hu, "Inflation and Extraordinary Returns on Owner-Occupied Housing: Some Implications for Capital Allocation and Productivity Growth," in *House Prices and Inflation,* eds. J.A. Tuccillo and K.E. Villani (Washington, DC: Urban Institute Press, 1981), pp. 11-33; and Harvey S. Rosen and Kenneth T. Rosen, "Federal Taxes and Homeownership: Evidence from Time Series," *Journal of Political Economy,* 88(1):59-79 (Feb. 1980).

FIGURE 2
IMPACT OF TAX CHANGES ON HOMEOWNERSHIP AND RENTAL HOUSING INVESTMENT

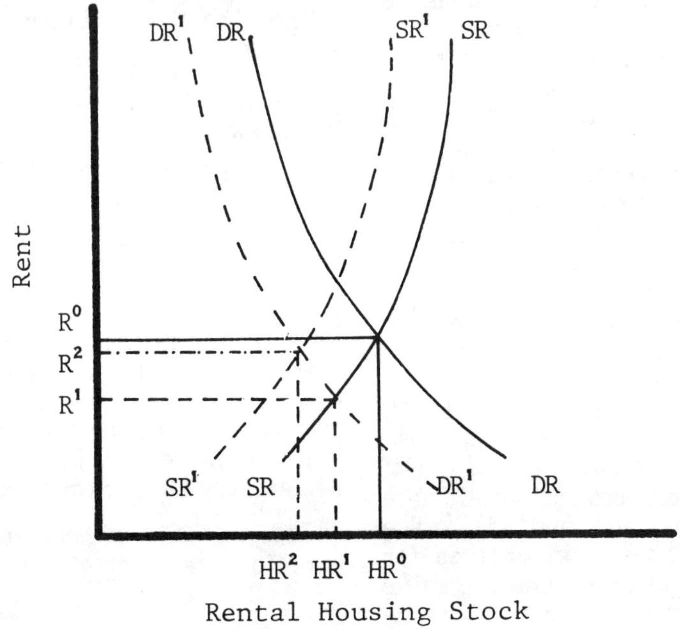

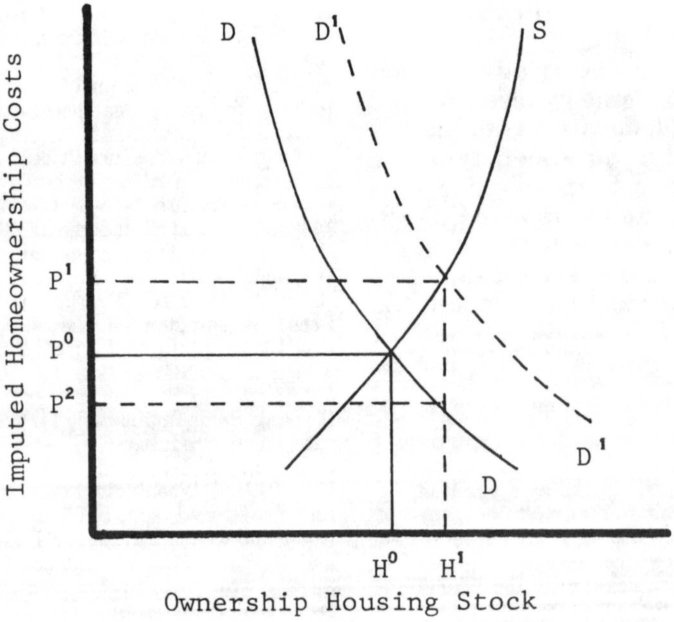

ship in Canada (UCH) may be defined over any time period as

$$UCH = O + M + D + (E)(i)(1\text{-}t) - \Delta^e PH \quad [1]$$

where O represents expected operating costs, M represents expected mortgage interest, D represents expected house depreciation, (E) (i) (1-t) represents the expected after-tax (1-t) foregone interest (i) on homeowner equity (E), and Δ^e PH represents the expected capital appreciation of the house from its depreciated value.[22] An increase in anticipated inflation thus affects expected user costs immediately by increasing Δ^e PH and O, which lowers UCH, since PH > O.

Higher anticipated inflation will, with a lag, be reflected in higher nominal interest rates,[23] which raise both the mortgage costs and foregone interest costs on homeowner equity. Under the assumption that both the nominal rate of interest and price of homes increase by the rate of inflation—that is, the expected rate becomes the realized rate and is fully incorporated with no tax or other premiums—the increase in interest rates will fully offset the increase in the price of the home for new homebuyers and existing owners with variable rate mortgages; and expected user costs will increase by the increase in expected operating costs and depreciation.[24]

Since operating costs and depreciation are typically less than the cost of renting equivalent housing services, if rents, operating costs, and depreciation all rise in proportion—that is, with inflation—for any anticipated positive inflation, the expected user costs of homeownership will rise less than the expected increase in the cost of renting equivalent housing services. This will increase the relative demand for homeownership and increase home prices, until the increase in user costs associated with the rise in home prices restores the user homeownership-rental cost balance, assuming housing and mortgage markets operate perfectly.

In reality, imperfections in the home finance market associated with the level payment mortgage impede the full price adjustment, as the tilt problem increases early-year real mortgage payments and prevents many households from qualifying for mortgage credit.[25]

22. This expression is simpler than the equivalent expression for the United States. The U.S. expression must recognize the tax deductibility of mortgage interest and property taxes, the taxability of capital gains subject to possible deferment via a home rollover, and the tax exemption on the first $125,000 of capital gain for persons over 55.

23. For evidence of this in Canada, see Jack L. Carr and Lawrence B. Smith, "Money Supply, Interest Rates and the Yield Curve," *Journal of Money, Credit, and Banking,* 4(3):582-94 (Aug. 1972); and Jack L. Carr, James E. Pesando, and Lawrence B. Smith, "Tax Effects, Price Expectations and the Nominal Rate of Interest," *Economic Inquiry,* 14(2):259-69 (June 1976).

24. This occurs since the sum of the mortgage and homeowner equity equals the value of the home. However, this ignores a number of effects, such as the tilt or cash-flow problem and possible increase in the variance in the expected house price inflation as inflation increases, which affect housing demand and may cause user costs to rise by restraining the actual and expected increase in house prices.

25. The tilt problem arises from an increase in the anticipated inflation rate because increased inflation affects the level of interest rates but only the rate of change of household income. As a result, although increased inflation does not alter the present value of future mortgage payments, it changes the time profile of real mortgage payments, increasing the income-to-payment ratio in the early years and reducing it in later years. For a discussion of this effect, see

Nevertheless, an increase in the anticipated rate of inflation will lower the preadjustment relative user cost of homeownership, and tenure choice will shift in favor of homeownership. This reduces the demand for rental accommodation and further weakens the rental housing sector.

Interacting with the tax system. The increase in the relative attractiveness of homeownership arising from an increase in the anticipated rate of inflation is reinforced by tax preferences for homeownership.[26] Higher inflation increases the benefits of the exemption from capital gains tax and of the nontaxation of imputed net rent. The latter benefit rises because the increase in the imputed net rent arising from inflation is not taxed, while the increase in income necessary to pay the higher cost of equivalent housing is taxed. Thus the after-tax increase in income necessary to enable an existing homeowner to maintain the same housing services equals the increase in operating costs—assuming mortgage costs are fixed—while the after-tax increase in income necessary to enable an existing tenant to rent the same housing services equals the full increase in gross rent. Consequently, the proportion of household income devoted to shelter falls for an existing homeowner relative to an existing tenant as a result of inflation,[27] and in anticipation of this, tenants are induced to shift their desired tenure form away from rental housing.

Since accelerating inflation increases the relative attractiveness of homeownership compared to renting, especially when it interacts with existing tax preferences for homeownership, expectations of accelerating inflation shift housing demand from the rental sector. This exerts downward pressure on rents and reduces the relative attractiveness of investment in rental housing. Moreover, this reduction is reinforced by the use of historic rather than market or replacement costs as the basis for depreciation for tax purposes. The use of historic costs causes depreciation to decline in real terms as a result of inflation, and this restrains the increase in net after-tax cash flows.

James R. Kearl, "Inflation, Mortgages and Housing," *Journal of Political Economy*, 87(5):1115-38 (Oct. 1979); and Kenneth T. Rosen, "The Housing Crisis and the New Homeowners Incentive Plan," *Journal of the American Real Estate and Urban Economics Association*, 5(3):366-78 (Fall 1977).

26. For a discussion of the impacts of inflation and the tax structure on homeownership preferences, see Diamond, "A Note on Inflation," pp. 438-50; Frank de Leeuw and Larry Ozanne, "The Impact of the Federal Income Tax on Investment in Housing," *Survey of Current Business*, 59:50-61 (Dec. 1979); Hendershott, "Real User Costs," pp. 401-44; Rosen and Rosen, "Federal Taxes and Homeownership," pp. 59-75; and Yoram Weiss, "Capital Gains, Discriminatory Taxes and the Choice between Renting and Owning a House," *Journal of Public Economics*, 10(1):45-56 (Feb. 1978).

27. This conclusion is likely to hold even if mortgage costs are variable, since homeowner equity increases with inflation and the interest foregone on this equity is not taxed. The relative decline is larger if the tax system is not indexed and inflation causes the household to move through marginal tax brackets. In the United States, the benefit is further enhanced by the deductibility of mortgage interest and property taxes. Since these deductible items rise with inflation and the tax system is not indexed, the relative benefits of these deductions rise with inflation.

Changing philosophy behind housing policy

During the 1970s, the philosophy underlying housing policy in Canada shifted from one which encouraged the private sector by improving the efficiency of the real and home finance markets, to one which discouraged the private rental sector by direct intervention and regulation. This discouragement took many forms.

First, intervention occurred through large-scale construction of government housing and subsidization of nonmarket rental housing—primarily limited dividend corporations, nonprofit corporations, and nonprofit cooperatives—for low- and moderate-income households which directly competed with the private market sector. For example, between 1970 and 1974—that is, prior to rent control—government and nonmarket apartment starts accounted for 9.9 percent of total housing starts and 23.8 percent of total apartment starts, compared to 5.8 percent and 12.5 percent, respectively, in the preceding six years.[28]

Second, the government assisted private homeownership through a variety of subsidies, direct loans, and tax incentives. The most significant subsidy forms were cash grants provided by the federal government and some provinces in 1975 to stimulate the demand for homeownership;[29] federal interest subsidies offered between 1973 and 1978 under the Assisted Home Ownership Program (AHOP), which provided subsidies of up to $1200 a year to reduce mortgage payments on the purchase of a house to 25 percent of family income;[30] interest-free loans provided by the federal government and some provinces at various times; and land leases offered by various provinces at subsidized rents to low- and moderate-income families. Direct mortgage loans were made by the federal government under AHOP to purchasers who failed to qualify for private institutional funds.[31] A major tax incentive for homeownership was also provided by the introduction in 1975 of Registered Home Ownership Savings Plans, which allowed a nonhome-owning taxpayer to make tax-deductible contributions of $1000 a year up to a maximum of $10,000 to a plan whose income was not taxed and whose total contributions and accumulated income could be withdrawn without tax for the purchase of a home.

Third, regulation arose in many forms, including rent control; Landlord and Tenant Act revisions, which generally increased tenant security and imposed additional re-

28. Calculated from Smith, *Anatomy of a Crisis*, p. 36, and Canada Mortgage and Housing Corporation, *Canadian Housing Statistics, 1981* (Ottawa: Canada Mortgage and Housing Corporation, 1981), p. 9.

29. In Ontario, for example, the province provided a $1500 cash grant to first-time home purchasers, and the federal government provided an additional $500 cash grant to first-time home purchasers of a newly constructed dwelling, subject to a price constraint. The combined grants represented 4-5 percent of the price and 20-80 percent of the required downpayment for an average-priced home. For a discussion of this and other programs, see Smith, "Canadian Housing Policy in the Seventies," pp. 338-52, and George Fallis, *Housing Programs and the Distribution of Income in Ontario* (Toronto: University of Toronto Press for the Ontario Economic Council, 1980), pp. 58-103.

30. A partial offset to this was the Assisted Rental Program (ARP) introduced in 1975, which provided interest-reducing loans for the construction of rent-controlled multiple rental dwellings.

31. Similar loans were also made under ARP.

strictions on landlords; controls on foreign investment; and an unearned increment land tax in Ontario, which discriminated against investment in rental housing compared to nonresidential investment real estate.[32]

By subsidizing and directly providing the competition to private rental housing, and by imposing additional regulations on the private rental sector, government policy restrained rents in the private sector, created an unfavorable atmosphere for housing investment, and clearly discouraged the private ownership of and investment in rental housing.

Rent control

Rent control was introduced in Canada in 1975, mainly in conjunction with the federal Anti-Inflation Program, and provided the ultimate discouragement for the rental housing market.[33] Since rent control is a provincial responsibility, the form and substance of the controls varied between provinces, but the discouragement for the rental sector was universal.

Regardless of their specifics, rent control measures will, if effective, depress the real value of existing rental units, substantially inhibit new rental construction, even if such construction is exempt from controls, and promote deterioration in the quality and quantity of the existing housing stock. A recent study of rent control in Ontario, for example, indicated that during the first five years of controls, the real per unit value of rental apartments declined 39 percent and the nominal per unit value declined 8 percent.[34] Since the existence of controls in one segment of the market creates an unfavorable environment and generates expectations that controls will be extended to the uncontrolled segment, the commitment of additional resources for rental housing through new construction, renovation, and repairs and maintenance is severely discouraged.[35] This effect on new construction was clearly demonstrated in Ontario, where private unassisted rental starts in 1980 declined to 3842 units, or to only 13 percent of their 1970-74 precontrol level.

SUMMARY

The foregoing analysis indicates that a variety of forces combined during the past decade to weaken the private rental sector. These forces exerted downward pressure on rents, reduced the relative after-tax net yield associated with any given gross rent, introduced market distortions prejudicial to rental housing, and created an unfavorable investment climate.

The investment boom in rental construction in the late 1960s and early 1970s restrained rents at the beginning of the 1970s and held the

32. For an analysis of this tax, see Lawrence B. Smith, "The Ontario Land Speculation Tax: An Analysis of an Unearned Increment Land Tax," *Land Economics*, 55(1):1-12 (Feb. 1976).

33. Actually, a form of rent control existed prior to 1975 in Quebec, and rent control was introduced in British Columbia and promised in Ontario in 1975 prior to the Anti-Inflation Program.

34. Lawrence B. Smith and Peter Tomlinson, "Rent Controls in Ontario: Roofs or Ceilings?" *Journal of the American Real Estate and Urban Economics Association*, 9(1):93-114 (Summer 1981).

35. An exception occurs if renovation or upgrading expenditures create an exemption from controls.

rent-to-income ratio for tenants to 18.0 percent.[36] Thereafter, downward pressure on rents was exerted by a shift in household preferences in favor of homeownership as a result of increased tax incentives for homeownership, expectations of rising inflation, and sharply increased government grants and subsidies for homeownership; and by increased competition from government and subsidized nonmarket housing forms. This downward pressure was reflected in a persistent decline in real gross rents, which fell 34 percent between 1971 and 1981 as measured by the Consumer Price Index, and in a sharp squeeze in net rents exclusive of financing costs, which remained relatively constant in nominal terms but declined 58 percent in real terms between 1971 and 1981.[37] The squeeze on net rents associated with new nonsubsidized construction was even larger in the 1970s and early 1980s, since mortgage costs rose 100-150 basis points during the 1970s, an additional 300 basis points in 1980, and another 150 basis points in 1981.

Although the rental component of the Consumer Price Index is often considered downward biased,[38] the direction and approximate magnitude of these declines are supported by an analysis of rents in Ontario based on survey data. This analysis indicates that real gross rent declined 9 percent and real net rent exclusive of financing costs declined 22 percent between 1974 and 1980.[39]

Given the extraordinary squeeze on real net rents and after-tax returns on rental housing investment, and expectations of even further declines associated with the imposition and/or continuation of rent controls, the collapse of the private rental sector was inevitable.

POSTSCRIPT ON MYTHS ASSOCIATED WITH THE RENTAL CRISIS

Despite this analysis, which indicated that the crisis in rental housing is clearly attributable to insufficient rents and declining net returns for rental housing, the views are often expressed that high interest rates are responsible for the crisis, and that the real crisis is the decreasing affordability of rental housing.

High interest rates

Since housing is typically a highly levered long-term asset where profitability depends on the cost of credit, the decline in rental construction is often attributed to the sharp increase in interest rates in the 1970s. Although this is an intuitively appealing argument, it is incorrect because variations in the rate of interest primarily affect cyclical fluctuations in housing construction and not secular trends, because the real mortgage rate declined during the 1970s, and

36. Walker, "What Are the Facts?" p. 25.

37. Based on an index of rental apartment expenses estimated by weighting the property tax, repair and maintenance, insurance, utility and fuel, and miscellaneous shelter cost components of the Consumer Price Index by .20, .10, .01, .12, and .05, respectively.

38. Ann Dougherty and Robert Van Order, "Inflation, Housing Costs, and the Consumer Price Index," *American Economic Review*, 72:154-64 (Mar. 1982); and Larry Ozanne, "Expanding and Improving the CPI Rent Component," in *House Prices and Inflation*, pp. 109-21.

39. Smith and Tomlinson, "Rent Controls in Ontario," pp. 93-114.

because the increase in the conventional mortgage rate was relatively small prior to the end of 1979.

In the longer run, interest rates move with inflation and, in the absence of structural or demographic changes, or non-neutral tax or tilt effects, it is reasonable to expect rents to do so as well. Since the value of a rental investment essentially depends on its expected discounted cash flow, an inflation-induced increase in the rate of interest, and hence in the discount rate, normally would not affect the investment value, because it would usually be offset by an equivalent increase in the expected net rent.[40] Consequently, inflation-induced increases in the rate of interest should affect neither the profitability nor the volume of rental construction.[41]

Of course interest rates may move independently of the rate of inflation, either as the result of temporary short-run fluctuations or of long-term changes in the real rate of interest. Since short-run fluctuations in the rate of interest are normally incorporated into long-term mortgage contracts, these variations affect expected profitability and hence the volume of rental construction. However, these fluctuations are usually short-lived and hence explain cyclical fluctuations but not the longer-term downward trend in rental construction.

Similarly, long-term changes in the real rate of interest on mortgages cannot explain the decline in rental construction, because the real mortgage rate—using an ex post facto definition: the current nominal mortgage rate minus the current inflation rate or minus the previous year's actual inflation rate—declined for much of the 1970s, and although it rose at the end of the 1970s, the real mortgage rate was 300 basis points lower at the end of the 1970s than at the beginning. Finally, changes in the nominal mortgage rate cannot explain the severe decline in new rental construction, since the nominal mortgage rate rose from a monthly average of 9.91 percent during 1969-71 to only 10.98 percent during 1977-79.[42]

Consequently, interest rate changes were not responsible for the downward long-term trend in rental construction during the 1970s, although at times they may have had a minor impact via the tilt effect.[43]

40. Since the present value PV can be defined as

$$PV = \frac{R_1(1+\dot{p})}{(1+i)(1+\dot{p})} + \frac{R_2(1+\dot{p})^2}{(1+i)^2(1+\dot{p})^2} + \cdots\cdots$$

$$+ \frac{R_n(1+\dot{p})^n}{(1+i)^n(1+\dot{p})^n} + \frac{S_n(1+\dot{p})^n}{(1+i)^n(1+\dot{p})^n},$$

where R_j is the expected rent at the end of the jth period with no expected inflation, S_n is the residual or scrap value at the end of period n, i is the discount rate with no expected inflation, and $\dot{p}$ is the expected inflation rate, it is clear that a change in the expected rate of inflation, if incorporated into both rents and the discount rate, will leave the present value unaffected.

41. Inflation does, however, affect profitability and rental construction in other ways, as discussed in this article's section on increasing inflationary expectations.

42. However, the nominal rate did rise sharply to 14.32 percent in 1980 and 18.15 percent in 1981.

43. This impact, if any, would have been relatively small because of the relatively small increase in the nominal rate of interest in the 1970s, and because the tilt effect affects only cash flows and not expected profitability, and most Canadian developers had

Increases in the real rate of interest, however, would have significantly affected rental housing starts in the early 1980s, had other factors not already virtually destroyed this market.

On the other hand, the shift from long-term fixed-rate mortgages to variable-rate short-term mortgages probably had an adverse effect on rental construction by shifting the risk associated with interest rate variability from the financing institution to the investor.[44]

Affordability

The increase in the median rent-to-income ratio from .21 to .25 in the United States and in the shelter-cost-to-income ratio for tenants from .18 to .22 in Canada are often cited as evidence for a decline in the affordability of rental housing. The preceding analysis suggests, however, that the rent-to-income ratio is inappropriate as an indicator of changing rental affordability. This inappropriateness stems from the demographic changes and increase in household preferences for homeownership which probably altered the characteristics of the typical renter by lowering the average age and relative income of the typical renter. As a result, the increase in the rent-to-income ratio is likely to be simply a reflection of the decline in tenant incomes associated with the falling average age of tenants and shift of higher-income tenants to homeownership.[45] This interpretation is supported both by the 34 percent decline in real gross rents during the 1970s, and by the 54 percent decline in the ratio of rents to median family income between 1971 and 1980.[46] The increase in the rent-to-income ratio for tenants, therefore, is indicative not of a decline in the affordability of rental housing but of a decline in the average income percentile of tenants—which itself may be a reflection of the problems facing rental housing.

THE FUTURE OF PRIVATE RENTAL HOUSING

The preceding discussion indicates that the current rental housing crisis is the product of a complex set of factors, the foremost being the change in tax preferences for homeownership, expectations of accelerating inflation, substantial government support for alternative housing forms, and rent control, which interacted to restrain rents and reduce the attractiveness of investment in new residential construction. The future of private rental housing depends on the extent to which the effects of these forces persist and the impact of new structural shifts, such as the changing age composition of the population. Although the negative impacts of a number of these forces are likely to dissipate, the outlook remains relatively pessimistic because of the probable continuation of rent control and unfavorable demographic influences.

sufficient internal and/or external financing to be unconstrained by this.

44. The shift to short-term variable-rate financing for homeowners should have somewhat offset this by increasing the risks associated with homeownership and reducing household preferences for homeownership.

45. This point is made by Lowry, "Rental Housing in the 1970s," p. 28, and by Rosen, "The Affordability of Housing in 1980 and Beyond," p. 10.

46. Calculated from Canada Mortgage and Housing Corporation, *Canadian Housing Statistics, 1981*, pp. 74, 76.

The introduction of additional tax preferences for homeownership and expectations of accelerating inflation in the first half of the 1970s shifted tenure preferences in favor of homeownership from rental housing, and thereby reduced the desired stock of rental housing in the economy. This exerted downward pressure on rents and substantially reduced the volume of new rental construction as the market sought to adjust to the new equilibrium. As this equilibrium is approached, the depressing effects of these forces will diminish, and upward pressure on rents and new rental construction should reappear, although the new growth paths will be lower than they were previously. In addition, if the expected inflation rate declines or homeownership tax preferences are reduced, the previous process would be reversed as the relative attractiveness of homeownership would decline and the desired stock of rental housing would increase.

The downward pressure from government support for alternative housing is also likely to diminish as government reduces its active intervention in the housing market as a result of the large and growing budgetary requirements of such intervention[47] and changing public attitudes. Such a reduction has already begun: public funds authorized for these activities were cut approximately 73 percent between 1977-78 and 1980-81.[48]

On the other hand, the effects of these favorable market forces are likely to be largely nullified by continuing rent control and increasingly unfavorable demographics. Since the economic consequences of rent control are so clearly negative, the imposition and continuation of rent control would appear to be primarily political.[49] As a result, its future is difficult to predict. Assuming, however, that rent controls remain throughout most of Canada, they will override the corrective market mechanisms and exacerbate the crisis in rental housing. This will occur even if new rental construction is exempt from controls, because the existence of controls in one segment of the market generates expectations of an eventual extension and hence depresses new rental construction.

Finally, although the elimination of rent control and the threat of its reintroduction would enable a normal market recovery and avert a prolonged rental housing crisis, recovery in rental construction would be tempered by increasingly unfavorable demographics in the 1980s. Average annual net household formation in the 15-34 age bracket, the dominant bracket for new rental demand, is expected to decline from 103,250 households in 1971-81 to 62,100 households in 1981-86, and only 13,700 households in 1986-91;[50]

47. For a discussion of these requirements, see Lawrence B. Smith, "Federal Housing Programs and the Allocation of Credit and Resources," in *Government in Canadian Capital Markets: Selected Cases*, J.E. Pesando and L.B. Smith (Montreal: C.D. Howe Research Institute, 1978), pp. 20-67, and Task Force on Canada Mortgage and Housing Corporation, *Report on Canada Mortgage and Housing Corporation* (Ottawa: Canada Mortgage and Housing Corporation, 1980), pp. 43-76.

48. Based on appropriations for Public Housing, Federal-Provincial Housing, and Non-Profit Corporations and Cooperative Housing. If ARP is included, the decline is 78 percent.

49. For an excellent discussion of rent controls, see *Rent Control: Myths and Realities*, eds. W. Block and E. Olsen (Vancouver: Fraser Institute, 1981).

50. Philip W. Brown, "The Demographic Future: Impacts on the Demand for Housing

meanwhile, little change is expected in net household formation aged 65 and over. Assuming no sustained increase in real incomes, the net demand for rental housing is unlikely to grow substantially, although there will be a shift in the age composition of this demand and an increase in replacement demand. On the other hand, these unfavorable demographics in the long run may offer hope for avoiding a prolonged crisis in the rental housing market, although not in new rental construction, since the depressing effects of rent control on supply may be substantially diluted by the negative demographic influences on demand.

in Canada, 1981-2001," in *Symposium on North American Housing Markets into the 21st Century*, eds. G. Gau and M. Goldberg (Cambridge, MA: Ballinger Publishing, forthcoming).

ANNALS, *AAPSS*, **465**, January 1983

The Coming Crunch in Rental Housing

By ANTHONY DOWNS

ABSTRACT: Is there a rental housing shortage? Not yet, but one may arise soon—especially in fast-growth areas. Rental housing still accommodates over one-third of all U.S. households, with eight out of nine rental units provided by private owners. Yet recent moves of many better-off households to homeownership have shifted the composition of renters toward higher fractions of the poor. Residential rents have lagged behind living costs for 20 years. Even so, investing in rental units has been kept profitable by tax shelter and other factors. Higher real capital costs will weaken most of these factors in the 1980s, while making homeownership more difficult. This will raise demands for rental housing. But developers will not supply much more until rents rise or interest rates fall. Hence rents will soon begin rising rapidly, penalizing the poor. Rent controls would aid them at first but would only aggravate shortages in the long run. A better policy would be letting rents rise enough to motivate developers to build new units, while aiding the poor through a nationwide housing voucher program. This could be paid for by moderately reducing existing tax benefits enjoyed by more affluent homeowners.

Anthony Downs is a senior fellow at the Brookings Institution in Washington, D.C. For 18 years a member and then chairman of Real Estate Research Corporation, a nationwide consulting firm, he has served as a consultant to corporations, private foundations, major developers, and local, state, and national government agencies, including the Department of Housing and Urban Development and the White House. Among those with whom he currently consults are Aetna Life and Casualty, the Ford Foundation, the American Council of Life Insurance, and the Federal National Mortgage Association. Dr. Downs received a Ph.D. in economics from Stanford University. Author of seven books and over 200 articles, he is currently working on a study of the causes of urban decline and the future of American cities.

NOTE: The views in this article are solely those of the author and not necessarily those of the Brookings Institution, its Trustees, or any of its other staff members.

FOR the last few years, a controversy has raged among housing practitioners and experts concerning whether there is or will be a crisis in U.S. rental housing markets. Many practitioners believe an acute shortage of rental units already exists, mainly because of recent low production of new unsubsidized multifamily rental units. In contrast, most academic and government housing experts believe there are plenty of rental housing units, as shown by relatively slow increases in rents and no substantial decline in national vacancy rates.

To resolve this controversy and to analyze desirable future housing policies, I recently completed an in-depth study of the economics of rental housing during the coming decade. It includes projections of demand and likely future new production, plus an analysis of any indicated shortfalls in such production. This article summarizes the major conclusions of my study, soon to be published as a book by the Brookings Institution.

BASIC FACTS ABOUT U.S. RENTAL HOUSING

Rental housing still plays a major role in the United States, sheltering over one-third of all households. The vast majority of such housing—eight out of nine units—is not subsidized but is furnished by private owners acting for profits. Private rental markets are dominated by small-scale operators, since about 60 percent of all rental units are in structures with fewer than five units, including 31 percent that are single-family homes. Although the rental housing inventory increased 15 percent in the 1970s, it grew only about half as fast as the owner-occupied inventory.

More and more heads of households with economic resources have become homeowners. This is partly because of the widespread belief that investment in owner-occupied housing is the best possible use of wealth and the most easily available hedge against inflation. As a result, the composition of the renting population has shifted toward higher fractions of households with low earning power. Notable among these are female heads of households, who now comprise over 40 percent of all renters, the largest single group. The average income of female-headed renter households is less than half that of husband-and-wife renter households, which are shifting to homeownership as rapidly as they can. The number of husband-and-wife renter households is actually declining. This change in composition means that a rising share of the rental market will be severely constrained by the declining ability of consumers to pay rent.

KEY TRENDS CONCERNING RENTAL HOUSING ECONOMICS

The ability of private rental owners to continue providing good-quality housing services to their 24 million tenants depends on the future profitability of rental housing. If it is profitable enough to pay for adequate maintenance, its quality may continue to rise as it has during the past 30 years. If profitability falls, quality may deteriorate. But profitability is not evenly distributed through the inventory, and so deterioration is most likely to occur in areas where rental housing is not profitable, such as many low-income neighborhoods in large cities. Profitable units, as in many newer suburbs, will be kept in good condition.

Residential rents have not increased as fast as consumer incomes, operating costs, or construction costs during the past 20 years, particularly the past few years. This is true even after correcting for substantial underestimation of rent increases by the Bureau of Labor Statistics' (BLS's) Consumer Price Index (CPI). The best estimate, by Ira Lowry, is that real rent levels have fallen about 8.4 percent in the past 20 years, or roughly 4.2 percent per decade—compared to the BLS estimate that they have fallen 25 percent in the past 20 years.[1] As a result, rents would have to be much higher than they are now to make creation of new rental properties economically feasible, given high construction costs and interest rates. Construction costs will surely not fall or even cease rising much, though interest rates might come down.

In fact, rents would have to rise substantially just to support the same real values of rental properties that existed in the past when interest rates and operating cost ratios were much lower. Putting that same conclusion another way, it appears that the real value of rental housing properties in the United States sustainable from their rents alone has fallen substantially since 1960—perhaps by as much as 50 percent. This fall results from large increases in operating costs and interest rates but slow increases in rents. Yet equity investments in rental housing seem to have been profitable up until 1980, based on investors' experiences.

This paradox results from the impacts on both equity yields and market prices of four factors other than current net operating income—rents less operating costs. These factors are (1) tax shelter, (2) leverage, (3) low real interest rates on mortgages during the 1970s, and (4) anticipated price appreciation. Each factor contributed to yield on equity, and therefore to demand for rental properties, even though it did not directly affect net operating incomes.

Tax shelter helped offset low net operating incomes because losses benefit high-bracket investors. Leverage resulted from borrowing most of the cost of each investment; it multiplied the positive effects of depreciation and increases in property values. Low real rates of interest occurred when lenders offered long-term, fixed-rate mortgages in the late 1960s and throughout the 1970s at low rates, failing to foresee rising inflation. Anticipated appreciation resulted from possibilities of converting rental units to condominiums, and from the self-fulfilling nature of rising beliefs among investors that real estate was a good inflation hedge. All four factors not only aided yields on equity but also persuaded investors to pay higher prices for rental units than could be justified by their current earnings from rents alone.

Moreover, in the late 1970s, apartment syndicators were skimming the cream off the rental market, building small units with high annual turnovers. They were able to raise rents faster than the CPI went up and to pass most operating cost increases on to tenants. Hence the market values of their

1. Ira S. Lowry, *Inflation Indexes for Rental Housing*, Rand Note N-1832-HUD (Santa Monica: Rand Corporation, January 1982).

units rose faster than those of the average units in the rental inventory as a whole.

RECENT CHANGES IN ECONOMIC CONDITIONS

In 1980 and 1981, high real interest rates changed three of these four key factors in ways adverse to rental housing. These changes are likely to persist for several years, and perhaps throughout the 1980s. They reduce past beneficial effects of leverage, interest rates, and anticipated appreciation on equity yields and market prices. Therefore in the future, the yields and prices of rental housing will depend more on profits from current operations, and thus on rents, than in the past decade.

The real cost of capital for housing and other real estate will be much higher in the 1980s than in the 1970s, with many important effects. The advantage of low real rates caused by unanticipated inflation will no longer benefit borrowers, since lenders have adopted new forms of instruments that will pass rising interest costs on to borrowers. This removes one factor raising equity returns from rental housing.

Homeownership will be more difficult to attain. Higher interest rates can no longer be offset by stretching out loan terms or increasing the share of incomes devoted to housing, since such tactics have already gone about as far as they can. Therefore heads of households who would, on a purely demographic basis, become homeowners will be forced to rent instead. This is especially true of first-time buyers; thus the demand for rental housing will rise faster than in the 1970s.

Home prices will rise more slowly than in the past, increasing at about the same pace as the general inflation rate, except in high-demand areas with strong restrictions on new housing supply. Hence the profitability of investing in homeownership will be less. This will also reduce investors' anticipation of appreciation in the market price of rental units—another key factor that increased equity yields and market prices of such units above the level sustainable from rents.

Interest costs will remain too high to make production of many new rental units feasible for up to several years, or whenever rents rise much higher. Moreover, lenders will refuse to supply the capital equity investors need for leveraging, except in the form of joint ventures, variable-rate loans, or renegotiable loans. Hence the huge benefit-multiplying power of leveraging will be greatly reduced, and many small-scale investors will be unable to obtain long-term funds. The supply of rental housing, therefore, will not grow as fast as the demand. Also, there will be pressure to economize on space generally, resulting in the use of smaller housing units, especially among those newly built.

At present there is a gap between actual rents and those needed to sustain existing market prices without capital losses to rental owners. Therefore the weakening of key factors other than rent that aided yields and increased prices will simultaneously (1) pressure owners to raise rents rapidly, more nearly to support present prices, and (2) cause a softening of market prices when owners must sell. Most owners will be able to raise rents because of increasing market tightness as demand rises faster than supply. Consequently, rents will rise faster than prices generally. This is a reversal of the situation prevalent in the past two decades. Exceptions will occur in markets where large numbers of added units are created through means other than new construction, or where rent controls are adopted.

PROJECTIONS OF FUTURE DEMAND AND PRODUCTION

The number of additional households formed 1980s will be held below its pure demographic level by the high costs of housing. Hence this number will not average 1.83 million, as it would if household formation remained at 1970 levels. Rather, it will be much lower, perhaps as low as 1.5 million per year. Estimates of the average number of new renter households over the whole decade vary from 2.9 million to 5.8 million. However, the most probable estimate appears to call for about 4.3 million added rental households, an average of 430,000 per year.

Converting this demographic estimate into the total demand for rental housing requires estimating the number of units required for replacement purposes. Assuming a low replacement rate, the number of units needed under the most likely household projection—low growth, slow decline of renting—is 2.01 million total units per year, including 641,000 rental units and 1.369 million ownership units.

Construction of new rental units in the late 1970s averaged about 480,000 units per year from all sources. Construction of new ownership units averaged about 1.425 million in the same period, including condominium conversions and mobile homes. Non-new creation was very significant for rental units, exceeding new construction in the late 1970s. This includes conversion of nonresidential space into housing, retrieval of units temporarily removed from use, and division of large units into smaller ones. This source of added supply was less significant for ownership housing, relative to total needs. However, since it involves obtaining more units from the existing inventory, and since making better use of that inventory is likely to be the most effective strategy for expanding the rental supply in the near future, non-new creation will be very important in the 1980s.

Production of new rental housing units will be very low in the next few years because of continued high interest rates and the continuing lag of rents far below levels needed to support new building. If interest rates remain high, new production will remain low indefinitely. If a slackening of inflation brings interest rates down, production might rise toward the end or even the middle of the decade. The timing depends on how fast rents rise in relation to construction costs and interest rates.

In addition, refinancing or selling existing rental properties will be difficult because of high financing costs. These high costs reduce the ability of existing owners to take funds out of their properties to pay for renovating or maintaining them and will cause the deterioration of many older rental buildings.

Low production of new rental units will cause major shortfalls in the supply of such units in the 1980s as compared to potential future demand. This will lead to significant rental housing shortages in many areas. However, entry of additional rental units into the market through non-new creation will reduce the impact of these shortfalls considerably, especially in areas where there are large older inventories of housing and nonresidential properties. Hence the major rental shortfalls will be in fast-growth areas, especially those where rent controls have been adopted and new construction has ended.

To balance the market in the face of this tendency, fewer separate households will be formed. More people will double up, in a reversal of the recent tendency for more spreading out in housing space. Another balancing factor will be faster increases in rents where no rent controls are adopted. As previously noted, rents will start rising faster than operating costs or the costs of homeownership, and will rise relative to the costs of homeownership significantly during the decade. Eventually, if not constrained by controls, rents will become high enough to make some new construction of rental properties feasible. A third major balancing factor will be more intensive use of the existing inventory, including non-new addition of rental units.

Upward pressure on rents will cause widespread political agitation for local and even state governments to adopt rent controls, especially in large cities containing large renter populations and many elderly residents. The more such controls are adopted, the greater the eventual rental shortage. Although most cities will probably remain free from controls, enough could adopt them to cause a major constraint on new rental housing development.

FUTURE POLICIES CONCERNING RENTAL HOUSING

Public policies in response to this situation are justifiable to increase equity and efficiency in housing markets. The need for such policies is especially great in urban areas, which are affected by many externalities. Externalities are impacts which flow directly from one person to another without going through markets. An example is the failure of an apartment owner to prevent drug addicts from gathering in vacant units in his building; their presence reduces the security of surrounding households. Private markets often cannot handle such direct impacts equitably or efficiently, because they affect people involuntarily, rather than through voluntary transactions as in markets. Hence nonmarket interventions from the public sector are often required to deal with such relationships justly.

Public policies concerning rental housing should aim mainly at achieving three goals: (1) stimulating production of new rental units, (2) using the existing inventory more intensively, and (3) helping poor renters cope with rising rents. However, any housing policies requiring federal subsidies must be weighed against the fact that direct income maintenance of the poor is being cut back. Hence those housing subsidies should provide benefits comparable to the ones being reduced, or housing subsidies should be given lower priority than restoring income-maintenance cuts.

Stimulating new rental housing production

The best way to stimulate new rental housing production is to create conditions under which interest rates generally would decline. This could be accomplished through less stringent monetary policy and less expansive fiscal policies. Subsidies aimed at aiding housing alone are not desirable, considering that there are more urgent demands on federal funds. Other subsidies, such as extending more tax advantages to rental housing, would have relatively little impact on new building, compared to lowering interest rates.

To reduce a major inhibition blocking new rental production, the federal government should pass a law prohibiting local rent controls, or create strong financial incentives for local governments not to adopt such controls, in case such a law is unconstitutional. Such a prohibition is probably necessary to persuade major sources of capital to invest heavily in financing badly needed new rental apartments. But if rent controls were banned and rents rose rapidly, poor households would suffer major economic setbacks, since rents are the largest item in their budgets. Hence fairness requires accompanying that ban with a housing voucher program operated as an entitlement—that is, all low-income renter households would be eligible, though they would have to live in decent-quality units to get the payments. This will be discussed further.

In the near future, state housing agencies should be permitted to continue using tax-exempt bonds for financing construction of new rental apartment projects in key locations, even though this type of subsidy is not very efficient economically. The locations involved should be either in the suburbs, where such units would achieve more socioeconomic integration, or in deteriorating central-city areas that need infusions of new construction as part of an overall renovation plan. Also, limited numbers of new public housing units could be built for very large families and for the elderly in communities where the latter could then be induced to move out of the large single-family homes they now occupy.

Local governments could greatly encourage new rental housing production in several ways, though few have strong incentives to do so. For one thing, they could raise allowable densities in areas already zoned for multifamily housing. In addition, all local governments should reduce the complexity and time required in the process of getting permission to build or renovate rental housing.

Making more intensive use of the existing inventory

Local governments can also employ several effective tactics to encourage better use of existing structures for rental housing. They should postpone increases in property taxes on rehabilitated properties to prevent such increases from discouraging renovation. They should also change zoning laws and housing codes to encourage division of large, older single-family homes into multiple dwellings. Such cutting up of older homes is already a major source of added rental units, even where illegal. Regulating it in a sensible manner is a much better policy in most neighborhoods than trying to prevent it altogether.

Experience shows that rental buildings in which owners reside are much better maintained than absentee-owner units, especially in low-income neighborhoods where most deterioration occurs. Therefore local governments should develop specific rewards for owners who reside on the premises of their rental properties, such as tax credits or rebates. No such policies are now in effect, but they might help reduce deterioration in older areas dominated by sizable apartment buildings.

Concerning housing code enforcement, local governments should use a selective, differential approach that recognizes varying levels of quality in differing neighborhoods and aims at encouraging owners to maintain their properties. Hence code enforcement efforts should be combined with counseling about how to rehabilitate units in violation, and even with financial assistance to help owners renovate. Low-interest loans could be made available for rehabilitating rental housing, both from the federal government directly through an interest-rate subsidy and from local governments with Community Development Block Grant funds.

Helping poor renters meet the rising costs of occupying decent-quality units

As noted previously, the federal government could modify the Section 8 existing program and expand it into a comprehensive housing voucher program for households with very low incomes. This program should have about equal status with restoring food stamp cuts, unless a federal prohibition of rent control is adopted. In that case, it should have slightly higher priority. The feasibility of housing vouchers has already been demonstrated by the Experimental Housing Allowance Program.[2]

Financing a housing voucher entitlement program would add several billion dollars per year to the federal budget, even though only about half of all eligible households would actually participate.[3] This added cost could be offset by reducing the present tax benefits homeowners enjoy from deducting mortgage interest and property taxes from their taxable incomes. Those benefits aid mainly high-income households, whereas housing vouchers would aid mainly the poor. Reduction of such tax benefits could best be done by transforming homeowner deductions into tax credits at one uniform tax rate somewhat lower than the average rate now prevailing. This shift would also redistribute the remaining homeownership tax benefits so that more of the benefits would go to low- and moderate-income families. This would help offset higher costs of homeownership for many such families, enabling more to buy homes than under present deductibility. Yet this change would retain major tax advantages for homeownership, since it should be encouraged by public policy.

LIKELY FUTURE ADJUSTMENTS IN HOUSING MARKETS

Once any of these policies is adopted and has affected the market, some further adjustments to future conditions will have to be made by many households of all types. These will include behavior changes they will regard as undesirable. For example, many renters

2. For an analysis of the feasibility of housing vouchers, see Katherine L. Bradbury and Anthony Downs, eds., *Do Housing Allowances Work?* (Washington, DC: Brookings Institution, 1981).

3. Participation in housing allowances was lower than in direct income maintenance programs. This was true even on the part of the Experimental Housing Allowance program, lasting 10 years, that made all low-income households in the entire metropolitan area eligible. See Bradbury and Downs, *Do Housing Allowances Work?* pp. 21-27, 121-35.

and homeowners will be paying higher fractions of their incomes for housing because of higher rents and homeownership costs than in the past. Also, many heads of households who would like to own will be renting because they cannot afford the higher costs of homeownership. And many persons who would like to form separate households will be living with other persons because they cannot afford separate housing.

Owners of rental property will be keeping it in use longer than they might otherwise, so the inventory will be older on the average. It may also be more deteriorated, but that is not clear, since higher rents may enable owners to maintain their properties better. Persons who buy or rent new accommodations will be living in smaller units than in the previous decade.

The total share of capital flowing into home mortgages for both rental and ownership units will be somewhat smaller in the 1980s than in the 1970s. One reason is that owning housing seems less likely to produce high profits, given slower appreciation and higher real interest rates. Hence the demand for home mortgages will be lower. In addition, the 1981 Economic Recovery and Tax Act improved the relative attraction of investing in corporate equities and small businesses by increasing the tax benefits of doing so, compared to the benefits of investing in homeownership and rental housing.

RENT CONTROLS, FEDERAL ANTIPOVERTY AIDS, AND THE FUTURE OF RENTAL HOUSING

As noted before, rapid future rent increases would injure the poor, many of whom already pay high fractions of their incomes for housing. Rent increases would weaken the overall effectiveness of federal transfer programs in aiding the poor. Such programs include food stamps, welfare, Medicare, and Social Security. One way the federal government could offset such weakening would be through a housing voucher program providing added purchasing power to the poor, as described earlier. But that would require large expenditures and so seems unlikely in the near future. Hence poor households squeezed by rising rents will create strong pressures on many local governments to adopt rent controls. Some governments will enact such controls to gain their short-run benefits, even though in the long run rent controls aggravate rental housing shortages. They both halt almost all building of new rental units and discourage many owners from maintaining existing ones in good condition.

This analysis indicates that federal policies concerning antipoverty transfer programs and local government policies concerning rent controls ought to be considered together, even though they are operated by two different levels of government. Theoretically, combining these elements into a single integrated housing strategy for the poor may not actually influence either government to take the other into account. But it does show how interdependent these elements are and what impacts each might have on the other.

The physical and financial housing deficiencies of poor households as a group are caused mainly by poverty. Hence those deficiencies cannot be remedied without major and costly expansion of existing federal assistance to the poor. Even full employment would not eliminate poverty or urban problems, as shown by high unemployment rates in urban ghettos when overall unemployment was under 4 percent. Current federal policies that reduce aids to the poor or prevent their growth will therefore perpetuate present rental housing deficiencies.

If the federal government does not respond to rising rents with added aid to the poor, rent controls will be the only public policy relief available to them. But the longer rent controls are in effect, the harder it is to get rid of them. Prolonged controls in the face of rising demand for rental housing will generate crowding, deterioration of existing rental units, and overall shortages affecting middle-income renters as well.

The political pressure on the federal government to respond to such a situation would eventually become compelling, especially since much of it would come from nonpoor renters. Experience in other Western democracies shows that government responses often take the form of expanding publicly subsidized housing, rather than allowing the private sector to meet rental needs. This is politically easier than ending rent controls and letting rents rise high enough to make private development of new rental units feasible again. If the federal government responds to future pressures to do something about rental housing shortages by subsidizing more public housing, the private rental inventory may shrink enormously within a few decades, as it has in Great Britain. In 1947, 61 percent of all British housing consisted of privately owned rental units; today, such units comprise about 11 percent of the total.[4]

This analysis is admittedly quite speculative. However, it indicates that relying entirely on a free market approach to solve rental housing problems in the short run might paradoxically cause a greatly expanded dependence on public housing in the long run. Such a free market approach in the near future would combine a national ban on rent controls—which I believe is desirable—with refusal to expand federal aids to the poor in spite of soaring rents. This might start the long-run decline of private rental housing. And that might lead to major expansion of publicly subsidized and operated housing, even though the latter is less desirable and more expensive for all income groups, including the poor, than rental housing furnished by the private market.

It would therefore be much better to attack likely future rental housing shortages by combining a nationwide ban on rent controls with a federal housing voucher entitlement program focused on low-income renters. That would allow rents to rise high enough to encourage new private rental development without imposing severe costs on the poor. The added federal costs of this approach could be paid for by changing the form of existing homeownership tax benefits to a tax credit, and modestly reducing the total size of those benefits. In my opinion, this would be the best strategy for combating the coming crunch in rental housing markets.

4. Joel F. Brenner and Herbert M. Franklin, *Rent Control in North America and Four European Countries* (Washington, DC: Potomac Institute, 1977).

ANNALS, *AAPSS*, **465**, January 1983

Declining Neighborhoods: Problem or Opportunity?

By WILLIAM G. GRIGSBY and THOMAS C. CORL

ABSTRACT: Widespread deterioration and squalid living conditions in many older residential areas in the United States stand in dramatic contrast to the large, comfortable, and attractive residences in the suburbs. The disparity in living environment is not easily explainable in terms of differences in household incomes, since real incomes in many of our older and now unsightly central-city neighborhoods have been generally increasing, not falling. A variety of explanations, none very convincing, have been offered for the anomaly of rising income and expanding decay. Over the years, various remedies have been tried without particular success. The only real hope for reversing the process of decay lies in altering the expectations of those who live and work in the affected neighborhoods, but the prospects for this are not bright. In any event, suburbanization is likely to continue draining population from the urban core because most city dwellers still aspire to joining the movement outward, and the trend of rising income will allow them to achieve this goal.

William G. Grigsby is professor of city and regional planning at the University of Pennsylvania. He has held appointments at the University of Pennsylvania as associate professor of city planning and finance, assistant director of the Institute for Urban Studies, and chairman of the Department of City and Regional Planning. He received a B.S. in business from the University of Colorado (1948), an M.S. in business and economics from Columbia University (1950), and a Ph.D. in economics from Columbia University (1958).

Thomas C. Corl is a lecturer in the Urban Studies Program and the Department of City and Regional Planning at the University of Pennsylvania. He served as the university's director of community relations from 1978 to 1981 and has worked with several Philadelphia community organizations. Mr. Corl has a B.A. in sociology from the University of Illinois (1967) and an M.A. in sociology from Princeton University (1969).

FOR nearly every metropolitan area in the United States, there is a remarkable range of houses and living environments. Widespread deterioration and squalid living conditions in many older residential areas stand in dramatic contrast to the large, comfortable, and beautifully landscaped residences of the new suburbs. This range and the contrasting segments within it begin to frame our understanding of housing problems. The housing market mirrors the nation's social structure. Those with higher incomes are consistently well housed. Those with the lowest incomes are generally poorly housed. While there are exceptions to this relationship, the overall pattern is clear enough. In this sense, the housing market works. It produces and distributes housing according to the capacity of occupants to buy or pay rent.

This is only half the story, however. If the immense variation in housing quality and living environments were entirely the consequence of the unequal distribution of income, an exploration into the question of what to do about substandard residential conditions would be either relatively simple or totally unnecessary. But more than income would appear to be involved. In few North American and Western European urban regions having income levels and distributions roughly comparable to those in this country are there the deplorable physical environments found here. The worst sections of Canadian cities are luxurious by comparison. Even Glasgow, once infamous for its horrible slums, has almost no neighborhoods as depressing as many of ours. And within the United States itself, the range of housing and neighborhood quality across cities having similar income profiles is quite large.

Most housing and neighborhood programs designed to improve residential conditions in deteriorated areas emanate from the federal government. Though there have been temporary successes, these programs generally have not been able to alter the dynamics of inner-city decay permanently. A few programs are even alleged to have accelerated decay. As a consequence, such improvement in conditions as has occurred is frequently ascribed to rising incomes and housing programs for the population in general, rather than to efforts aimed directly at lower-income groups.

Complementing the top-down efforts of the federal government have been the steadily increasing activities of neighborhood organizations. Against formidable market forces and with limited governmental support, these organizations have won small but important victories. Anti-redlining campaigns, local credit unions, community development corporations, and political pressure have been used to good effect by many neighborhood groups. However, outward movement of stable households has adversely affected the capacity of many neighborhoods to attract capital to stabilize or improve their character.

Despite the mixed record of various remedial programs, it is widely felt that for a number of reasons, inner-city decline is in the process of being reversed and that stabilization and renewal will embrace an expanding portion of the central city. To facilitate renewal, more and more housing and community programs have a neighborhood focus. This article briefly explores the likely future of declining neighborhoods and the efficacy of policies to revive them. It does so by approaching questions regarding neighborhood decline and revival within the larger context of current metropolitan social, economic, and political trends. City governments must understand these broad movements in order to get a sense of where history is taking their communities, whether today's problems are likely to abate or increase, and, therefore, what broad strategies might be successfully employed and what maximum gains can be expected. Since the trends themselves vary sharply across metropolitan areas, our observations are not equally applicable everywhere. They have most relevance for the large old urban centers in the northeast and midwest, especially those with significant concentrations of racial minorities. At least superficially, the neighborhood problems in newer, growing areas seem both less severe and, along some dimensions, different.

HOUSING CONDITIONS, NEEDS, AND PREFERENCES

There is not very good correspondence between the powerful impressions formed by observations of inner-city decay and the data used to document these conditions. In terms of traditional measures of housing conditions, such as lack of plumbing facilities and dilapidation, the U.S. housing stock has been steadily improving for many years and is of remarkably high quality. According to one complicated definition, less than 5 percent of the inventory is seriously substandard.[1] The number of households with more than one person per room—another traditional indicator of housing conditions—is also under 5 percent, and much of this overcrowding is temporary in nature. Impressions of housing need, however, embrace more factors than quality and space. The cost of shelter, level and reliability of services, neighborhood conditions, and degree of locational choice are all perceived as important, and improvement has not been recorded on all these dimensions. Perhaps most important is the fact that needs are defined with reference to what most members of society can afford, not by comparing today's conditions with those of previous generations. So as rising real incomes yield correspondingly better housing, rising expectations partially nullify the sense of progress.

Whatever the figures say, no one disputes the fact that serious housing problems do exist. They are largely concentrated in neighborhoods and among households plagued by other problems that make solutions to inadequate housing alone extremely difficult and sometimes irrelevant. In a complex milieu of adverse circumstances, housing is one important item on the agenda of lower-income families, but other conditions may be more threatening than substandard or insecure shelter. It is this overlapping but less than complete correspondence between housing and other personal problems, between housing problems and neighborhood problems, and between substandard housing and low income that has served to divide analysts on questions regarding which remedial strategies should be pursued and, therefore, which populations should receive priority for assistance.

1. Congressional Budget Office, U.S. Congress, *Federal Housing Policy and Recurring Issues* (Washington, DC: Government Printing Office, 1978), Table 1, p. 6.

INTRAMETROPOLITAN POPULATION AND EMPLOYMENT TRENDS

Rising incomes do more than push up the standards against which housing adequacy is judged. They actually cause a great deal of perceived central-city decline by facilitating the so-called flight to the suburbs. Although most suburban growth has resulted simply frcm disappearance of buildable land inside central cities, it also reflects a long-standing preference for residential environments that central cities do not provide. A national survey by the Department of Housing and Urban Development (HUD) in 1978 on "The Quality of Community Life" found that people living in cities did not like city life as much as people living in suburbs and rural areas preferred those locations. In fact, almost half of the city dwellers wanted to live in suburbs and rural areas, while rural residence was the top choice among people in both suburbs and rural areas.[2] Not surprisingly, there has been a steady exodus of households from central cities as a larger and larger proportion of the urban population obtains the wherewithal to express its preference for the higher-quality, more expensive housing away from the metropolitan core. And as these groups have moved to the periphery, lower-income households have spead outward behind them, creating a moving edge of real and apparent decline as well as abandonment of excess stock.

Thus cities are experiencing two apparently opposing trends with respect to population and housing. According to certain objective indicators of physical quality already described, housing conditions have been steadily improving for several decades. At the same time, however, as the total number of households in parts of the city declines, as the spread between city and suburban family income increases, and as the proportion of city households that have serious problems or that make problems for others increases, stable families see a worsening of housing and neighborhood quality.

It could be, of course, that the objective measures of quality either are inaccurate or do not sufficiently embrace downward trends. Or it could be that perceptions of residential decline in specific neighborhoods do not correctly describe the direction of change for a city as a whole. Regardless, it is clear that the continuing outward movement of households adds a special dimension to a city's housing and neighborhood problems beyond those associated with low income alone. It causes the city to suffer from, as well as be helped by, rising incomes. City strategies must be based, therefore, on judgments as to how long this thinning-out process will continue and on whether, realistically, very much can be done about it. If thinning-out has just about run its course, neighborhood stabilization and upgrading in still viable—however defined—neighborhoods should meet with more success than in the past. If, however, thinning is likely to continue, we can expect a repetition of program failures

2. Office of Policy Development and Research, U.S. Department of Housing and Urban Development, *A Survey of Citizens' Views and Concerns about Urban Life* (Washington, DC: U.S. Department of Housing and Urban Development, 1978), p. 17 and chapter 6. See also Office of Policy Development and Research, U.S. Department of Housing and Urban Development, *The 1978 Survey of the Quality of Community Life: A Data Book* (Washington, DC: U.S. Department of Housing and Urban Development, 1978).

except in neighborhoods with special locational advantages. And if a sizable net return of middle- and upper-class families to the central city is probable, greater frictions between income and racial groups may be forecast.

Interestingly, both more thinning-out and recentralization are predicted with equal vigor. Each view is premised on different explanations of why decentralization has occurred in the first place and of what forces are operating at the moment. For this reason, it is useful to make explicit our own assumptions about the dynamic factors at work, first looking backward in time and then projecting ahead to the year 2000.

The first thing to emphasize with respect to historic decentralization trends is that the phrase "flight to suburbs" is a misleading notion. Outward movement in all metropolitan areas began long before central cities fell on such hard times and long before business and industry began to suburbanize. Several studies document that the thinning-out process began at least as far back as the 1890-1900 decade but was submerged from view because growth at the fringe was still largely inside city limits. It preceded the automobile, the Federal Housing Administration (FHA), and black inmigration to central cities by many years.

The second point to stress is that although thinning-out was greatly accelerated by the emergence of the automobile society, the primary effect of the highway networks was to make it possible for development that would have occurred outside the city anyway to take place at lower densities than previously expected.

The final point to mention in our look to the past has to do with the suburbanization of employment which occurred as manufacturers and wholesalers sought locations on or near major highway thoroughfares and as retailers and service industries moved closer to expanding residential markets. These movements served to reduce to a fairly low level the direct dependence of suburban households on central-city jobs and services. As long ago as the mid-1950s, about two-thirds of workers who lived in the suburbs also worked there. The long journey to work from suburb to city which planners frequently deplored was a myth even then. It was one of several wrong assumptions on which urban revival strategies were then based.

These dynamics of the thinning-out process were not well understood when urban renewal began in the 1950s. Efforts were based on explicit forecasts showing growing central-city populations and on associated worries about residential crowding. Nevertheless, worry was simultaneously being expressed about the loss of middle- and upper-income households to the suburbs. Well before 1960, however, planners, in response to these pessimistic pronouncements, were already noting that their urban renewal projects had precipitated a counterflow which, although still a trickle, would soon become a large stream. The residential renaissance of central business districts, already receiving widespread attention, was expected to spread to other parts of the city. But a return to the city could not reach appreciable proportions, because there were neither residential nor employment opportunities for households to return to, and such opportunities could be created only very slowly, if at all.

PREDICTIONS FOR THE EIGHTIES

As the nation moves into the 1980s, it is confronted with conflicting predictions. One prescient group of commentators argues that the days of abandonment are drawing to a close. The forces of decentralization have played themselves out, and the rising cost of energy will, along with the changing age composition of the population and a rejection of suburban lifestyles, cause the trickle of middle-class families back to the city to become, at last, the large flow predicted over 20 years ago. After a critical mass of new middle-class residents has been created at the center, growth will feed on itself, and the expanding frontiers of decay which were characteristic of most of the postwar period will be replaced by a growing perimeter of renewal activity. One of the major impediments to central-city revival, urban crime, will be partially removed by a decline in the high-crime age group, 15-24. A second related barrier, inferior public education, will not be a concern to the increasing proportion of childless households, already over 60 percent nationwide and growing each year. The gentrification of neighborhoods encircling the downtown areas of our cities is cited as evidence that the return flow has already reached the proportions that were forecast.

Another group of urban futurologists with equally impressive credentials is less sanguine. If middle- and upper-income households had nothing to return to in 1960, they have even less to attract them back to central cities today. Two decades ago, the city was good but the suburbs were better. In the intervening years, the quality of city schools has declined, crime has increased, an even smaller proportion of the city's housing stock can appeal to today's affluent suburbanites, and employment opportunities in the city have decreased. With declining racial prejudice and discrimination, cities are now losing large numbers of black residents as well as white. To the extent that the cost of energy is a factor, it favors a suburban location for the now 70-80 percent of the suburbanites who work there, and there is no indication yet that these costs are causing business and industry to rethink their suburban locations. Until employment recentralizes, households in large numbers will not. And until then, gentrification will remain confined almost entirely to areas immediately adjacent to downtown, or so it is argued. The large amount of suburban residential and nonresidential development in slowly growing metropolitan areas would appear to support that argument.

So two movements in opposite directions may be observed—gentrification and suburbanization. Is the former steadily replacing the latter, or will the two continue in tandem, with thinning-out the dominant trend, though perhaps not to quite as great an extent as before? We opt for the thinning-out prognosis. Long-term trends do not suddenly abate and reverse themselves. The century-long outward tide is still clearly visible and for that reason alone could not be expected, barring an event of cataclysmic proportions, to lose its entire momentum in just a few years.

But there are less metaphysical reasons for not expecting decentralization to reverse itself soon. Numerous forecasts for a large number of metropolitan areas indicate only modest population and employment growth but a spectacular rise in real income. These two trends operating together argue for a continuing decline in central-city populations overall. Four-day work weeks, progress in telecommunications, smaller and more fuel-efficient automobiles, retrofitting of modern heating systems and, at worst, recapitalization of home values will more than counteract whatever weak recentralization tendencies result from rising energy costs. Moreover, not many households want to be urban pioneers, and not many can become pioneers without creating formidable political resistance by the city residents they would displace. A decline in the number of live births after 1985, stemming from the preceding decline that began in 1962, will contribute further to population loss in central cities.

In brief, the metropolitan environment within which today's housing problems are being tackled will not markedly change. Certainly it will not improve for central cities. If today's solutions for inner-city areas have been inadequate, tomorrow they will be so too. This does not mean better solutions are readily available. Indeed, it is now popular to argue that the public sector must be more realistic and lower its sights. Some problems are thought to be insoluble. Regardless of one's views about establishing more modest goals, it would seem wise to recognize the formidable forces that are creating the outcomes public policy is trying to alter.

THE CHANGING POLITICAL ENVIRONMENT WITHIN CITIES

While discussions of central-city housing problems frequently allude to the competing political interests between city and suburb and among levels of government, some of the most visible conflicts occur within cities between housing program managers and housing activists. These conflicts have developed in part because emphasis on community development and citizen participation has broadened the base of participation in program implementation, if not policy formation. The Neighborhood Housing Services begun in 1973, the Community Development Block Grant program created in 1974, the Community Reinvestment Act of 1975, the National Neighborhood Policy Act of 1977, and the Neighborhood Self-Help Development Act of 1978 exemplify this trend.

The emphasis on neighborhood in general and on neighborhood-based organizations in particular derives in part from a sense that some of the desirable features of small-town living environments can be created in large cities through appropriately designed small-scale residential settings. Such settings provide opportunities for face-to-face contact and knowledge of neighbors. These opportunities, in turn, are thought to lead to the development of mutual support networks and political influence by residents on behalf of the neighborhood interests. Efforts to create physical environments that nurture support networks have had only marginal success in general. Strategies aimed at building neighborhood organizations have been more successful.

The major reason why neighborhood and community development issues are politically charged is that these matters are closely tied to the struggle for the empowerment of the poor, the minorities, and the disenfranchised who live in the city. The importance of neighborhood is closely linked to the idea of decentralization of power to these groups. It is argued that if this were done, program effectiveness as well as individual satisfaction, self-esteem, and sense of belonging would be increased.

Cities vary substantially with respect to governmental decentralization. Seattle and Birmingham, to name two, have models of citizen participation in housing and community development programs that are highly regarded. Other cities maintain tight control in the mayor's office. No doubt part of the resistance to further decentralization of housing programs comes from elected politicians who fear a political structure that would parallel ward politics but be relatively independent and not directly responsive to elected officials. More generally, politicians and bureaucrats at all levels are likely to favor decentralization if it does not diminish their own power and authority. HUD policies, for example, tend to favor decentralization to neighborhood organizations that would entail a loss of authority for local officials but not federal officials.

An additional barrier to decentralization is lack of leadership and interest in many of the neighborhoods most in need of help. And since, as already suggested, many problems that manifest themselves in neighborhoods do not originate there and thus cannot be solved by neighborhood groups, even the strongest of such groups frequently become frustrated. For these reasons, decentralization unaccompanied by greater investment in comprehensive planning at the top would be a mixed blessing. Without a strong central planning function, shifting public power to quasi-governmental units at the neighborhood level is not likely to increase either equity or program effectiveness.

The political effectiveness of many neighborhood organizations sometimes leads their members and leaders to believe that they should move into actual program management and resource allocation in a variety of areas from housing to economic development. A few have been successful at this, but most have been frustrated when understaffed agencies with democratic procedures flounder in the face of bureaucratic responsibilities and large-scale problems. One must have reservations, therefore, about the ability of neighborhood organizations and community development corporations to operate programs effectively. Neighborhood organizations may materially contribute to a sense of community, and they are often politically effective, but these contributions should not be confused with the capacity for management. The promising examples that are cited seem altogether too rare and special. More often, community groups have only enough power and resources to fail.

POSSIBLE DIRECTIONS FOR NEIGHBORHOOD STRATEGIES AND PROGRAMS

People who live in poor housing in undesirable locations also tend to have less education, more illness, higher unemployment, and lower-paying jobs. This fact begins to explain why housing programs have been expanded to deal with other kinds of problems that occur in neighborhoods with poor housing. In the past two decades various combinations of housing and nonhousing programs have been directed at these problems. The war on poverty conducted by the Office of Economic

Opportunity used the Community Action Program to foster community development. Similarly, Model Cities employed more social services than had been typical of previous HUD programs. Current activities, in addition to purely physical improvement programs, include everything from extra police protection to neighborhood festivals. Each of the programs and services was designed to address problems beyond the substandard housing conditions that occur in deteriorating neighborhoods. Consequently, while they do not serve directly to improve houses, they are intended to upgrade both the social and physical quality of the environment.

Failure of these programs to achieve greater success is frequently ascribed to the huge gap between available resources and those that are necessary to raise the quality of life in declining neighborhoods to an acceptable level. But before we ascribe too much of the problem to too few resources, it is worth bearing in mind that if neighborhood conditions in some cities are indeed worsening in tandem with rising incomes, inadequate resources are not the problem. Nor is it simply organizational or administrative inefficiency. Much of the difficulty is due to lack of understanding of the nature, magnitude, distribution, and causes of housing and neighborhood problems.

The need for better understanding can be seen most clearly by referring again to intrametropolitan trends, and in particular to the theoretical confusion caused by the ever-widening ring of social problems and physical blight associated with the outward movement of population. If this decentralization had been the consequence only of rising incomes, then neighborhood succession should not have been accompanied by decline, except in neighborhoods close to the very bottom of the distribution, where households still in poverty were able to inherit the homes of the upwardly mobile near-poor. Instead, however, despite a decreasing low-income population, many neighborhoods well above the bottom rung are experiencing social and economic problems.

Several theories have been advanced to explain this apparent anomaly of rising incomes and expanding decay. One is that mortgage lending practices and inadequate maintenance by landlords bring down the neighborhoods. But if the real income of neighborhood residents did not fall as neighborhoods filtered—and, as just noted, this generally appears to have been the case—then there would be no reason for housing suppliers and market intermediaries to alter their customary practices. Another explanation frequently offered is racial change, particularly if it is rapid. There may be special situations in which transition from white to black precipitates decline. Several studies have concluded, however, that racial change by itself has often brought neighborhood improvement. Still another popular theory emphasizes the intractable problems caused by large concentrations of lower-income households. These concentrations do appear to account for part of the severity and durability of poverty in urban areas, but they do not provide a very good explanation for the spread of neighborhood decay. Public policy itself is often blamed for the widening ring of blight and decay, though the precise reasons vary widely, ranging from charges of ineptitude to favoritism of suburbs and excessive investment in highway infrastructure. Finally, the most durable myth of all is that houses simply deteriorate as they grow older today. If this were true, many of the nation's finest old houses would have been condemned and demolished long ago.

To explain neighborhood decline in the face of rising incomes, it is necessary to accept one or more of the following assumptions, and we are not sure ourselves which one or ones might be correct:

1. Physically and economically, most neighborhoods perceived to be in a process of decline are actually in better condition, in absolute terms, than they were in the past, but either rising standards of adequacy or increasing social problems explain perceptions of decline.

2. There is a confusing mixture of physical decline, caused by housing abandonment and the boarding-up of neighborhood commercial structures, and physical improvement, associated with rising real income.

3. The statistics on rising real incomes are misleading. A larger-than-average proportion of households that can afford to move into stable neighborhoods have various personal problems which draw their attention away from home maintenance or spill over into their neighborhoods.

4. Households are dispersing at such a high rate that prices have become depressed, enabling lower-income groups to migrate to neighborhoods somewhat distant from the boundaries of the old poverty areas.

Depending on which theory seems most plausible, an improved environment, in other than the very worst neighborhoods, might be achieved by (1) no appreciable change in present policy, (2) a shift in resources away from housing assistance to employment and social service programs, (3) containment of the poor in the inner city through programs that would reduce incentives to outmigrate to still stable areas, or (4) more rapid removal of vacated structures accompanied by land reuse.

Ultimately, however, the creation and preservation of both decent housing and the physical structure of neighborhoods requires a favorable investment climate, broadly defined. Landlords have to expect to receive profits commensurate with those which can be obtained on investments of comparable risk elsewhere. Owner-occupants must anticipate that money spent on upgrading and maintenance will be recouped though a better living environment and stable property values. Merchants must be persuaded that modernization of storefronts will help sales. City government must feel confident that street signs that are repaired will not be immediately vandalized. Ordinarily citizens who sweep their streets or paint their walls or clear vacant lots must have similar confidence that their efforts will not be offset by youths who make graffiti or people who dump worn-out family belongings on the nearest available piece of open space.

There are two partially overlapping prerequisites to a favorable investment climate (1) adequate current and expected resident income and (2) desire by residents and government to commit resources to home and neighborhood. The income prerequisite is universally recognized. But, as already mentioned, if income were the only factor, we would be at a loss to explain why average real income in many neighborhoods that are thought to be deteriorating is the same or higher today than 30 years ago, when the neighborhoods were regarded as stable middle-class communities. Missing in these neighborhoods is the necessary willingness to care for and invest in the physical environment.

Why this is so is not well understood, but public policy may in some respects have aggravated the problem. Rather than working to improve the inner-city investment climate, government for more than a decade has simply viewed the private inner-city investor as the enemy. While officials, for example, ascribe intolerable conditions in some of the public housing projects to poor building design, or a non-middle-class clientele, or the failure of the federal government to provide sufficient funds for building maintenance and social services, the same conditions in the private sector are said to be caused by slumlords trying to make excessive profits. Landlords who fail to pay real estate taxes, usually on overassessed properties, in order to keep their dwellings in use are publicized as tax dodgers. If they abandon their properties because they cannot maintain them in decent condition and earn a profit, they are similarly chastized. While slumlords do exist, present approaches to the problem do nothing to improve the desire of people to live or invest in the inner city, and it creates an atmosphere not conducive to reasoned exploration of inner-city problems.

Lip service not to the contrary, there is no housing or neighborhood strategy either in existence or proposed that would appreciably improve the investment climate in the inner city. Modest rehabilitation is not such a strategy. Indeed, it is not a strategy at all; it is simply an objective, one which by itself does almost nothing to improve the investment climate. Maximum rehabilitation is alleged to be a strategy that improves investor confidence by removing visible signs of blight. Investors, however, are not so naive.

What about neighborhood economic development, including enterprise zones? This approach could be aimed at only a few neighborhoods. Moreover, most household heads who are in poverty are either not potentially in the labor force or already employed full-time. They are elderly, handicapped, required to be at home to care for children, or are the breadwinners for a large number of dependents. As for nonheads who are unemployed or underemployed, particularly teenagers, experience has shown that even very large businesses provided with considerable financial incentive to create jobs are able to absorb only a small number of unskilled workers into their organizations. Experience in Third World squatter neighborhoods has taught us that it is exportable skills of the residents, together with social networks within the neighborhoods, that foster prosperity and upward mobility.

What, then, about the drive to grant broader decision-making powers to neighborhood groups? Certainly, this would seem to be a desirable objective in its own right. If towns of 10,000 to 50,000 population can have a measure of self-rule, why not neighborhoods of comparable size in large cities? Yet one should be cautious about assuming that just because neighborhood residents recognize symptoms of illness they can also correctly diagnose and treat the problem.

Finally, what about opening up the suburbs, or at least making a greater effort to enable subsidized households to disperse out of the inner city? In the short run, this obviously does not contribute to either a stable investment climate or a better social climate in the neighborhoods from which the assisted families depart. Over the longer term, perhaps greater stability is achieved throughout the metropolitan area, but greater stability can be approached in other ways as well.

Are we to conclude, then, that there is no short- or medium-term solution to neighborhood decline? A number of astute observers of the urban scene have come to such a conclusion, not with respect to central cities generally, but certainly with respect to many of the nation's large, old cities. Yet between now and the year 2000, several billions of dollars will be spent by the public sector to improve the living conditions in less desirable neighborhoods. Even today a billion dollars is not a small sum of money. Is it difficult to believe that proper planning of such a high expenditure of funds cannot attract private investment of several times that amount and produce a residential environment substantially superior to those which exist today.

Whether federal, state, and local governments have the will, knowledge, and understanding necessary to develop such plans and implement them is the question. On the whole, we think they do not have these qualities at the present time. With public resources increasingly constrained, however, rhetoric as a basis for planning is gradually being replaced by thoughtful inquiry and recognition of better ways to mediate conflicting local interests. Without, therefore, being able to suggest specifically in what direction policies to improve neighborhoods should head, we are somewhat hopeful that out of the present confusion of ideas, new organizational arrangements between city government and neighborhood groups will emerge, and that these arrangements will provide the opportunity for the creation of more coherent and efficacious neighborhood physical and social programs than now exist.

ANNALS, *AAPSS*, **465**, January 1983

Mortgage Lending in Older Urban Neighborhoods: Lessons from Past Experience

By LYNNE BEYER SAGALYN

ABSTRACT: At a time when policy initiatives of the Reagan administration are reducing government regulations and relying increasingly on private markets, a look at how home mortgage credit was supplied in areas redlined by institutional lenders offers a historical perspective on how the market works in credit-short neighborhoods. The evidence from Chicago shows that credit was available from professional investors using land installment contracts. But the cost to black homebuyers in these neighborhoods undergoing racial change was remarkably high. Investors realized high returns from race- as well as risk-related factors. Without sacrificing the high investment return, they shifted the lending risk to financial institutions. In effect, these institutions' only recourse was the value of the mortgaged property, the element conventionally considered most uncertain in these neighborhoods. The problems of an imbalance between lending risk and return highlight the importance of the structure of lending incentives as well as the availability of credit in these neighborhoods.

Lynne B. Sagalyn received her Ph.D. from the Massachusetts Institute of Technology, where she is assistant professor of planning and real estate development. Her research and publications have been on race discrimination in urban housing markets, exclusionary land-use controls, and rental housing investment. She is currently investigating public-private relationships in downtown redevelopment.

NOTE: This article is based on Lynne B. Sagalyn's dissertation, "Housing on the Installment Plan: An Economic and Institutional Analysis of Contract Buying in Chicago" (Massachusetts Institute of Technology, 1980), partial financial support for which came from the Joint Center for Urban Studies of MIT and Harvard University.

IN April 1982, the President's Commission on Housing issued its final report setting forth its recommendations based on the belief that the housing sector can most efficiently deliver services at a lower cost if government participation is kept at a minimum.[1] Less government involvement in residential credit markets may affect the flow of credit into urban neighborhoods through changes in policy affecting the volume of Federal Housing Administration (FHA)-insured home mortgage loans, or in regulations targeted at eliminating redlining, the Home Mortgage Disclosure Act (HMDA), and the Community Reinvestment Act (CRA). FHA-insured mortgages have been an important source of credit in urban areas, particularly in neighborhoods undergoing racial transition.[2] The HMDA and CRA, by requiring financial institutions to disclose information on mortgage lending activities and by creating a regulatory incentive to evaluate lending procedures and provide credit services in older, often poorer urban neighborhoods, have sought to increase the flow of funds to these areas and thereby stem neighborhood decline.

Redlining emerged as a policy issue in the 1970s, but the lack of mortgage credit in older urban neighborhoods, particularly those undergoing racial change, was a more serious problem in the preceding two decades. During this period, when both forms of institutional credit—loans insured by the FHA and uninsured, conventional loans made by financial institutions—were generally unavailable in these areas,[3] home purchases were commonly financed with alternative instruments, such as land installment contracts. In light of current initiatives to reduce government involvement in private markets, a look at how this credit gap was filled, in the absence of specific programs or targeted regulations, offers a historical perspective on how the private market works in credit-short neighborhoods.

The land installment contract market in Chicago is an important example of this. Although noninstitutional sources of credit financed homeownership in many cities, the costs of these transactions, unrecorded in public records at the time of sale, have been largely undocumented. Data collected for a major class action lawsuit[4] on behalf of

1. President's Commission on Housing, *The Report of the President's Commission on Housing* (Washington, DC: Government Printing Office, 1982), p. xvi.

2. C. Duncan MacRae, Margery Austin Turner, and Anthony M.J. Yezer, "Determinants of FHA Mortgage Insurance in Urban Neighborhoods," *Housing Finance Review*, 1:55-71 (Jan. 1982). The President's Commission on Housing cited the continuing need for FHA to provide mortgage insurance where the private market is unable or unwilling to do so. The impact on loan volume will depend on the type of FHA program change or budget changes reducing commitments for FHA loans or for Government National Mortgage Association mortgage-backed securities.

3. David McEntire, *Residence and Race* (Berkeley: University of California Press, 1960); Alfred Avins, ed., *Open-Occupancy vs. Forced Housing Under the Fourteenth Amendment* (New York: Bookmailer, 1963); U.S. Commission on Civil Rights, *1961 Report: Part IV, Housing* (Washington, DC: Government Printing Office, 1961); Chicago Commission on Human Relations, *Mortgage Availability for Non-Whites in the Chicago Area* (Chicago: Chicago Commission on Human Relations, 1963).

4. *Contract Buyers League* v. *F & F Investment*, 300 F.Supp. 210 N.D. Ill. (1969).

black families purchasing homes between 1952 and 1968 presents a unique opportunity to study this market.

THE MARKET RESPONSE TO REDLINING

In the conventional way we would expect markets to respond, when institutional lenders redlined or refused to supply credit in older, racially changing neighborhoods in Chicago in the 1950s and 1960s, professional investors moved into these areas to make loans on profitable terms and to service the unmet demand. They filled the credit gap by virtue of their expertise in uncertain lending situations and their specialized access to mortgage credit or their available cash for investment. In doing so, these investors acted as nonfinancial intermediaries between outmigrating white families who could not finance the transactions themselves and at the same time buy another home, and incoming black families who did not have cash to cover the purchase price.

Market conditions in neighborhoods undergoing racial transition offered investors a number of opportunities to profit by filling the credit gap. As a consequence of the reduced supply of mortgage credit, homes could be acquired at depressed prices and, when subsequently sold, financed at above-market rates. Racial change afforded an additional opportunity to profit from differences in housing prices which resulted from prejudice among departing white resident-owners[5] and discrimination against prospective black buyers with limited housing choices.[6] Through arbitrage—buying in one market and selling at a higher price in another—investors could profit from these constraints hindering direct property transfers. The key element was the price difference that resulted from buying for cash at a discount in the white market when racial change threatened, and then selling on credit at a premium in the black market during so-called neighborhood invasion.

By providing a means for existing owners to liquidate and for prospective buyers to purchase homes, these investors, or arbitrageurs, provided a needed market service. Yet it was a remarkably costly and disruptive process in the short run, contributing to neighborhood instability. Many arbitrageurs, stimulated by potential profits from servicing this market, did not just passively broker the transaction but actively initiated neighborhood change through blockbusting and panic-selling tactics.[7] Further, with con-

For a discussion of the Contract Buyers League and some of the arguments involved in the litigation, see James A. McPherson, "In My Father's House There Are Many Mansions—And I'm Going to Get Me Some of Them Too," *Atlantic Monthly*, 229:52-82 (Apr. 1972); Gregory L. Colvin, "Discriminatory Housing Markets, Unconscionability and Section 1988: The Contract Buyers League Case," *Yale Law Journal*, 80:514-66 (1971).

5. Martin J. Bailey, "Effects of Race and Other Demographic Factors on the Values of Single-Family Houses," *Land Economics*, 42:215-22 (May 1966).

6. John Kain and John Quigley, *Housing Markets and Racial Discrimination* (New York: National Bureau of Economic Research, 1975), pp. 62-82; Rose Helper, *Racial Policies and Practices of Real Estate Brokers* (Minneapolis: University of Minnesota Press, 1969).

7. For a firsthand account of these well-known practices in Chicago, described by one of the area's most active speculators using a

trol over the capital necessary for transition, they—and financial institutions—played an important role in funneling excess housing demand among black households into certain neighborhoods which concentrated the market impacts that might have been dispersed across a number of neighborhoods.[8]

Not only did different housing market suppliers fill the credit gap, but they financed purchases with an alternative instrument, one traditionally used in lending situations where down payments were low and the perceived risks high. The land installment contract (LIC), legally referred to as "articles for agreement for warranty deed," and "trustee's deed," or simply "contract for deed," provided the buyer with immediate possession of the property for which he made a down payment and, like a mortgage, agreed to pay a specific monthly installment payment which included interest and principal and amortized the loan balance over the term of the contract.

Two characteristics of the LIC are important for understanding its use in this alternative credit marke First, unlike a conventional deed sale financed with a mortgage, the seller in an LIC transaction retained title to the property until the loan balance had been paid completely or until a certain proportion of equity had accrued and a mortgage secured. On this type of contract, if the borrower defaulted on his payments, the costs and delay of foreclosure proceedings, in Illinois, were minimal.[9]

The second important feature of the LIC was that a high interest rate could be easily hidden. Because the seller, and not a third party, provided financing, he could cover the high cost of long-term credit by inflating the sales price. In a market dominated by such sales, there was no need to quote the buyer without this credit premium.[10] Further, by overstating the value of the property, the seller-lender circumvented state usury laws which limited the contract interest rate, one commonly noted restraint on conventional mortgage lending in older urban neighborhoods.

HOW COSTLY IS NONINSTITUTIONAL CREDIT?

Buying a home on an installment contract in transitional neighborhoods in Chicago between 1956 and 1968 was a remarkably costly experience. One measure of this cost is the markup between the contract seller's acquisition costs and subsequent sale price on an LIC. In a sample of nearly 300 LIC transactions during this period covering more

pseudonym, see Norris Vitcheck (as told to Alfred Balk), "Confessions of a Blockbuster," *Saturday Evening Post*, 235:15-19 (14-21 July 1962).

8. See Kerry D. Vandell and Bennett Harrison, "Racial Transition Among Neighborhoods: A Simulation Model Incorporating Institutional Parameters," *Journal of Urban Economics*, 5(4):315-33 (1978); John Yinger, "Racial Transition and Public Policy," Policy Note P78-1, Department of City and Regional Planning, Harvard University, Mar. 1978.

9. The legal remedy available to the contract seller in Illinois in the event of default resulted in one of the less costly and most rapid foreclosure proceedings on LICs in most states. Because a contract buyer could be evicted through the forcible entry and detainer procedure applied in rental eviction cases, the entire process could take as little as 60 days, as compared to nearly three years for a conventional mortgage.

10. See Michael A. Stegman, *Housing Investment in the Inner City: The Dynamics of Decline* (Cambridge: MIT Press, 1972), pp. 199-202, for a discussion of LIC activity in Baltimore.

than 105 neighborhoods in Chicago, buyers signed contracts that obligated them to pay, on average, 69 percent more than what investors—contract sellers—paid for acquiring, fixing up, and transferring one- to four-family properties. Generally, contract sellers made few improvements and turned over the property in a relatively short period, less than six weeks. White families who were forced to sell at depressed prices suffered an immediate loss of accrued equity. However, because housing demand was strong, credit short, and black mobility into new residential areas restricted,[11] these price reductions were not passed on to the black homebuyer. Under these conditions, contract sellers had some monopoly power which allowed them to charge black families the higher, inflated prices.

The inflated price of LIC transactions not only misled the buyer about the market value of the home, but it also distorted his purchasing power and reduced further the slim odds of securing institutional mortgage financing. Because contract sellers quoted a single price that included a premium for supplying credit, the disparity between the LIC price and the appraisal value by a mortgage lender would have required a larger down payment from the buyer and thereby decreased the likelihood that he would qualify for a loan. Since the market value of the home was insufficient to support a conventional or FHA-insured mortgage which could refinance the balance of the contract, LIC financing effectively locked the buyer into high-cost credit.

How large was this credit premium? Based on the previously cited sample of LIC transactions, I estimated that contract sellers inflated prices an average $5300—in 1957-59 dollars—to cover the costs associated with providing long-term credit.[12] Between 1956 and 1965, the 10-year period of most active LIC sales, this premium, expressed as a proportion of the LIC price, declined only a little, from 28 percent to 24 percent.

How should we interpret this credit adjustment? Consider the 69 percent arbitrage markup reported previously. This represents the deferred profit the seller expected to collect over the life of the contract. If he did not finance the sale but instead was able to buy and sell for cash immediately, what profit would he have received in this hypothetical situation? About 22 percent. However, this option was unlikely because the appraised value for lending purposes was much lower.[13]

11. Otis D. Duncan and Beverly Duncan, *The Negro Population of Chicago* (Chicago: University of Chicago Press, 1957); Chicago Commission on Human Relations, *Mortgage Availability for Non-Whites in the Chicago Area;* David McEntire, *Residence and Race* (Berkeley: University of California Press, 1960).

12. This credit premium represents the difference between the actual LIC sale price and a hypothetical sale price a seller might have been willing to accept if he sold without supplying credit. This latter cash-equivalent price was derived by summing the seller's cost of acquiring the property and the discounted value of the income stream—the difference between what the contract buyer pays to the contract seller and what he pays to the lender who granted him a mortgage on the property—he expected to receive over the life of the contract. See Lynne B. Sagalyn, "Housing on the Installment Plan: An Economic and Institutional Analysis of Contract Buying in Chicago" (Ph.D. diss., Massachusetts Institute of Technology, 1980), pp. 166-70.

13. Stegman, *Housing Investment in the Inner City*, p. 206, makes this point, and the lending documents for the conventional loans given to contract sellers in Chicago included an appraisal statement that reaffirms it.

Overstating the market value is the traditional means by which sellers have adjusted for the costs of financing low-equity, high-risk purchases. In Chicago, the average down payment in these LIC transactions was small, 6 percent. However, if the estimated adjustment for the risk and liquidity of the LIC noted before represents over two-thirds of the large transaction markup, broker profit from arbitraging racial differences in market prices would account for the residual.

The inflated LIC price combined with the characteristic low down payment and short contract payment period camouflaged a high rate of interest. When LIC monthly interest payments were evaluated against the contract seller's total costs for the investment, the average yield to the seller paid by contract buyers between 1956 and 1961 was over 15 percent. By 1962, increasing internal competition among contract sellers, higher investment costs, and lower markups forced the average rate down to its 13-year low point, 13 percent. Yet this was still twice the stated LIC interest rate and twice the prevailing rate on conventional mortgages.

While these financial terms of LIC credit were set in a market, albeit a restricted one, many of the risks to the contract buyer were neither negotiable nor subject to the laws of supply and demand. Nor were they clearly understood by the buyers. Without title ownership or equity rights specifically defined by law, the contract buyer lacked the institutional protection otherwise afforded by a standard deed and mortgage transaction. First, in the event of default, his interest was not protected by the costly legal expenses of a foreclosure, or by a reasonable redemption period during which he could satisfy his debt and retain his home, or by the right to any equity proceeds from a judicial sale.[14] Second, even if the contract buyer was not delinquent in his payments, his interests were vulnerable to actions by the contract seller that might cloud good title. Furthermore, over time as the contract buyer's equity increased and the contract seller's risk decreased, this mismatch between rights and risks became more distorted.

The size of the markups and credit premiums on LIC transactions in transitional neighborhoods underscores the high costs of the market adjustment borne by both resident sellers and homebuyers on the margin. The high costs of LIC credit further spilled over into the neighborhood, as new contract buyers, overburdened by the inflated loan payment charges, deferred home maintenance and increased the number of occupants in the units, whereby housing deterioration accelerated.

SHIFTING THE RISK

By financing these LIC purchases, contract sellers appeared to be capturing a high return for accepting the risks of lending in these neighborhoods, risks which financial institutions would not consider or otherwise could not profitably take. Yet appearances in this market were deceptive. Contract sellers operating successfully in this alternative market complemented

14. John Mixon, "Installment Land Contracts: A Study of Low Income Transactions, With Proposals for Reforms and New Programs to Provide Home Ownership in the Inner City," *Houston Law Review*, 7:535-54 (May 1970).

high returns with a strategy to minimize risk. The land installment contract was the most obvious, but not sole, element of this strategy. By owning property through a blind land trust[15] and by financing the LIC sale with a conventional mortgage, contract sellers in Chicago skillfully limited their personal liability and shifted the lending risk to those individuals and institutions financing their speculative activities.

As a consequence, without sacrificing the high investment return, the contract seller rarely had much capital at risk. For the sample of arbitrage transactions I studied, the average cash equity invested by the contract seller represented only 5 percent of his total investment costs. Another 10 percent of these costs was financed by the contract buyer's down payment, while the lending institution, by financing over 85 percent, held the greatest share of the risk that the underlying value of the property might be insufficient to cover the outstanding mortgage balance in the event the contract seller defaulted on the loan. Lending institutions, by implication, financed these transactions based on the security of the LIC's hybrid economics as a cross between an absentee-owner income-producing property and a resident-owner unit.

15. Nearly all contract sellers conducted property transactions—acquisition, mortgage finance, LIC sale—within this legal framework, identifiable only by bank number. In addition to concealing his identity and the extent of his property holdings, the trust format allowed the investor to limit his personal or business liability, since the trust entered into all transactions and its resources were limited, generally to a single property.

Incentives in financing speculation

In accepting this lending risk, these savings and loan associations and commercial banks—55 in number, or nearly 19 percent of those in the Chicago metropolitan area—played a pivotal, if not unorthodox, role in the large-scale development of the LIC market in Chicago. Although few regulations licensed entry into the market, contract sellers depended on access to a continuous and reliable source of capital to finance a large portfolio of LIC properties. Without this capital, speculative activity would have been limited by an investor's smaller personal investment resources. Additionally, unlike private, informal investment groups and individuals who otherwise supplied capital to these markets, financial institutions tapped a larger and lower-cost pool of investment funds: savings deposits.

Financing low-equity, speculative sales in transitional neighborhoods deviated from the industry's model of good lending behavior. However, many of these financial institutions were responding to the same high-risk, high-profit economic incentives motivating contract sellers. Assuming reasonable payment performance on these loans, lenders expected significantly higher returns to be paid back in a shorter time than those available on conventional mortgages during this period. For example, in 1965, a year of declining LIC activity, but one when the differences in loan characteristics were relatively small, the average interest rate on mortgage loans financing LIC properties was 13 percent higher, the loan origination fees nearly three times greater, and the amortization or pay-back period 29 percent shorter than for conventional mortgages on existing one- to four-family homes in Chicago.

The key element among these terms was the difference in the loan origination fee. By withholding a portion of the mortgage loan when the loan was issued, the lender in effect charged the borrower—or contract seller—an additional interest payment. In this way, lenders effectively raised the average interest rate on mortgages for LIC properties over 7 percent to 6.75 percent, as compared to a 3 percent increase to 5.74 percent for conventional loans.

Although this overall loan yield is an important indicator of expected economic return, to understand the structure of incentives underlying these speculative loans, we again need to look more closely at the sources and timing of this return—that is, at the loan fees. First, unlike the contract seller, the financial institution could not shift the lending risk on these conventional loans. Instead, by discounting the loan through high initial fees rather than by raising the interest payments, the lender reduced the amount of his capital at risk by minimizing his front-end commitment. In effect, this fee income increased the short-term return from the mortgage loan.

Second, the aggregate impact of many such high-fee loans magnified an institution's earnings and, in particular, the officers' income, in cases where these two were linked. In the case of one notable mutual association with the largest concentration of speculative loans, $161,000—or about 25 percent of gross income for one year, 1959—consisted of premium income. With an additional $180,000 of deferred premium income from 1959 reported on the association's balance sheet, the president of the association could expect in subsequent years to collect a $40,000 bonus, more than twice his salary, based on income collected from loan premiums in that year alone.[16]

For some institutions heavily involved in the LIC market, the dynamics of high-risk, high-yield investments could have created an internal self-sustaining rationale for making additional such loans. Initially, financial institutions might have sought out these loans as an accommodation to decreasing profit margins. Caught in an earnings squeeze between 1959 and 1962—the years when large numbers of mortgages backing LIC properties were made—from the rising cost of savings deposits and the declining interest rate on high-quality mortgage loans, these institutions might have sought higher yielding loans to increase their earnings and to pay the higher dividends necessary to attract depositors. Subsequently, as slow-paying or delinquent loans reduced the earnings of those associations with particularly large portfolio concentrations of speculative loans, earnings needed to pay savings dividends and for deposit reserves,[17] high loan premiums would have generated substitute income.

These dependencies on high loan fees, in addition to the not uncommon side payments and affiliated

16. H. Robert Bartell, Jr., "An Analysis of Illinois Savings and Loan Associations Which Failed in the Period 1963-1968," in *Study of the Savings and Loan Industry*, ed. Irwin Friend (Washington, DC: Government Printing Office, 1970), p. 377.

17. Bartell, "An Analysis of Illinois Savings and Loan Associations," pp. 415-17.

business interests associated with these speculative financings, represented obstacles to making conventional mortgage loans directly to the contract buyer. Although the contract buyer carried the higher costs of LIC payments, which included the contract seller's considerable intermediary profit, his relatively low down payment suggests that the large, up-front loan discounts would have been unaffordable. Of course, because of the complicity, cash payments presented a different problem and situations of conflicting interest represented a longstanding regulatory problem for the industry.[18] In short, by spreading the higher-than-average loan fees attached to these conventional mortgage loans over a longer period and by knowing the right sources, contract sellers became catalysts for financial institutions to make high-risk, high-return mortgage loans.

But ironically, by depending on investors selling homes on LICs in transitional neighborhoods to generate high-fee, high-return loans, lenders in effect placed major emphasis on the element considered most uncertain in these neighborhoods: the value of the real estate as security for the loan. In the conventional loan process, lenders impose down payment requirements and standards for the credit-worthiness of the borrower, both of which were absent in speculative mortgage financings. First, as an intermediary transaction where the contract seller was interposed between the lender and the contract buyer whose income provided the payment, the lender had no control over the key borrower criterion, the loan payment-to-income ratio.[19] Second, both contract seller and buyer had little equity at risk. But most important, the blind land trust held title to the property and generally the beneficiaries were not required to make additional personal guarantees on the loan. Therefore in the event the contract seller defaulted, the lending institution's only recourse behind the loan became the property itself. And having shifted all the risk, the contract seller had little incentive not to default on his mortgage payment if the contract buyer defaulted, unless he could continue to profit from maintaining his relationship with the lender and securing additional loans or from managing the property as a rental or by finding another buyer.

The lack of institutional credit in urban neighborhoods created a market niche not only for professional investors but also for those financial institutions that remained in the market to earn above-market returns from supplying credit in these areas. However, the experience suggests that financial institutions may have accepted greater risks than lending directly to homebuyers.

DRAWING ON THE LIC EXPERIENCE

When homebuyers in transitional neighborhoods in Chicago were unable to secure conventional or FHA-insured mortgages, the private market responded with an alternative supply of credit, but as we have seen, the cost was remarkably high. Although the high cost reflected expected high lending risk, it also

18. Edward S. Herman, "Conflict of Interest in the Savings and Loan Industry," in *Study of the Savings and Loan Industry*, pp. 833-47.

19. Bartell, "An Analysis of Illinois Savings and Loan Associations," p. 385.

reflected the additional profits the contract seller captured because of his access to a limited commodity—mortgage credit—in a housing market where he benefited further from racial discrimination against black families seeking to move into white neighborhoods. After 1966, when changes in FHA underwriting policies permitted loan insurance in older urban neighborhoods, credit conditions changed.[20] FHA-insured mortgages replaced land installment contracts as the common means of home finance. With the change in FHA policy, institutional mortgage credit became available directly to homebuyers, but the imbalance between the risks and rewards to the lender exerted a significant influence on the market dynamics in these neighborhoods, as it did in the LIC market.

What does the LIC experience tell us about the structure of lending incentives in these neighborhoods? What happens when lenders who initiate and manage high-risk loans hold little of the risk yet retain the high profit? In the typical LIC transaction, the contract seller, not personally liable for the mortgage loan and having little capital at risk, had little to lose by defaulting on the payments, which many did, if the contract buyer defaulted. The experience with FHA-insured mortgages during the late 1960s and early 1970s in urban neighborhoods, which resulted in widespread defaults and foreclosures, reemphasizes the consequences of completely shifting the lending risk. With the loss on a defaulted loan covered by insurance, lenders had little incentive to minimize the risk of default by carefully evaluating the credit strengths of borrowers or working out payment problems, as would a conventional lender with an uninsured loan.[21] Since the mortgage lending process involves a long-term financial commitment, the implication is that if lenders retain a share of the risk, they will have an incentive to remain involved through the term of the risk, and in protecting their interest reduce the overall costs of high-risk lending.

The LIC experience also emphasizes the importance of understanding the role of high loan fees in high-risk lending. Although high up-front loan fees represented a rational means to increase the return on loans when otherwise limited by interest rate ceilings, the fees too became part of the problem. For a number of financial institutions in the LIC market, high-interest, high-fee loans became not only a means to boost short-term earnings, and for officers a way to profit personally, but a threat to institutional solvency when loan portfolios accumulated large concentrations of these loans. For lenders using FHA-insured mortgages, high discount points in combination with the insurance protection created an incentive to finance risky borrowers and properties and to foreclose quickly in the event of default. The sooner the loan was repaid, the larger the return on the loan; the larger the number of

20. For a discussion of these changes, see P. M. Greenston, C. D. MacRae, and C. I. Pedone, "The Effects of FHA Activity in Older Urban, Declining Areas: A Review of Existing, Related Analysis," Research Report 220-1 (Washington, DC: Urban Institute, 1975).

21. "The Role of the Mortgage Banker in the FHA-Insured Single-Family Home Loan Process," in *The Role of Mortgage Lending Practices in Older Urban Neighborhoods* (Evanston: Center for Urban Affairs, Northwestern, 1975), pp. 121-62.

points, the greater the incentive.[22] The implication here is that if regulations on interest rates were removed, FHA-insured high-risk lending would be more prudently administered, since the loans would yield risk-related profits directly from market-level interest rates and not indirectly from high loan fees and fast foreclosures.

Further, the LIC experience emphasizes the role played by the intermediary in overcoming the barriers to direct lending in older urban neighborhoods. Financial institutions in the LIC market actually took the risk of lending in these neighborhoods, but the contract seller, capitalizing on his understanding of the dynamics of the neighborhood, originated and managed the LIC loan and thereby served as a vehicle for the investment. The market role a facilitator plays in creating the context for investment goes beyond the particular example in the LIC market, but the implication is that without some intermediary, financial institutions would be less likely to identify opportunities and to participate in the urban lending market.

Other researchers evaluating the way current federal regulations and programs affect the flow of credit to urban areas have made a similar point.[23] While the development of new risk-sharing programs for investment has proven successful in promoting investment, facilitators, community groups, and advisers have been an important part of an institutional structure necessary to take advantage of lending opportunities.

Although the conditions in Chicago in the 1950s and 1960s which fostered the LIC market are unlikely to occur again, the lesson we can draw from this market response is not that credit was supplied. Rather, the lesson is how the interaction between the participants, profit incentives, and market instruments affected the balance between lending risk and return, and thereby affected the cost of credit restrictions to consumers.

22. Susan M. Wachter, "The 1968 Congressional FHA Amendments to the National Housing Act: Their Impact on Urban Areas," in *The Urban Impacts of Federal Policies*, ed. Norman J. Glickman (Baltimore: Johns Hopkins University Press, 1980), pp. 432-34.

23. John A. Tuccillo, "Federal Regulations, Housing Programs, and the Flow of Urban Credit," Contract Research Report for Department of Housing and Urban Development (Washington, DC: Urban Institute, Aug. 1980). The facilitator also plays an important role in reinvestment strategies such as Neighborhood Housing Service partnerships. See Urban Systems Research and Engineering, Inc., *Creating Local Partnerships: The Role of the Urban Reinvestment Task Force in Developing Neighborhood Housing Services Organizations* (Washington, DC: Department of Housing and Urban Development, Mar. 1980).

ANNALS, *AAPSS*, **465**, January 1983

Housing the Poor in a Postshelter Society

By GEORGE STERNLIEB and JAMES W. HUGHES

ABSTRACT: The United States has completed a vast three-decade-long sweep of unprecedented housing achievement. While a relatively small proportion of record production levels was targeted directly to America's poverty population, the latter's housing condition improved markedly as a result of the much-maligned filtering process. But this success will face very serious inhibitors in the future. The breakdown of the traditional political housing alliance, the stagnation of real median family incomes, the growing number of persons under the poverty level, and a housing finance system subject to full market forces and credit competition—for the first time since the New Deal—characterize the early 1980s. Within this context, housing for the middle class is an issue of much more political potency than the housing needs of the poor. But without the reformation of a broad-based housing constituency, one of the great achievements of the last generation—the improvement in the shelter provisions of the poor—must quickly abort.

George Sternlieb is founder and director of the Center for Urban Policy Research, Rutgers University, and professor of urban planning and policy development. James W. Hughes is professor of urban planning and policy development at the Rutgers School of Urban and Regional Policy. They have jointly authored and edited 15 books and more than 30 articles. Their most recent works include America's Housing: Prospects and Problems, The Future of Rental Housing, Shopping Centers, U.S.A., *and* Demographic Trends and Economic Reality: Planning and Markets in the 1980s, *all published by the Center for Urban Policy Research.*

THE housing accommodations of the poor in the United States are practically unique among major industrial countries in their dependence on the vigor of the private housing economy. In the main this has yielded positive results. A rising tide may not float all boats, but the history of the last three decades of general housing advances in the United States contains a striking level of improvement in the shelter provisions for the needy. Direct publicly owned housing plays a relatively minuscule role. As of 1980, for example, only 1.3 million units, out of a total housing inventory of 88 million dwelling units, were publicly owned and operated. In total, about 4 million low- and moderate-income households were receiving some form of federal housing subsidy in 1980, only 5 percent of the nation's 80 million households. While state and municipal financing aid has grown in importance, their total input is still small—and spread to a variety of income groups, as indeed holds true for the federal input as well.

Thus government-aided housing for the poor has been of much less importance than the much-maligned process of filtering down. This is the provision of improved housing for the lower socioeconomic sectors of society through the trading-up of those more affluent.

It is the thesis of this article that this process has been much more successful than many of its critics have been willing to acknowledge, but that this success is subject to, and will face, very serious inhibitors in the future.

THE WELL-HOUSED SOCIETY

The process of widespread housing improvement was spearheaded by the unrelenting expansion of America's housing inventory during the post-World War II period. This was predominantly the result of a 50 percent net growth—approximately 20 million units—in the nation's housing stock over the 20-year period, combined with selective demolition and rehabilitation of deficient dwellings. Between 1950 and 1970, the proportion of substandard housing in the United States declined from 37 percent to 9 percent.[1]

But in retrospect, this achievement served only as a prelude to the remarkable housing events that were to come. As shown by the data in Table 1, the 1970s was the most prolific housing decade ever, with a 20 million unit net housing addition. In 10 years the absolute expansion of the preceding 20 years was replicated. This was accomplished by record production levels of owner-occupied single-family units and also by unparalleled gains in rental facilities. The sheer magnitude of the absolute quantities of housing delivered to America's housing consumers ensured that this period would be remembered as the nation's Golden Housing Era.

Inventory counts, however awesome in scale, reveal only the broadest dimension of the decade's housing achievement. Equally impressive are the statistical tabulations revealing the quantity of housing delivered per person. As detailed in Table 2, internal housing unit densities dramatically improved. Indeed, overcrowding—whether measured by standards of either 1.51 or 1.01 or more persons

1. A substandard housing unit is one which was either rated dilapidated by a census enumerator or lacked some or all plumbing facilities.

TABLE 1

CHANGES IN THE HOUSING INVENTORY, U.S. TOTAL: 1960, 1970, AND 1980

(numbers in thousands)

				CHANGE: 1960-70		CHANGE: 1970-80	
	1960	1970	1980	Number	Percent	Number	Percent
All housing units	58,326	68,672	88,397	10,346	17.7	19,725	28.7
Year-round units	56,584	67,699	86,678	11,115	19.6	18,979	28.0
Occupied units	53,024	63,445	80,378	10,421	19.7	16,933	26.7
Owner occupied	32,797	39,886	51,787	7,089	21.6	11,901	29.8
Percentage of total	61.9	62.9	64.4	—	—	—	—
Renter occupied	20,227	23,560	28,591	3,333	16.5	5,031	21.4
Percentage of total	38.1	37.1	35.6	—	—	—	—

SOURCE: U.S. Department of Commerce, Bureau of the Census, *Census of Housing: 1970*, Detailed Housing Characteristics, Final Report HC(1)-B1, United States Summary (Washington, DC: Government Printing Office, 1972); U.S. Department of Commerce, Bureau of the Census, *1980 Census of Housing*, Selected Housing Characteristics, Supplementary Report HC80-S1-1 (Washington, DC: Government Printing Office, October 1981).

TABLE 2

PERSONS PER ROOM, TOTAL OCCUPIED HOUSING UNITS: 1970 AND 1979

(numbers in thousands)

			CHANGE: 1970-79	
	1970	1979	Number	Percent
U.S. Total				
Total occupied:	63,446	78,571	15,125	23.8
.50 or less	31,729	47,518	15,789	50.0
.51 to 1.00	26,655	27,906	1,251	4.7
1.01 to 1.50	3,782	2,358	−1,424	−37.7
1.51 or more	1,280	789	−491	−38.4
Central Cities				
Owner occupied:	10,300	11,787	1,487	14.4
.50 or less	5,650	7,648	1,998	35.4
.51 to 1.00	4,015	3,765	−250	−6.2
1.01 to 1.50	518	293	−225	−43.4
1.51 or more	117	80	−37	−31.6
Renter occupied:	11,095	11,911	816	7.4
.50 or less	5,119	6,654	1,535	30.0
.51 to 1.00	4,849	4,510	−339	−7.0
1.01 to 1.50	785	525	−260	−33.1
1.51 or more	342	221	−121	−35.4

SOURCE: U.S. Department of Commerce, Bureau of the Census, *Current Housing Reports*, Series H-150-79, *Annual Housing Survey: 1979, Parts A and C* (Washington, DC: Government Printing Office, 1981).

TABLE 3
HOUSING INADEQUACY, 1970-79
(numbers in thousands)

	UNITED STATES TOTAL				CENTRAL CITIES			
			CHANGE: 1970-79				CHANGE: 1970-79	
	1970	1979	Number	Percent	1970	1979	Number	Percent
Owner occupied	39,886	51,411	11,525	28.9	10,300	11,787	1,487	14.4
Lacking some or all plumbing facilities	1,662	731	-931	-56.0	123	29	-94	-76.4
No bath or share	1,923	855	-1,086	-55.5	177	55	-122	-68.9
Renter occupied	23,560	27,160	3,600	15.3	11,095	11,911	816	7.4
Lacking some or all plumbing facilities	1,849	984	-865	-46.8	494	254	-240	-48.6
No bath or share	2,176	1,160	-1,016	-46.7	681	340	-341	-50.1

SOURCE: U.S. Department of Commerce, Bureau of the Census, *Current Housing Reports*, Series H-150-79, *Annual Housing Survey: 1979, Parts A and C.*

per room—has been rendered a national housing problem of minimal proportions.[2] The classic vision of the urban housing problem—the trauma of severe overcrowding depicted by the multiple persons per room syndrome in the literature of the 1950s—has substantially been relegated to history.

And these quantitative improvements were paralleled by substantial reductions in levels of housing inadequacies. Reliable measures of housing conditions that are field operational are sadly lacking.[3] Within this limited state of the art, however, as shown in Table 3, a vast upgrading clearly took place. From 1970 to 1979, fully three-quarters of central-city owner-occupied units which in 1970 had lacked some or all plumbing facilities were removed from the market. And the same held true with nearly equal vigor for central-city renter-occupied facilities, with nearly half of the deficient units gauged by this criterion either removed from the market or upgraded.

So vast were the improvements in the housing arena that by the end of the decade, questions were being

2. Over time there has been an escalation of the criterion of overcrowding, from a historical benchmark of 1.51 or more persons per room to the more recently employed threshold of 1.01 or more persons per room.

3. The 1980 census did not attempt to measure structure condition (dilapidation) directly. Thus the plumbing facilities standard must stand as a surrogate indicator of condition. For an analysis of the difficulty of measuring structure condition, see U.S. Bureau of the Census, *Measuring the Quality of Housing: An Appraisal of Census Statistics and Methods*, Working Paper no. 25 (Washington, DC: Government Printing Office, 1967).

TABLE 4
1973 MONTHLY GROSS RENTS OF HOUSING UNITS REMOVED FROM CENTRAL CITY INVENTORY 1973-79 (numbers in thousands)

1973 RENT LEVEL	TOTAL 1973	REMOVALS: 1973-79	REMOVALS: PERCENTAGE OF 1973 TOTAL
Specified renter occupied	11,405	973	8.5
less than $100	3,128	423	13.5
$100 to $149	3,881	324	8.3
$150 to $199	2,658	137	5.2
$200 to $299	1,203	43	3.6
$300 or more	266	11	4.1
No cash rent	269	34	—
Median rent (dollars)	130	107	—

SOURCE: U.S. Department of Commerce, Bureau of the Census, *Current Housing Reports*, Series H-150-79, *Annual Housing Survey: 1979, Parts A and C.*

raised as to whether Americans were overconsuming housing, with too great a share of the nation's resources earmarked—to the detriment of more essential sectors of the economy—to shelter functions. Whatever the validity of such concerns, this monumental upgrading brought in its wake substantial physical housing gains for America's poverty population.[4]

THE COST OF IMPROVEMENT

The success of the powerful political housing constituency that lasted through the long generation from the end of World War II to Watergate raised the housing standards of the nation as a whole directly—and those of the nation's poor as well, at least as a byproduct. But for the latter, the improvement of the physical conditions of housing units, as best as can be measured, was accomplished at some level of impact. Much of this revolved around the scrap-page issue.

In the United States, approximately 500,000 housing units a year typically are removed from the market. As would be expected, much of this represents low-cost housing. The process is typified by the data shown in Table 4, which indicates the proportion of 1973 rental housing units by rent level that were removed from the central-city inventory by 1979. In the six-year period under consideration, 13.5 percent of all renter-occupied units renting for less than $100 in 1973 were taken out of use. An additional 8.3 percent of the units renting between $100 and $149 similarly disappeared.[5]

4. Other deficiencies external to the dwelling unit—neighborhood conditions, access to employment opportunities, adequacy of public services, and the like—have become much more important than housing per se. See George Sternlieb and James W. Hughes, *America's Housing: Prospects and Problems* (New Brunswick, NJ: Rutgers University Center for Urban Policy Research, 1980).

5. Further analysis of *Annual Housing Survey* data reveals that the bulk of the removals sheltered low-income occupants.

The process of demolition and/or conversion to nonresidential purposes, while varying in scale with the business cycle, is inevitable. Over and above this is the competition for units vacated by the more affluent. The basic model of the American housing market is one in which the stock of shelter units is augmented substantially at the top in terms of price, with the bottom strata continuously being eliminated. The issue in terms of the housing conditions available for the poor are the relative speeds of growth of the lower end of the stock through filtering down versus the actual physical attrition level, tempered by absorption/competition from new household formations. But all of this must be placed in the context of costs within an inflationary era. In general, the last three decades have seen a positive physical condition relationship emerge, as witnessed by the physical improvements in the stock, but also price increments frequently in excess of the resource growth among the less affluent.

THE END OF THE OLD HOUSING ALLIANCE

We have come a long way from Franklin Delano Roosevelt's realistic description of "America as a nation—one third ill housed." The vigor of the first generation of crusaders for adequate shelter for the poor and the pioneer advocates of public housing who were their leading element have passed from the scene.

The definition of government's role in housing of the late 1940s and 1950s was epitomized by the bonuses offered the returning heroes of World War II. Housing for the conquering hero has a long tradition. Just as the Duke of Marlborough was given Blenheim by a grateful nation, so did our own armed services disband to a smorgasbord of housing aid. The GI Bill and the VA mortgage were just part of the feast spread on the housing table. In part, this was recompense for service. But it was fortified by a felt necessity to continue to prime the economic pump lest we return to the depression which, at least in some eyes, had merely abated in the course of the hostilities.

A long tide of enabling legislation continued to evolve in the decades that followed. While some of it was merchandised in the cause of the poor, the bulk of it—the below-market interest rate mortgages, the government guarantees, the state housing finance agencies, and all the other elements—was basically dedicated to generating construction for the broad sweep of the middle class.[6] The major federal housing programs of the 1970s are detailed in the appendix to this article.

As the reservoir of housing improved, however, as we moved from the 1940s era of a nation dominated by renters to one of homeowners, the hunger for housing as shelter abated. And with the abatement came a whole new ordering of priorities. Somewhere in the middle to the late 1960s, the very term "government housing program" became synonymous with the poor. The broad-based housing constituency of the earlier postwar era

6. In retrospect, the favored treatment granted to housing finance in the nation's credit markets was perhaps the greatest impetus to the overall housing progress of the last generation. The impact of the virtually complete removal of this priority status—and the subjection of housing to full market forces and credit competition the past three years—has not been fully appreciated.

split; the majority were those who were relatively complacent about their holdings but fearful that they would not continue to increase in value, versus the poor who were still looking for basic shelter.

The breaking point was reached not so much with the scandals that were attached to some of the assistance programs as with the realization by the major post-Roosevelt figure of the right, Richard Nixon, that there were more votes against housing programs than there were objectors to their demise. The housing moratorium of 1973 on federally subsidized homeownership and rental assistance programs was implemented.

Nixon's success at doing so reflected the breaking up of the political alliance for housing that had dominated the congressional scene for more than a generation. In its heyday this was embodied by a conjunction of the thrift institutions—the savings and loan associations and mutual savings banks, which were dedicated by law very largely, if not exclusively, to lending on housing; the mortgage bankers—who served as intermediaries between the lenders and the homebuilders; the homebuilders—who were perhaps the most powerful of the several constituents; and a substantial add-on of liberal groups dedicated to the needs of the poor. And this says nothing of the growing potency of minority groups, particularly the National Council of Negro Women. This broad political base had maintained the unparalleled level of housing development which characterized the United States. In so doing, they merely served as the visible edge of a generalized American consensus which gave first priority to housing. And it was this coalition which dissolved in the early 1970s.

The very success of homebuilding led to a dissolution of the bonds between the elements that represented the needs of the poor and a market grouping that felt secure without them. The homebuilders no longer felt that they needed participation by the government in the low-income sector. The thrift institutions were most anxious to reduce their participation in housing—particularly government-aided housing—for more profitable ventures. The wave of conscience that characterized postriot America clearly had ebbed; the political clout of minority groups and the poor in general suffered defeats from which neither has fully recovered. And perhaps most important of all, the United States had moved from a country of renters in the early post-World War II era to a nation of homeowners, with nearly two-thirds of all households in this latter category. This group seemingly did not suffer from the hungers of the past in terms of shelter but was much more concerned with postshelter considerations—that is, housing as investment, housing as forced saving and tax refuge, and housing as a form of protection from the inflationary ravages which were beginning to be viewed as chronic rather than merely transient.

In the years subsequent to 1973, the level of subsidized starts drifted down—the little that was constructed typically occurred under programs of relatively light subsidy aimed at more affluent sectors than held true in the past. Within the private domain, the homebuilders tended to focus on the up-scale, trade-up market rather than first-time homebuyers. Indeed, by 1981, profiles of new homebuyers indicated that nearly five out of six were trading in—and up.

TABLE 5
MEDIAN FAMILY INCOME: 1950-80

	MEDIAN FAMILY INCOME	
	ACTUAL DOLLARS	CONSTANT 1980 DOLLARS
1950	3,319	11,361
1960	5,620	15,637
1970	9,867	20,939
1973	12,051	22,346
1980	21,023	21,023

	GAINS IN REAL INCOME	
	CONSTANT 1980 DOLLARS	PERCENTAGE GAIN
1950-60	4,276	37.6
1960-70	5,302	33.9
1970-80	84	0.4
1970-73	1,407	6.7
1973-80	−1,323	−5.9

SOURCES: U.S. Bureau of the Census, *Current Population Reports*, Series P-60, No. 127, "Money Income and Poverty Status of Families and Persons in the U.S.: 1980 (Advance Data from the March 1981 Current Population Survey)" (Washington, DC: Government Printing Office, 1981).

While an abortive surrogate for the formerly earmarked low-income construction programs was developed in the later 1970s—the Section 8 program—its total contribution to the present has yielded less than a million units. Its provision of open-ended operating subsidies was an invitation to excess. The very costs of the program in turn have brought it virtually to an end.

In 1982 the United States faces a future in which the flow of unaided housing units has been substantially reduced by a new cost calculus, while at the same time, the targeted programs for low-income groups have essentially withered.

7. By the beginning of 1982, the contractual obligations for outstanding reservations in the program over their potential life were estimated at over $100 billion.

PIVOTAL SHIFTS

Underlying the transition of 1973 were basic shifts in the American economy whose full weight is still being felt—and which may well bear the seed of even more consequential future change. For in that year median family incomes peaked in the United States. The post-World War II era was one of overwhelming growth in real family incomes. As detailed in Table 5, between 1950 and 1960, for example, median family income—in constant 1980 dollars—increased by $4276. From 1960 to 1970, the real gain totaled in excess of $5000. Indeed from 1970 to 1973, the surge forward continued with an increment of $1407. But the 1973 median family income of $22,346 represented the terminal point in the parade to ever-increasing affluence. The energy shocks that were felt

TABLE 6
PERSONS BELOW THE POVERTY LEVEL: 1960-80

YEAR	PERSONS BELOW POVERTY LEVEL: ALL PERSONS	PERSONS BELOW POVERTY LEVEL: PERSONS IN FAMILIES WITH FEMALE HOUSEHOLDER (NO HUSBAND PRESENT)	ALL FAMILIES, MEDIAN FAMILY INCOME (CONSTANT 1980 DOLLARS)
1960	39,851	10,663	15,637
1970	25,420	11,154	20,939
1973	22,973	11,357	22,346
1980	29,272	14,649	21,023

SOURCE: U.S. Bureau of the Census, *Current Population Reports,* Series P-60, No. 127, "Money Income and Poverty Status of Families and Persons in the U.S.: 1980."

through the remainder of the decade—as well as other economic traumas—aborted the historical trend: the median family income in America by 1980—$21,023—was more than $1300 below the level of 1973. And with this has occurred a parallel decline in general housing buying power.

As America's 1982 housing starts hover close to a post-World War II low, with the housing finance market in shambles, as reflected by the increasing level of virtual bankruptcies among institutional lenders, the shrinkage in housing opportunities for middle America becomes evident.[8] Will the needs of the poor secure direct attention in a newly housing-conscious political calculus? The issues at this point can be raised in only rhetorical fashion. In any case, the housing constituency of yesterday can be viewed in retrospect as a victim of affluence. One of the issues of today and tomorrow will be whether it will be reconstructed—and if so, whether the housing necessities of the poor will be incorporated into whatever composition the new coalition may have.

POVERTY: FALL AND RISE

Clearly the shape and dimension of who make up the poor are central to the answers that will evolve. In Table 6 are shown data on the number of persons below the poverty level as established by the Census Bureau for each of several years.[9] It should be noted that the definitions have changed over time—and certainly there is no agreement on the adequacies of the criteria.[10] Accepting these, however, suggests first a substantial shrinkage in poverty levels, corre-

8. As of this writing, it appears that 1982 housing starts will barely exceed 1 million units. During the decade of the 1970s, annual housing starts in excess of 2.0 million units were achieved four times.

9. For poverty-level incomes according to household size, see U.S. Bureau of the Census, *Current Population Reports,* Series P-60, No. 127, "Money Income and Poverty Status of Families and Persons in the United States (Advance Data from the Mar. 1981 Current Population Survey)" (Washington, DC: Government Printing Office, 1981).

10. Census-defined poverty statistics do not include the value of noncash benefits in determining income. Food stamps, subsidized housing, Medicaid, and other "in-kind" benefits are not counted as income. Inclusion of the latter may lower the poverty totals but would probably not alter the trend depicted in Table 6.

TABLE 7
FAMILIES, BY TYPE, TOTAL AND MEDIAN FAMILY INCOME, 1975 AND 1979

	TOTAL FAMILIES (numbers in thousands)				MEDIAN FAMILY INCOME (dollars)			
			CHANGE: 1975-79				CHANGE: 1975-79	
	1975*	1979†	Number	Percent	1975	1979	Number	Percent
Total	56,245	58,426	2,181	3.9	13,719	19,661	5,942	43.3
Married-couple families	47,318	48,180	862	1.8	14,867	21,503	6,636	44.6
Male householder, no wife present	1,444	1,706	262	18.1	12,995	16,867	3,872	29.8
Female householder, no husband present	7,482	8,540	1,058	14.1	6,844	9,927	3,083	45.0

SOURCES: U.S. Bureau of the Census, *Current Population Reports*, Series P-60, No. 105, "Money Income in 1975 of Families and Persons in the United States" (Washington, DC: Government Printing Office, 1977); and U.S. Bureau of the Census, *Current Population Reports*, Series P-60, No. 127, "Money Income and Poverty Status of Families and Persons in the U.S.: 1980."

*14 years and over.

†15 years and over.

sponding to general income gains, from 1960 through 1973. In that latter year—a high point of prosperity and a low point of poverty—approximately 10 percent of all Americans, or 23 million persons, were under the threshold condition. But as median incomes have declined generally, the number of persons below the poverty level has increased to beyond 29 million.

Within these overall data, however, the composition of the poor has been markedly altered. Persons in families headed by females with no husband present made up approximately 25 percent of the total poverty population in 1961. By 1980, they accounted for half. The significance of this demographic phenomenon is revealed in Table 7: the fastest-growing family type in America from 1975 to 1979 comprised female householders/no husband present, a household configuration whose median income level in 1979 was under $10,000.

RENT-INCOME RATIOS

The growing differential between shelter costs and income levels as a function of demographics highlights the dilemma: improved physical condition of housing achieved at the cost of reduction in low-rent accommodations, within the context of select low incomes. This is shown in Table 8, which indicates median rents as a percentage of median income for various demographic groups. Male-headed households with wife present—married couple families—spent less than one-fifth of their incomes for rent through 1976 and barely exceeded that level in 1979. Other male-headed households over the same six-year span moved from spending 21 percent of their incomes for rent to spending

TABLE 8
RENTER HOUSEHOLDS, MEDIAN RENT AS A PERCENTAGE OF MEDIAN INCOME: 1973, 1976, AND 1979

HOUSEHOLD COMPOSITION BY AGE OF HEAD	1973	1976	1979
2-or-more-person households	19.6	22.6	24.1
Male head, wife present	18.2	18.9	20.0
under 25 years	19.8	20.3	21.3
25-29	17.4	18.3	19.0
30-34	17.0	17.8	18.6
35-44	17.1	17.7	19.0
45-64	16.4	17.5	19.1
65 and over	29.6	29.6	27.8
Other male head	21.0	26.3	28.3
under 65 years	20.7	26.2	28.1
65 and over	28.0	28.8	31.0
Female head	26.9	35.8	37.2
under 65 years	26.6	35.4	38.3
65 and over	31.0	33.2	32.4
1-person households	30.7	31.0	30.2

SOURCE: U.S. Department of Commerce, Bureau of the Census, *Current Housing Reports*, Series H-150-79, *Annual Housing Survey: 1979, Parts A and C*.

28.3 percent, while female-headed households shifted from 26.9 to an oppressive 37.2 percent.

The housing buying power of most of America has been affected by lags in real income. Two-income households have emerged as a new elite which, at worst, are much more buffered than holds true of the balance of our society.[11] The poor, in terms of housing buying power, have become even poorer. Yet the fiscal squeeze on middle America has left much less room for concern about the shelter provisions of the less fortunate.

THE FUTURE

Time lags between concept and reality, of legislation and ameliorative measures predicated on the past rather than the shape of today and tomorrow, are far from unique to shelter. But they are exemplified in the issues of policy toward housing the poverty-stricken in America. At this writing, for example, the major shelter initiatives proposed by the administration revolve around some form of housing voucher—that is, an earmarked income supplement to meet the gap between some appropriate portion of income—typically 25 percent, subject to certain allowances—and the market cost of extant housing. This in turn is predicated on housing conditions as they have evolved in the last decade. These shelter initiatives assume a bountiful supply of housing, if at increased prices. Thus the perspective is that the shelter limitations of poverty are not a function of the limited number of physical accom-

11. The median family income in 1979 totaled $19,661. In contrast, married-couple families with wives working full-time had a median income of $26,196.

modations available to the needy, but rather their costs.

We would suggest, however, that while this held substantially true through the late 1970s, the functional realities of the housing market of today—and even more pointedly of tomorrow—must blight this vision. The relative availability of shelter described so forcefully in the Experimental Housing Allowance Program in such communities as Green Bay, Wisconsin and South Bend, Indiana may or may not have held true for the rest of the country even at the time of the fieldwork—but in any case it will not hold true in the future.[12]

The end is at hand for the sheltered housing finance industry of specialized lending institutions for shelter predicated on long-term fixed low-interest mortgages. It was this element in concert with rising incomes which permitted the vast three-decade upgrading of America's housing inventory. Not all of the poor found their shelter improving, certainly. The sad realities of rural poverty—as in the Mississippi Delta—and hard-core slum areas cry out against complacency. But these areas, as best as we can tell, have thinned out quite markedly, the sheer number of individuals caught within them substantially reduced.

But this is a tribute to the past, not of things to come. Within the latter context, the decline in housing starts—even if these are largely devoted to occupants of affluence—has harsh implications for the needy when the housing delivery is viewed as a total system. The tool of housing allowances or rent supplements or whatever they may be called, without complementary support for housing unit construction, will prove to be self-defeating. The housing needs of the poor—indeed, any of their requirements involving significant public expenditure—have lost their political potency. The priorities of reindustrialization, at least as of this writing, are clearly paramount.

From a political perspective, one of the more intriguing questions of tomorrow is the potential reinvention of a broader-based housing constituency—spearheaded by the tastes and desires of the latter stages of the baby boom generation, supported by the hard-hit classic members of the housing industry—which might also serve to benefit the poverty stricken. Without this essential juncture, however, the improvement in the shelter provisions for the latter group—one of the great achievements of the last generation —must quickly abort.

APPENDIX

A few words remain to be said about the major housing programs of the 1970s.[13]

Conventional Low-Rent Public Housing

Under the conventional public housing program, local public housing agencies (PHAs) develop, own, and operate low-rent public housing projects

12. See Katharine L. Bradbury and Anthony Downs, *Do Housing Allowances Work?* (Washington, DC: Brookings Institution, 1981). Though somewhat overbroadly titled, this provides a full description of the research.

13. The descriptions were secured from Morton Schussheim, Susan Vonhorenbeck, and Grace Milgram, "Descriptions and Evaluations of Selected Housing Subsidy Programs" (Washington, DC: Congressional Research Service, Library of Congress, 1980).

financed through the sale of tax-exempt bonds. Debt service on these bonds is paid by the federal government under annual contributions contracts (ACC) for up to 40 years. Construction is normally financed through the sale of tax-exempt project notes of the PHA, backed by a federal guarantee.

In the early years, federal contributions were limited to the amounts required to amortize the full capital costs of the projects. However, operating subsidies became necessary as operating expenses increased and maximum rents were limited to 25 percent of the tenant's adjusted income. The 1979 Housing Authorization Bill authorized that operating subsidies could still be paid after the original annual contributions contracts had expired, so long as the project continued to serve low-income families. Additional contributions have been made available in recent years to amortize the costs of modernizing older public housing projects.

Section 8—New Construction

Assistance is provided to rental households living in dwellings newly constructed under prior commitment from the Department of Housing and Urban Development (HUD). HUD pays owners the difference between the contract rent established by agreement with HUD and the payment made by the household. The household locates its own apartment in an eligible structure and is accepted by the landlord, who verifies its income. The household pays between 15 and 25 percent of its income, depending on income and household size.

Except for projects specifically built for the elderly and the handicapped, the only eligibility criterion is income. Preference is to be given to families who occupy substandard housing or who are involuntarily displaced from their current residences.

The maximum income, set by HUD in each market area, is generally 80 percent of median for four-person families, up to 100 percent of median for families of eight or more persons, and down to 50 percent of median for one-person households. Thirty percent of assisted households must be of very low income—that is, below 50 percent of median, adjusted for household size.

Approximately two-fifths of households in the country were potentially eligible.

Section 8—Existing Housing and Moderate Rehabilitation

Rental assistance is given to households that are certified by a public housing agency (PHA), for units in existing structures. The PHA, authorized to provide housing, is awarded the authority to issue certificates through a HUD allocation system. Each certified family finds its own apartment—which may be the one in which it currently resides—in the private market at no more than the fair market rent. The owner must agree to participate and to meet HUD requirements. The apartment also must meet HUD-established standards.

The existing housing program also includes a moderate rehabilitation program, for which regulations were issued effective 24 May 1979. This program is also to be administered by public housing agencies, which are to select proposals from owners in such a way as to promote one of three objectives: freedom of housing choice and spatial deconcentration of assisted housing, prevention of displacement of lower-income families in neighborhoods undergoing private revitalization, and neighborhood preservation and revitalization. A minimum expenditure of $1000 per unit is required. The upper limit on expenditures is controlled by the fair market rents, which are set at 120 percent of the existing housing rent schedule for the area. Currently the Section 8 program for New and Substantially Rehabilitated Units is being phased out.

Section 235—Homeowners' Assistance Program

Section 235 provided homebuying assistance to low- and moderate-income families. Direct cash subsidy payments were made by HUD to reduce mortgage interest costs to as low as 4 percent under the revised Section 235 program—1 percent under the original, and 5 percent from 1976 to January 1978. The homeowner must contribute at least 20 percent of adjusted gross income toward monthly mortgage payments, insurance, and tax payments on the house.

The original Section 235 program was suspended in January 1973. A revised Section 235 program was implemented in early 1976. The program is now essentially defunct.

Section 236—Rental Housing Assistance Program

The Section 236 program was a major source of new rental housing from 1969 to 1973. Since the latter year, the government has been phasing out new construction under this program, with only a handful of projects expected to be built in 1980-81 under earlier commitments. Subsidies continue, however, on behalf of some half-million tenant households which occupy Section 236 housing built in prior years.

Mortgage interest reduction payments are made by the federal government to the lender on behalf of the owner of qualified multifamily housing. The Housing and Community Development Act of 1974 authorized additional rental housing assistance—deep subsidies—to be provided on behalf of low-income tenants whose rental charges exceed 25 percent of income, and required that 20 percent of tenants in a project be of such a low income.

Section 202—Housing for the Elderly and Handicapped

Under the Section 202 program, HUD makes long-term direct loans to sponsors of housing for the elderly and the handicapped at an interest rate based on the average interest rate of all interest-bearing obligations of the United States forming a part of the public debt. The original Section 202 program provided loans at a 3 percent interest rate. This original program was considered very successful financially, producing approximately 45,000 units during its 10 years of operation, with only one foreclosure, but it was phased out in favor of construction financed by Section 236.

An important aspect of the revised Section 202 program is that all projects receive the benefits of leased housing assistance payments under the Section 8 program. This means tht eligible tenants will not pay more than 25 percent of their incomes for rent. To guarantee their availability on approval of the financing, reservations for Section 8 funds are set aside at the time a Section 202 reservation is made.

ANNALS, *AAPSS*, **465**, January 1983

The Exclusionary Effect of Growth Controls

By BERNARD J. FRIEDEN

ABSTRACT: Local government regulation of land development and homebuilding has become more complicated and more demanding in recent years. Most of the new control techniques can be used either to manage growth in an orderly way or to limit and discourage growth. A review of experience in Northern California reveals many instances in which techniques such as utility moratoria, development fees, growth quotas, environmental impact reviews, and environmental lawsuits have been used in ways that increase the cost of new housing. Among the direct cost impacts of growth controls, the most important result from the rapidly increasing development charges levied by many communities, and from the stretch-out of development time caused by local review procedures. Many growth controls also generate a series of indirect impacts likely to lead to far greater increases in the sales prices of new homes. Four indirect impacts likely to have major effects on house prices are redesign of housing developments to make them more acceptable to local interest groups; restriction of the supply of land available for homebuilding; restriction of competition among homebuilders; and reduction in the ability of homebuilders to increase their output during cyclical increases in consumer demand.

Bernard J. Frieden is a professor in the Department of Urban Studies and Planning at the Massachusetts Institute of Technology and former director of the MIT-Harvard Joint Center for Urban Studies. He has served as adviser on housing and community development to federal agencies and White House task forces during three presidential administrations. His most recent book, The Environmental Protection Hustle *(1979), is a study of growth controls and housing in California. He is also coauthor, with Marshall Kaplan, of* The Politics of Neglect: Urban Aid from Model Cities to Revenue Sharing *(1975), and has written extensively on housing, public policy, and urban planning.*

NOTE: From *Resolving the Housing Crisis*, copyright 1982, Pacific Institute for Public Policy Research. Reprinted with permission from Ballinger Publishing Company.

BETWEEN the mid-1960s and the mid-1970s, communities across the country tightened governmental controls over land development and homebuilding. In some cases, local governments made major changes at one stroke by enacting new growth management ordinances. More typically, however, they put into place a series of new review procedures and permit requirements, one at a time but with striking cumulative effects. The result was that by the mid-1970s new housing developments required more permits and more reviews by public agencies than in the past. In addition, at many stages of the review public agencies would commission time-consuming technical studies and hold public hearings, which were often drawn-out and often abrasive. Two of the best-known titles in the literature on development controls characterize the changes of this period succinctly and accurately: *The Quiet Revolution in Land Use Control*, and *The Permit Explosion*.[1]

The stated rationale for most of the new review and permit requirements was a concern for managing new growth carefully to protect the quality of the local environment. Although the controls proliferated during a time when public awareness of environmental issues was rising, environmental motivations alone probably cannot account for the permit explosion. In the political controversies that surround homebuilding proposals, other motivations have also come to the surface—particularly fiscal, social, and ideological motivations. These other motivations predate public and media discovery of the environmental crisis, and indeed supplied much of the impetus for earlier land use controls in suburbia. The mix of motivations varies from place to place and over time, making it hard to generalize about what prompted the spread of new controls. But it would not be accurate to attribute the exclusionary impacts of these controls entirely or even mostly to environmental considerations.

GROWTH CONTROL TECHNIQUES

This review of exclusionary effects of the new regulation focuses on California, where communities have made especially active efforts to control growth. Growth control measures take many different forms, with no single pattern predominant. Each community has worked out its own combination of control measures, and different measures tend to generate different impacts in local housing markets. To understand how these controls limit the options available to housing consumers, it is useful to identify the main approaches being used.

Measures to preserve farmland are one important way of limiting growth by reducing the supply of land available for development. Many California communities have established agricultural preserves under the provisions of the state's Williamson Act, which offers property tax reductions for owners of farmland who agree not to sell their land for development. The state makes funds available to reimburse local governments for part of the tax

1. Fred P. Bosselman and David Callies, *The Quiet Revolution in Land Use Control*, prepared for the Council on Environmental Quality (Washington, DC: Government Printing Office, 1972); Fred P. Bosselman, Duane A. Feurer, and Charles L. Siemon, *The Permit Explosion: Coordination of the Proliferation* (Washington, DC: Urban Land Institute, 1976).

revenues they lose as a result of reduced farmland assessments.[2] Some local governments make use of agricultural zoning to achieve the same purpose, either in conjunction with the establishment of Williamson Act preserves or independently.

Another way to freeze land from development is to require exceptionally large minimum lot sizes for new homes. Large-lot zoning is not recent and not a California invention, having been used for many years to limit suburban growth in other parts of the country. But earlier large-lot restrictions in places such as New Jersey meant minimum lot sizes of two, three, four, or sometimes five acres. Local officials might have liked to go further, but judicial decisions suggested that the courts would strike down requirements that went beyond this range. California communities have now gone from large-lot zoning to superzoning, by creating zoning districts that require minimum lot sizes of 20, 40, and even 60 acres per single-family home. Much of western Marin County is zoned for 60-acre lots, known locally as ranchettes. This regulation is a formidable way of blocking homebuilding throughout large areas, where only the wealthiest of homebuyers can afford the cost of a 60-acre site.

A local government can also limit growth by establishing a moratorium on new connections to public utility systems. The usual legal justification for a utility moratorium is that the community has come dangerously close to reaching the limits of its water supply or its sewage disposal capacity, so that additional connections threaten to overwhelm the system. In areas of rapid growth, these circumstances do occur from time to time, and a moratorium on new connections can be used legitimately to give local officials time to expand their utility systems. However, once a moratorium exists, many communities delay the necessary expansions or else extend their systems only enough to handle slight additional growth, thus setting the stage for more moratoria in the near future. And if there is no shortage of utility capacity, it is possible to create one. In the early 1970s, Marin County slowed the expansion of its water system to provide just enough reserves to take care of its existing population. The thin margin of safety in Marin's reservoirs made it possible to declare a moratorium on new water connections in 1973, even while rainfall was still normal. The two years of drought that followed, from 1975 to 1977, not only kept the moratorium in effect but also forced the county's water district to resort to water rationing and the use of an emergency pipeline, and earned Marin's residents a great deal of sympathy in the press as victims of a natural disaster. In reality, the drought in Marin County was mostly artificial, resulting from a growth control tactic that backfired.

A related method of controlling growth through utility connections

2. For an account of the Williamson Act and other California provisions for reduced assessments to preserve open space, see the following: Gregory C. Gustafson and L.T. Wallace, "Differential Assessment as Land Use Policy: The California Case," *Journal of the American Institute of Planners*, 41: 379-89 (1975); State of California Legislative Analyst, *Report on Open Space Taxation* (Sacramento: State of California Legislative Analyst, 1971); Valerie C. Kircher, "The Legislative Battle Over Preserving Agricultural Land," *California Journal*, 7: 155-57 (May 1976); and California Land Conservation Act of 1965, California Government Code, secs. S1200-S1295.

involves staging the extension of water and sewer lines and establishing public service boundaries for these extensions. Formalizing extension plans in this way puts developers on notice that land beyond the boundaries will not receive public services and directs their attention instead to land within the service area. This technique can be a reasonable way to plan for the orderly timing and location of new utility lines to accommodate growth. But it can—and frequently is—a way to limit growth by withholding services. By drawing service boundaries close to areas that are already built up, a community can ensure that little vacant land will be available for development. When San Jose decided to limit its growth in the early 1970s, one method it used was to reduce the supply of vacant land within its delineated urban service area.

A more direct way of increasing the cost of new houses, and thereby limiting production and shifting it into higher price brackets, is to impose development charges. Many communities have established a schedule of fees levied on new homes, including charges for water and sewer connections, park fees, school fees, and charges for processing various kinds of permit applications. In many cases, local governments require developers to build or pay for facilities that will benefit the community at large as well as the residents who will live in a proposed development. A frequent example is the requirement that a builder provide a site for a new school or install utility lines with greater capacity than his or her development alone would justify. Several studies have found a clear national trend toward requirements for developers to build or pay for public facilities that were previously provided by local government. The U.S. Department of Housing and Urban Development's Task Force on Housing Costs—whose members included a mix of federal and local officials, and representatives of both the private and public sectors—reported in 1978:

> We find that local governments are steadily transferring from the community at large to the developer, and thence to the new housing consumer, a greater share of the public capital costs of growth. This is being done through the imposition of fees and charges as well as through requirements for construction and dedication. In many areas this trend has proceeded beyond what is equitable and reasonable.[3]

As is true of other growth controls, this technique is used with great variations from place to place. Some communities try to assess charges that local officials believe represent legitimate costs of servicing new developments exclusively. Others set charges and requirements as revenue-raising devices to protect the fiscal interests of established residents. In still others, development fees are part of a growth control tactic to discourage new construction by raising the cost of homebuilding and levying a special tax on newcomers who are not yet able to vote.[4]

3. U.S. Department of Housing and Urban Development, *Final Report of the Task Force on Housing Costs* (Washington, DC: Department of Housing and Urban Development, 1978), pp. 25-26. Another study that reached the same conclusion is Stephen R. Seidel, *Housing Costs and Government Regulations* (New Brunswick, NJ: Rutgers Center for Urban Policy Research, 1978); see p. 127.

4. For a fuller discussion of this subject, see Bernard J. Frieden, "Allocating the Pub-

Perhaps the most direct method for limiting growth is to establish an explicit quota for the number of new building permits to be issued each year. Petaluma is best known for this technique, having set an annual quota of 500 new homes per year starting in 1972. Several other communities in the San Francisco area have also made use of annual quotas, and Petaluma's success in meeting a court challenge to its system will undoubtedly encourage others to use similar controls in the future.

The growth control technique in widest use in California is the environmental impact review, mandated by state law for all but very small new developments. By 1976, California communities required 4000 environmental impact reports a year—four times as many as all federal agencies combined. The original justification for environmental impact reviews was to provide public officials with good information on the environmental consequences of proposed developments, so that they could make more informed decisions. It is hard to take issue with the desirability of having a good base of information for local decision making. However, environmental impact reviews in practice also create important opportunities for stopping or restricting growth. Developers, operating with borrowed money, are especially vulnerable to delays, and environmental reviews almost always stretch out the time needed for governmental reviews. Furthermore, environmental legislation has created new rights for local residents to challenge developments both at public hearings and in the courts. In California, environmental impact reports are at the heart of the permit explosion mentioned earlier.

Finally, an important growth control technique is the environmental lawsuit. It is always possible to find some fault in an environmental impact assessment, because environmental analysis is a blend of science, judgment, and values. And almost any growth opponent has standing to bring a lawsuit to block a development on the ground that the environmental review was inadequate. Groups hostile to suburban growth have seized on environmental lawsuits as an effective weapon against developers. A handbook for community activists prepared by the Stanford Environmental Law Society sums up the reasons for bringing lawsuits:

> First of all, there is obviously a chance of winning the suit. However, the mere threat of a suit can also be an impressive political tactic.... And finally, suits can be an effective delaying tactic in order to force compromises. Developers may want to postpone their project until the Court has cleared their status, or the Court itself may issue an injunction or temporary restraining order. Extensive delay may even force the developer to abandon his plans due to financing difficulties.[5]

The volume of California housing caught up in lawsuits is very impressive. Growth opponents seldom go to court against small projects, but they do challenge most of the big ones. In the San Francisco area, environmental lawsuits challenged proposals to build 29,000 housing units between 1971 and

lic Service Costs of New Housing," *Urban Land*, 39: 12-16 (1980).

5. Mary Cranston, Bryant Garth, Robert Plattner, and Jay Varon, *A Handbook for Controlling Local Growth* (Stanford, CA: Stanford Environmental Law Society, 1973), p. 77.

1975, or two-thirds of a year's normal housing production for the region.[6] Although some environmental lawsuits are brought to test legal principles or to seek redress of grievances, it is clear from the context of individual controversies that the lawsuit is very often a tactic for stopping growth.

DIRECT IMPACTS ON DEVELOPMENT COSTS

This formidable collection of growth control measures can affect the cost of new housing in many ways. Although there has been little systematic research so far on the cost consequences of growth controls, it is possible to identify the types of impacts and to reach preliminary judgments about the importance of each type.

Most research on the subject has focused on the direct impacts of growth controls on the development costs of new housing. These consist mainly of the cost of preparing environmental impact assessments, the cost of hook-up fees and other development charges, the cost of delays prior to construction, and the cost of plan revisions required as a result of environmental reviews.

In most jurisdictions, the developer is required either to prepare an environmental impact study or to pay the cost of having a consultant prepare one for the local government. Although environmental impact studies are often elaborate, particularly for large subdivisions, the cost per house is relatively minor—typically less than $100.[7]

Development charges imposed by local governments add substantially more to the cost of building new homes. Through the mid-1970s, development charges in most California communities were well under $2000 per home, except in places such as Livermore that used them as a key part of a growth control strategy. Livermore's schedule of fees included a residential construction tax, water and park fees, storm drain and sewer connection fees, and a school fee. The total added to about $4500 for a typical small home. After the passage of Proposition 13 in 1978, many localities moved quickly to add new fees as revenue-raising devices to replace property taxes they could no longer collect. Within a year after passage of Proposition 13, a survey by the California Building Industry Association found the median bill for construction-related fees up by 26 percent, with new charges ranging up to $3000 for an average three-bedroom house.[8] Recent surveys show that by mid-1979 fees amounted to several thousand dollars per home in many high-growth communities. In 26 cities within Orange County, total fees for a 1500-square-foot home averaged $4400 in July 1979, ranging from a low of $1300 in La Habra up to $7200 in Irvine and $7400 in San Clemente.[9] As of August 1979, average development fees for a house in a 100-unit

6. Bernard J. Frieden, *The Environmental Protection Hustle* (Cambridge: MIT Press, 1979), p. 143.

7. Seidel, *Housing Costs and Government Regulations*, p. 248.

8. Stephen J. Sansweet, "Catch-13: Californians Discover Tax-Cut Mania Has a Corollary: Fee Fever," *Wall Street Journal*, 1 June 1979, p. 1.

9. Alfred Gobar Associates, *Housing Cost Analysis: Orange County*, prepared for CEEED—Californians for an Environment of Excellence, Full Employment, and a Strong Economy through Planned Development (Brea, CA: Alfred Gobar Associates, 1980), Appendix.

subdivision totaled $4033 in the rapidly growing outer zone of the San Francisco Bay area, while the averages were $2520 and $1290 in the more built-up middle suburban ring and inner core cities.[10]

The stretch-out of processing time resulting from new growth controls also raises development costs. The time required for plan approvals prior to construction was less than a year for most California subdivisions around 1970; but by 1975 it had increased to about two years for typical developments in closely regulated areas and to five years or more for large developments with 500 or more homes. By 1980, the California Association of Realtors estimated the average lead time for a housing development at two-and-a-half years.[11] Developers operate with borrowed money, and longer processing times force them to pay higher carrying charges on their loans, as well as increased amounts for taxes, insurance, and property maintenance. Overhead costs for projects also increase, because staff salaries, office expenses, and other fixed items have to be carried for longer periods. During inflationary times such as the present, increases in construction costs also make delays expensive for the builder. The California Construction Industry Research Board estimated the combined costs of delay to the homebuilder as a range of 14 to 21 percent of the sales price per year in the mid-1970s.[12] More recently, with higher interest rates on borrowed funds and more rapid acceleration of construction costs, delays have become still more expensive.

Finally, there are direct cost impacts resulting from special conditions that are often attached to local government approval of housing developments. Developers may be required to set aside additional open space or to build extra facilities that were not originally in the plan. The cost of meeting approval conditions varies greatly from one project to another. A study commissioned by the California Legislature's Commitee on Local Government estimated that half of all housing developments subject to environmental reviews were required to make specific revisions in their plans and that the average cost of these revisions was no more than $2000 per project.[13] Another study of environmental reviews in the San Diego area estimated the cost of meeting approval requirements as $75 per house.[14] Both estimates are low, reflecting the fact that researchers considered only those changes resulting from formal conditions of approval and overlooked changes that developers made with-

10. Association of Bay Area Governments, *Development Fees in the San Francisco Bay Area: A Survey* (Berkeley: CA; Association of Bay Area Governments, 1980), p. 36.

11. Bay Area Council, *Housing: The Bay Area's Challenge of the '80s* (San Francisco: Bay Area Council, 1980), p. 15.

12. Construction Industry Research Board, *Cost of Delay Prior to Construction* (Los Angeles: Construction Industry Research Board, 1975), p. 14.

13. *The California Environmental Quality Act: An Evaluation Emphasizing Its Impact upon California Cities and Counties with Recommendations for Improving Its Effectiveness.* A report prepared for the Assembly Committee on Local Government, (San Diego, CA: Environmental Analysis Systems, 1975), 3:37.

14. Thomas Muller with Kathleen Christensen, *State-Mandated Impact Evaluation: A Preliminary Assessment* (Washington, DC: Urban Institute, 1976), p. 27.

out formal requirements in order to improve their chances of getting approval. These changes will be considered as indirect cost impacts, and they are very substantial.

INDIRECT IMPACTS ON HOUSING CONSUMERS

The direct cost consequences of growth controls are important contributors to inflation in housing prices, but they are only the tip of the iceberg. In addition to raising development costs, growth regulations create other conditions likely to lead to far greater increases in the sales prices of new homes. Four types of indirect impact are worth noting: (1) redesign of projects, (2) restriction of land supply, (3) restriction of competition, and (4) reduction of the ability of homebuilders to make adjustments to changing market conditions.

Project redesign

Case histories of housing developments in California show a very consistent pattern of changes during the long period of review and negotiation. Typically developers discover that they can make projects more acceptable to the opposition by building less housing than originally planned and leaving a greater part of the sites as open space. A compromise along these lines helps to placate nearby residents who are anxious to minimize the number of new neighbors they will have, as well as environmental groups that are committed to the preservation of open space. But once developers reduce the number of homes on the sites, they find that the cost per house goes up substantially, because land and overhead costs have to be allocated to fewer houses. Developers are concerned that homebuyers may be reluctant to pay for extra land unless the developers also upgrade the house itself. One revision leads to another, and later versions of the plan usually add space and extra features to the house itself, aiming for an upper-income market. Builders also learn that luxury housing is likely to be more acceptable to nearby residents and local officials than moderate-cost homes. A recent analysis of homebuilding under the Petaluma growth control system reached clear conclusions on this point:

> It appears that the substantial increase in floor area in Petaluma, from about 1,600 square feet before growth control to about 1,900 square feet after growth control . . . [was] due both to the incentive provided by the evaluation system under which allocations were awarded and to the economic response of builders who were faced with fixed quotas. . . . Builders learned after the first round of allocations that to compete successfully they had to provide high quality. Proposed subdivisions of fairly low quality were rapidly eliminated. The normal response of a builder, when faced with demands for high quality, is to build large units, since it is generally assumed that people who are willing to spend the extra money for high quality will also want larger homes. A second, and related, reason for larger size is that the builder, when faced with a fixed building quota, will try to obtain the maximum profit from each unit, which requires building the largest posible saleable house.[15]

In case studies of housing developments in the San Francisco area, I

15. Seymour I. Schwartz et al., *The Effect of Growth Management on New Housing Prices: Petaluma, California* (Davis: Institute of Governmental Affairs, Institute of Ecology, and UCD Kellogg Program, University of California, 1979), p. 55.

found one instance in which a developer reduced the number of houses in his plan to one-third the original volume while he tripled the sales price of each house. Another developer eliminated 90 percent of the homes he originally intended to build and divided most of his land into estate lots for custom-built homes.[16] There is evidence that environmental reviews typically lead developers to cut the number of houses in their plans. In a national survey of homebuilders in 1976, almost 90 percent in states with requirements for environmental reviews reported that they changed their plans because of these reviews. The most commonly cited change—by 59 percent—was a reduction in housing density.[17] Several case studies suggest, further, that these compromises not only change the number of homes on a site but also tend to shift the product from moderate-cost to more expensive housing.

Land supply

Growth controls have direct and obvious effects on the supply of land available for new housing. Many of the techniques mentioned earlier operate by preventing land from being developed for housing—through agricultural preservation measures, superzoning, and utility policies. When applied in communities where there is substantial demand for new housing, these techniques force developers to bid against each other for the limited supply of suitable land. Freezing some land from development makes the remaining sites more expensive. Growth controls further increase the cost of land for each new home when they mandate large minimum lot sizes. And many localities increase the cost of finished lots by imposing elaborate requirements for streets, sidewalks, and utility sytems.

The extent to which growth controls have raised land costs is unknown. But it is not surprising to find that during the early 1970s, when growth controls were multiplying and tightening across the country, the cost of land for new homes accelerated sharply and at a much faster rate than costs for materials or labor. National builder surveys indicate that from 1950 through 1969 the average annual increase in the price per square foot of finished lots was less than 8 percent, and from 1960 to 1969 it was only 5 percent. In contrast, from 1969 to 1975 the cost per square foot was up by an average of about 15 percent per year.[18] A more recent study of closely regulated Orange County estimates that the cost of a finished lot for a typical new single-family home went from $9800 in 1972 to $47,300 in 1978. Increases in lot costs alone accounted for 38 percent of the total increase in new home costs in Orange County, according to this analysis, which attributed much of the increase to regulatory restrictions.[19]

Growth controls affect the location of building sites as well as their cost. Restrictions in some communi-

16. Reported in Frieden, *The Environmental Protection Hustle*, chaps. 4 and 5.

17. Seidel, *Housing Costs and Government Regulations*, p. 242.

18. Michael Sumichrast and Sara A. Frankel, *Profile of the Builder and His Industry* (Washington, DC: National Association of Home Builders, 1970), p. 25; and National Association of Home Builders, *Economic News Notes*, 21:3-4 (1975).

19. Alfred Gobar Associates, *Housing Cost Analysis*, pp. 41-42.

ties lead builders to search for sites in less regulated places, as well as places where costs are lower. Both factors—the search for easier regulations and the search for lower land costs—typically shift development away from the already established suburbs to outlying communities that have not yet put new growth controls in place. This pattern is especially clear in the northern part of the San Francisco region. Marin County, just north of San Francisco, grew rapidly in the 1960s but still had 90 percent of its land open in the early 1970s. As the county's growth controls succeeded in discouraging further development, developers moved further north to Sonoma County, where the regulations were less demanding. Despite its favorable location and large supply of open land, Marin County reduced its share of the new growth in the San Francisco region after 1970, while Sonoma County's share doubled in the 1970s. The fact that Sonoma County's growth resulted in part from Marin County's growth policies did not escape the attention of local officials in Sonoma County. In June 1980, the city council of Rohnert Park asked other Sonoma communities to join with it in bringing a class action lawsuit against Marin County unless it revised its policies to allow the development of moderate-income housing.[20]

This deflection of growth created problems for housing consumers as well as for cities in Sonoma County. It meant that most people wanting to live north of San Francisco were shut out of places within short commuting distances of the central city, and had to buy homes 30 or 40 miles away. They pay for Marin County's growth controls by burning more gas and spending more time in their cars, while the region pays an extra cost in air quality for the longer distances they drive.

Restricted competition

The new regulation is likely to have major indirect effects on the housing industry, although there have been no major studies so far that might document the ways in which firms are adapting to changes in the regulatory climate. The scarcity of building permits in places where there is high demand for housing undoubtedly reduces competition among builders. Homebuilding has traditionally been a small-firm, highly competitive industry, and the competition among builders kept sales prices in check. The new regulation has changed this situation. Now builders compete against each other for permits, but whoever has a permit faces less competition in the marketplace and can sell houses at correspondingly higher markups. Builders have acknowledged this change in personal interviews, and their own recognition of reduced competition is one of the factors that explains why many persist in efforts to build in even the most tightly regulated areas. Informed observers have taken note of this situation. The Bay Area Council's recent housing report, for example, underlines the connection between growth regulation, risk, and competition:

> With fewer permits to be doled out, and more regulations to administer, local governments have accrued a good deal of unofficial power to accept, reject, or

20. Judson Snyder, "Rohnert Park to Marin County: A Little Housing Help!" *APA News* [American Planning Association], 15:1 (1980).

negotiate a proposal. The result is higher risk for the developer, because of greater uncertainty that his investment in a project will ever pay off—and of necessity, higher profit margins for those homes that do get built. The other side of the coin is that a tightly restricted housing supply limits competition, and allows developers to tack on as much profit as the market will bear.[21]

In addition to the scarcity of permits, other characteristics of growth regulation also reduce competition. The longer time period prior to construction and the more complicated review procedures make the entry of new firms difficult, particularly for small builders who lack the capital to survive long delays and lack the staff to manage technically demanding governmental reviews.

Reduced flexibility

One important feature of the housing economy is the marked instability of housing production. The frequent peaks and troughs of the homebuilding cycle reflect mainly the changing availability of mortgage financing and fluctuations in mortgage interest rates. The boom-and-bust character of market demand puts a premium on developer flexibility. Homebuilders have to vary their production often to keep pace with the market. If they build too many houses as a slump begins, they may be unable to sell them for long periods of time. If they are too conservative and fail to start homes before the upswing begins, they find themselves with nothing to sell during the peak period.

The longer lead time resulting from regulatory reviews poses a special problem, because developers cannot anticipate whether there will be a boom or a bust two or more years in the future. This problem hits consumers hardest during the recovery from a slump, as in the aftermath of the severe building slump of 1974-75. As the economy began to recover in 1975, depositors began to pour funds into California savings and loan associations, which meant that mortgage loans would soon be available on favorable terms. Consumer confidence was rising at the same time, and families that had put off home purchases during the past few years began to look for homes to buy. Even those builders who were able to recognize the turn of the market, however, were unable to build quickly enough to meet the new surge of demand: in the major market areas, they faced multiple growth restrictions and long delays in getting their permits. By the fall of 1976, people who wanted to buy new homes were waiting in long lines to bid for whatever was available. Several large builders sold their homes by lottery, while speculators began to enter the market in large numbers to earn quick profits by buying homes and reselling them. In the Los Angeles area, including Orange County, the average sale price of a new home jumped by 28 percent in a single year, from 1975 to 1976. And the price inflation spread to older homes as well. Between 1975 and 1977, average sales prices for existing homes were up by more than one-third in both Los Angeles and San Francisco.

These effects were especially severe in 1976 and 1977, because the preceding slump was deeper than usual and the recovery was very pronounced. But similar consequences, perhaps less extreme, are predicta-

21. Bay Area Council, *Housing*, p. 12.

ble for the future whenever there is an upsurge of demand. The combination of cyclical instability and time-consuming regulations adds up to a powerful inflationary force that will continue to trouble moderate-income families.

GROWTH CONTROLS IN AN INFLATIONARY ECONOMY

The exclusionary effects of growth controls are far-reaching, extending from direct cost impacts to indirect consequences affecting the decisions and behavior of firms in the housing industry. Growth controls are not the basic cause of high housing costs: an inflationary economy puts strong pressure on sales prices and interest rates even in areas where the regulatory climate is relatively favorable for homebuilding. But growth controls reinforce the underlying inflation and make it far more severe in places such as the major California markets than it is in the rest of the country. The cyclical nature of homebuilding in the United States, together with strong and sustained demand for additional housing in California, provide a market context in which growth controls are especially costly to the consumer.

Inflation has also affected consumer behavior in ways that help explain the consequences of growth controls. As consumers have become convinced that inflation will continue, they have tended to buy homes despite high prices, because they expect prices to be even higher in the future. Thus there is little consumer resistance to the kinds of compromises that developers strike with the regulators. Large, well-equipped, expensive homes attract buyers, even if the buyers must make great sacrifices to pay for them. As a result, many developers are able to build under costly regulatory systems and still make a profit.

Consumer surveys have revealed a widespread willingness to buy at a high price rather than postpone a purchase. Surveys conducted by the University of Michigan Institute for Social Research have regularly asked respondents whether the present is a good time to buy, and if so, why. Formerly, the usual reason people gave for a good time to buy was that prices were satisfactory or good buys were available. By 1977 few people gave these reasons. Increasingly, people who thought it was a good time to buy said that prices were going up and they wanted to buy before prices got any higher. In 1977 and later, almost half the families with incomes of $15,000 or more who thought it was a good time to buy houses gave as their reason that prices would go even higher in the future.[22] At the same time, surveys of business executives found that a majority were coping with inflation by trying to pass on cost increases more rapidly than before.[23] Homebuilders seem to be operating on the same principle. They are able to pass along to consumers most cost impacts of growth controls in California because demand is strong and people buy in anticipation of further inflation.

This brief look at the housing economy suggests that consumers beset by inflation and expecting more of the same are in a poor position to protect themselves against the development costs resulting

22. George Katona, *Essays on Behavioral Economics* (Ann Arbor: University of Michigan Institute for Social Research, 1980), pp. 72-73.

23. Ibid., p. 80.

from growth controls. A look at the politics of growth controls leads to a strikingly similar conclusion. Suburban governments that enact and implement growth controls are responsive mainly to already established residents who elect local officials. Potential homebuyers usually live elsewhere and have no representation in the regulatory proceedings. They are not organized as a political force, and indeed there is no way of knowing who they are until they turn up to look at model homes. Because the politics of growth control exclude families that want to move into the community, it is not surprising that compromises are struck at their expense. They arrive on the scene too late to influence the key decisions about their homes and neighborhoods. And in a market situation of strong demand and inflationary expectations, there is little they can do to resist the outcome.

ANNALS, *AAPSS*, **465**, January 1983

America's Persistent Housing Crises: Errors in Analysis and Policy

By JOHN F. KAIN

ABSTRACT: During the 1970s, the media headlined one housing crisis after another. Concern about these alleged crises tended to disappear as more dispassionate and less well-publicized follow-up studies demonstrated that the claims had been exaggerated. Nearly all comprehensive government and academic evaluations of housing problems and policies during the decade reached the same conclusions about the nature of the nation's housing problems and offered identical recommendations about desirable changes in housing policy. All found that housing conditions improved steadily in the postwar period, that the improvement was largely caused by a rapid growth in per capita and household incomes, that government programs made a minor contribution at best, and that existing housing programs and policies were both inequitable and inefficient. As the fraction of households living in substandard housing declined, moreover, the housing problems of poor persons were increasingly recognized as problems of poverty. All evaluations argued in favor of a reduction in housing subsidies for middle- and low-income households, a shift away from production programs, and greater reliance on cash grants that would provide assistance to low-income households in acquiring standard housing. In spite of this near unanimity of findings and policy recommendations, the nation's housing policy has consistently followed a different course.

John F. Kain is professor of economics at Harvard University, a member of the faculty of the Kennedy School of Government, and has served as chairman of the Department of City and Regional Planning. He is coauthor with John R. Meyer and Martin T. Wohl of The Urban Transportation Problem; *with John M. Quigley of* Housing Markets and Racial Discrimination: A Microeconomic Analysis; *and with Gregory K. Ingram and J. Royce Ginn of* The Detroit Prototype of the NBER Urban Simulation Problem. *He is currently researching a computer simulation model of urban neighborhood dynamics, described in a book just completed by him and William C. Apgar. He has been a consultant to numerous U.S. government agencies and foreign governments.*

THE 1970s began with a housing abandonment crisis, which was followed by a homeownership affordability crisis, a rental housing crisis, and a condominium conversion crisis. More recently, representatives of the construction unions have sought relief from the "worst depression in homebuilding since the great depression," and the financial pages have been filled with alarming stories about the near bankruptcy of the nation's thrift institutions, which have been the principal mortgage lenders. Even allowing for the media's tendency to exaggerate, the discrepancy between these views of America's housing and the facts is remarkable: between 1970 and 1980, real rents—that is, rents adjusted for inflation—fell by 18 percent; homeownership costs declined by more than 30 percent; the rate of homeownership rose from 65 to 67 percent; and virtually every other indicator of housing market conditions showed improvement. This article examines the five so-called housing crises of the past decade and offers suggestions for the nation's housing policy in the 1980s.

THE ABANDONMENT CRISIS

Housing abandonment was a major focus of the July 1970 hearings of the Senate Subcommittee on Housing and Urban Affairs,[1] and in February 1972, *Newsweek* reported that "housing experts agree . . . that the private housing market can no longer afford to shelter the poor," and that "in city after city, the phenomenon of abandonment—once regarded as a temporary and reversable aberration—has become a permanent disaster."[2] Even though the Department of Housing and Urban Development (HUD) implemented an extensive research program to document the extent of abandonment to identify its causes, it is probably true that a fully convincing explanation of the phenomenon still does not exist.

Several studies of areas with heavy abandonment identified the high levels of poverty and unemployment, racial unrest, deteriorating tenant-landlord relations, and the high levels of crime and vandalism that were prevalent in these neighborhoods as probable causes. Economists have tended to place more emphasis on declines in demand, resulting from the reduced convenience and attractiveness of many central-city neighborhoods, and have suggested that the high rates of federally subsidized construction may have created a surplus of low-income housing, with high vacancies, low profitability, and abandonment the inevitable result. High rates of abandonment and the default and foreclosure of thousands of subsidized low-income housing projects in central-city neighborhoods led President Nixon to suspend operation of the principal subsidy program in March 1973 and to order a comprehensive reassessment of all federal housing programs.

Although the subsequent review included no explicit policy recommendations, it strongly suggested

1. George Sternlieb, "The Abandoned Building as a Clue to the Future of the American City," testimony before the U.S. Senate Subcommittee on Housing and Urban Affairs of the Banking and Currency Committee, 23 July 1970.

2. *Newsweek*, 28 Feb. 1972, p. 60.

that the federal government should redirect its efforts from costly new construction programs to a system of cash assistance.[3] By enabling low-income households to consume standard market housing, housing allowances would maintain the profitability of rental property and thereby combat abandonment. In response, Congress enacted the Section 8 Existing Housing program, which leased existing units from private owners for low-income households.[4] Abandonment in American cities nonetheless continued throughout the decade. Although it is impossible to determine whether the rates decreased, increased, or remained the same, public perception and concern about the abandonment problem diminished as new crises emerged.

HOMEOWNERSHIP AFFORDABILITY

Researchers at the MIT-Harvard Joint Center for Urban Studies probably deserve most of the credit for publicizing the notion of a homeownership affordability crisis and for lending it academic respectability. Commenting on "the cost squeeze on homeowners" at a press conference in March 1977, Joint Center Director Bernard Frieden told media representatives: "The cost of single family homes is of special concern because . . . homeownership for the average family has been a cornerstone of national housing policy since the 1930s."[5] Paraphrasing the findings of a Joint Center report on the nation's housing needs, Frieden added that the average-income family had lost ground since 1970, "as costs of homeownership—the sales price of a house, mortgage and interest payments, taxes, insurance, maintenance and repair, and heat and utilities—have outstripped increases in income."[6] Noting that the sales prices of new housing almost doubled in the previous six years, Frieden estimated that the fraction of American families that could afford to buy a median-priced new house decreased from 46.6 percent in 1970 to 27 percent in 1976.

A less well-publicized analysis by the Congressional Budget Office (CBO) narrowed the crisis of

3. U.S. Department of Housing and Urban Development, *Housing in the Seventies: A Report of the National Housing Policy Review* (Washington, DC: Government Printing Office, 1974).

4. The Section 8 existing program was modeled on an earlier leasing program, Section 23. Although quite small, Section 23 was a valuable source of comparative data. Experience with this HUD program indicated that a leasing program using existing units could provide standard housing for low-income households at roughly half the subsidy per household as the larger new construction programs.

5. Harvard University and Massachusetts Institute of Technology News Offices, "Housing Problems Now Affecting Middle Class as Well as Poor, MIT-Harvard Study Shows," press release, New York, NY, 3 Mar. 1977, pp. 3, 4. The press conference was held to promote the Joint Center's report, *The Nation's Housing, 1975-1985* (Cambridge, MA: Joint Center for Urban Studies, 1977).

6. Harvard-MIT News Offices, press release, 3 Mar. 1977, p. 1. The authors of the Joint Center report further publicized the homeownership affordability idea in a series of articles in both scholarly and more popular publications. See Bernard J. Frieden, "The New Housing Cost Problem," *The Public Interest*, 49: 71, 73 (Fall 1977). Similar views are contained in Arthur P. Solomon, "The Cost of Housing: An Analysis of Trends, Incidence, and Causes," *Proceedings of the Third Annual Conference: The Cost of Housing* (Federal Home Loan Bank of San Francisco, 1978).

homeownership affordability to include primarily first-time homebuyers. The authors of the CBO report concluded that the ability of first-time purchasers, which account for about half of all homebuyers in a typical year, to buy a house decreased substantially between 1970 and 1975, as the costs of median new homes rose almost twice as fast, and the costs of existing homes at about one and one-half times as fast, as their incomes.[7] Even so, the CBO report notes that the proportion of young families—the bulk of first-time buyers—owning their homes continued to grow through 1974. Rising housing prices affect the ownership costs of repurchasers and nonmovers quite differently. While the housing costs of first-time homebuyers increased by 59.8 percent, the annual housing cost of a repurchaser buying a home in 1975 was only 27.3 percent higher than if the same household had bought an identical house in 1970. Similarly, the annual housing costs of nonmovers increased by only 22.6 percent. It should be noted that the median family incomes of all households increased by 39 percent during the same period.[8]

The Joint Center and CBO analyses made at least two mistakes. First, they overlooked—or at least attached too little importance to—the continuing growth in the rates of home purchase and homeownership. Indeed, there is some evidence that the decades-long trend toward higher homeownership actually accelerated during the period when the "affordability crisis" was supposed to exist.[9] In reaching their conclusions about homeownership affordability, the authors of the CBO report and the Joint Center study compared the rapid increases in sales prices of new and existing homes or the monthly dollar outlays for homeownership—mortgage payments, insurance, property taxes, maintenance and repair, and heating and utilities—to the increase in median family incomes over the same period. The pertinent measure of the price of homeownership, however, is the after-tax cost, including an appropriate accounting for property appreciation. Rapid increases in house prices, which the proponents of the homeownership affordability crisis emphasized so strongly, may actually reduce the economic cost of homeownership by creating larger capital gains.

A series of scholarly studies has since demonstrated that the notion of an affordability crisis was, at minimum, overstated. As John C. Weicher, the most persistent and effective critic of the so-called crisis, points out, the rapid rise of home prices was matched by even more rapid increases in new home starts and sales.[10] In addition, Weicher presents data indicating that the ratio of new home sales prices to median family income had been remarkably stable since the end of

7. Congress of the United States, Congressional Budget Office, *Homeownership: The Changing Relationship of Costs and Incomes, and Possible Federal Roles* (Washington, DC: Government Printing Office, Jan. 1977), p. xiii.

8. Ibid., pp. 13-18.

9. William C. Apgar, in unpublished analyses, contends that this and many other findings based on the 1970 census and *Annual Housing Survey* are in error because of problems of comparability of the two groups of data.

10. John C. Weicher, "The Affordability of New Homes," *Journal of the American Real Estate and Urban Economics Association*, 5(2):210 (Summer 1977).

World War II; the price-income ratio fell noticeably below 2.8 only once during the period 1949-77—that is, between 1970 and 1972. These two years, moreover, were characterized by abnormally high levels of production under Sections 235 and 502, programs specifically designed to permit low-income households to become homeowners. Excluding these subsidized units, the price-income ratios for 1963-75 all fall in the range of 2.7 to 2.9. These data are the basis of Weicher's conclusion: "It is probably no harder now than before for the typical homebuying family to save enough for a downpayment."[11]

Weicher also develops estimates of the after-tax and economic costs of homeownership that take into account the effects of inflation, higher interest rates, the deductibility of interest payments and property taxes from income, and capital gains. On the basis of these calculations, he offers qualified support for the CBO finding that the position of first-time homebuyers deteriorated during 1970-76. Like the Joint Center and CBO analyses, however, these calculations employ the convention that total monthly housing expense should not exceed 25 percent of a family's monthly income. Weicher admits that these traditional criteria may be misleading and points out that the "median incomes of new home buyers during 1973 and 1974 were several thousand dollars lower than conventional rules-of-thumb suggest they should have been."[12]

Subsequent analyses caused the widespread concern about homeownership affordability to dissolve into an overwhelming consensus that properly measured homeownership costs actually fell during the decade for both first-time homebuyers and homeowners. In a paper presented at a March 1980 HUD-sponsored conference, Patric Hendershott and Sheng-Cheng Hu concluded that during 1970-80, homeowners earned returns on their investments in housing amounting to nine percentage points above those available from investments in financial assets.[13] The authors also observed that at late-1978 expected inflation rates, the real user cost of capital—and thus the real implicit rents of owner-occupied housing for those in high tax brackets—were zero.

In a similar analysis of the effects of taxes, inflation, and capital gains on the cost of homeownership, Douglas B. Diamond, Jr. calculated expected homeownership costs during 1970-79 for the typical homebuyer. Using the average actual duration of occupancy of eight years, Diamond assumes that homebuyers act as though the average rates of inflation, house price increases, interest rates, and other costs experienced during the previous eight years will continue for the next eight. Noting that the use of an adaptive expectations framework would be even more favorable to homeownership, Diamond finds that before-tax ownership costs declined steadily from an index of 100 in 1970 to 82.7

11. Ibid., p. 213.

12. Ibid., pp. 219-21.

13. Patric Hendershott and Sheng-Cheng Hu, "Inflation and Extraordinary Returns on Owner Occupied Housing: Some Implications for Capital Allocation and Productivity Growth," in *House Prices and Inflation*, eds. J. A. Tuccillo and K.E. Villani (Washington, DC: Urban Institute Press, 1981), p. 31.

in 1975 and to 68.7 in 1979. After-tax average homeownership costs fell even more rapidly: from 100 in 1970, they decreased to 80.9 in 1975 and to 62.5 in 1979.[14]

Using the same method that Diamond devised, the President's Commission on Housing determined that the net effective cost of homeownership rose sharply after 1978 as higher real interest rates largely offset homeowners' expectations of appreciation in housing costs.[15] By 1982, the net effective costs of homeownership had thus been restored to 1970 levels, while the current cash costs—which are the major impediment to many first-time purchasers—were many times higher than 1970 levels. Not surprisingly, the sales and purchases of both new and existing homes between 1978 and 1982 were far below normal. The recent rise in the net effective cost of homeownership and the associated downturn in new construction activity and home sales have evoked new claims of an affordability crisis and demands for government intervention.

RENTAL HOUSING

While the alleged crisis in rental housing takes many forms, its most visible manifestations occur at the state and local levels, where various tenant groups have been successful in limiting the actions of rental property owners. The most common types of legislation include rent control, increasingly severe restrictions on evictions, and moratoriums, controls, or outright bans on condominium conversions. These measures have generally been justified by the claim that the continuing shortage of rental housing is causing rents to rise far beyond the ability of renters—and particularly low-income renters—to pay.

A November 1979 report by the U.S. Government Accounting Office (GAO) gave official sanction to the rental housing crisis:

> Millions of Americans cannot afford homeownership and cannot find affordable rental housing. Immediate national attention is necessary if an adequate supply of affordable rental housing is to be available. . . . The Congress and the Administration should take steps to mitigate this nationwide crisis.[16]

The report asserts that the primary causes of the crisis are (1) low levels of moderate priced, new private construction and (2) losses of existing units through abandonment and conversion to condominiums. Although the report does acknowledge that rents have increased less rapidly than prices generally, it never recognizes or attempts to resolve the apparent contradiction between the evidence of real rent declines and the claims that a rental housing crisis exists and that the plight of renters is becoming worse. GAO analysts refer to the real rent declines only in the context of explaining the low levels of rental housing starts—that is, that "according to various

14. Douglas B. Diamond, Jr., "Taxes, Inflation, Speculation and the Cost of Homeownership," *Journal of the American Real Estate and Urban Economics Association*, 8(3):281-98 (Fall 1980).

15. *The Report of the President's Commission on Housing, Advanced Edition* (Washington, DC: Government Printing Office, 30 Apr. 1982).

16. U.S. General Accounting Office, *Rental Housing: A National Problem that Needs Immediate Attention*, Report to the Congress by the Comptroller General of the United States, 8 Nov. 1979.

officials, market rents would have to increase about 25 percent above current levels in order to stimulate new investment in the private multifamily rental market."[17]

To justify its diagnosis of a rental housing crisis, the GAO report cites historically low and declining vacancy rates as well as worsening rent-income ratios.[18] The report particularly emphasizes statistics indicating that while median rents between 1973 and 1977 grew by an average of 9.6 percent per year, average renter income rose by only 5.6 percent. The authors of the GAO report add that median gross rents as a percentage of renters' incomes increased from 20 percent in 1970 to 25 percent in 1977, and that the percentage of renters spending more than 35 percent of their incomes for rent grew from 24.4 percent in 1973 to 30.3 percent in 1977.[19]

The difficulty with these income and rent data, however, is that the comparisons implicitly assume that the composition of the renter population remained the same over time. In fact, the characteristics of renter households changed dramatically over the decade, making simple comparisons of this kind seriously misleading. Declines in the real cost of homeownership induced more and more renters to buy their units. Since these former renters typically had higher average incomes than the households who remained renters, a statistical decline occurred in the average incomes of renter households. In addition, rising incomes, falling rents, and possibly the greater availability of rental units encouraged many individuals, couples, and small families to leave their extended living arrangements and establish separate households. Smaller households typically spend a higher fraction of their incomes on housing, thus contributing another statistical increase in the rent-income ratio of renters.[20]

CONDOMINIUM CONVERSIONS

In 1970, condominium and cooperative ownership of apartments were virtually unknown in the United States with the exception of New York City and a few resort communities. During the past decade, however, the condominium

17. Ibid., p. 13.

18. The GAO report states that "HUD has acknowledged that today's rental vacancy rate of 5 percent is dangerously low," and that "the national vacancy rate of 4.8 percent is the lowest since the Bureau of the Census began collecting the information." *Rental Housing: A National Problem*, pp. ii, 5.

19. Ibid., p. 9.

20. While a definitive analysis remains to be done, Ira Lowry states in a carefully reasoned article on the rental housing market during the 1970s that "the change in household structure and the shift of renters to homeownership was more than enough to account for the downward displacement of renter's median income and the rise of the median rent/income ratio during the decade." Lowry also points out that renters increased their per capita consumption of space and that the quality of their dwellings improved during the decade. Larry Ozanne supports Lowry's interpretation: "The increase in the aggregate rent-to-income ratio cannot all be a greater burden on the same households. The number of single person households has risen from 27 to 35 percent of all renter households in the 1970 to 1977 period, and single person households have always spent a larger fraction of their incomes for housing." See Ira S. Lowry, "Rental Housing in the 1970s: Searching for the Crisis," and Larry Ozanne, "Double Vision in the Housing Market and a Prescription for Correcting It," in *Rental Housing: Is There a Crisis?* eds. John C. Weicher, Kevin E. Villani, and Elizabeth A. Roistacher (Washington, DC: Urban Institute Press, 1981), pp. 23-28, 39-48.

form of homeownership has become widely accepted, and large numbers of rental units have been converted to condominiums. As part of the 1979 amendments of the Housing and Community Development Act, Congress therefore instructed the Department of Housing and Urban Development to carry out a comprehensive assessment of how this growth in condominium conversions would affect America's cities. In particular, the study was to assess the claims of anticondominium groups that conversions displace large numbers of long-term, elderly, and low-income tenants; that they destroy stable low-income neighborhoods; and that they seriously reduce the supply of affordable rental units in many housing markets.

The findings of the HUD study, which are broadly consistent with those of several earlier analyses of individual states and metropolitan areas, indicate that these fears are largely unfounded.[21] The study determined that a significant fraction of former tenants buy their units, that the buyers of converted units and the former tenants have similar characteristics, and that relatively few low-income renters are affected, because conversions tend to be concentrated in the highest-quality neighborhoods and buildings. Although long-term, elderly, and handicapped renters constitute a relatively small fraction of households displaced by conversions, all of the available condominium studies recommend that these groups should receive special protection.

The HUD study identified relatively few situations where condominium conversions were directly responsible for gentrification of previously stable low-income neighborhoods. It also emphasizes that the impacts of conversions on rental housing markets are much smaller than they may at first appear, because a large fraction of the buyers of converted units are former renters and often would have remained renters without the condominium ownership option. The impacts of conversions are further minimized by the fact that investors often continue to offer their converted units as rentals, often retaining current tenants. The authors of the HUD report thus conclude that "for every 100 rental units converted, there is a *net* increase of 5 units for sale to owners, and a net decrease of 5 available rental units," and that "when changes in demand and supply resulting from conversion are juxtaposed, the effect on the rental market is considerably less than the total of all units converted."[22] The

21. U.S. Department of Housing and Urban Development, Division of Policy Studies, *The Conversion of Rental Housing to Condominiums and Cooperatives: A National Study of Scope, Causes, and Impacts* (Washington, DC: Government Printing Office, June 1980); U.S. Department of Housing and Urban Development, *The Conversion of Rental Housing to Condominiums and Cooperatives: Annotated Bibliography* (Washington, DC: Government Printing Office, June 1980); Raymond, Parish, and Pine, Inc., Development Economics Group, "Condominium and Cooperative Conversions in the District of Columbia" (Washington, DC, 1979); John F. Kain, Herman B. Leonard, and Karl E. Case, *Condominium Conversion in Massachusetts: An Evaluation of Its Benefits and Costs,* report prepared for the Greater Boston Real Estate Board, Apr. 1980; and Herman B. Leonard, "Regulation of the Cambridge Housing Market: Its Goals and Effects," report prepared for the Cambridge, Massachusetts Chamber of Commerce, 1981.

22. *HUD Conversion Study,* p. iii.

report nonetheless contends: "There has been a shortfall of rental housing in the last several years . . . [and] . . . conversions have contributed to this shortfall."[23]

If the preceding assessment is accurate, it is difficult to explain the intense political opposition that has emerged in many communities where high levels of conversions have occurred. It is clear, however, that many former tenants are inconvenienced by having to move to new units. The fact that virtually every study of relocation has determined that all but a small minority of displaced renters find new units within one or two months, and that they usually prefer their new units to their old ones, apparently does not eliminate this source of opposition. Since conversions are likely to occur in the best buildings, those affected also tend to be among the most articulate and politically active of the renter population.

THE HOUSING DEPRESSION

The media are now promoting still another housing crisis, and Congress and the current administration are under heavy pressure to initiate major programs to stimulate new construction and to subsidize mortgage borrowing. During 1978-81, record-high interest rates, a steadily worsening economy, and growing uncertainty about whether inflation-driven increases in housing prices would continue sharply reduced the rates of both new construction and the sales of existing homes. In an article entitled "The Great Housing Collapse," *Newsweek* described the situation as "the worst depression in the housing industry since the 1930s," citing estimates by Jack Carlson, chief economist of the National Association of Realtors, to the effect that high interest rates had eliminated 3.2 million families from the homebuying market in the previous 39 months.[24] The article adds: "The number of housing related jobs has shrunk by 2 million, and the bankruptcy rate among real-estate firms and home builders has gone out of sight."

The persistence of high interest rates has also eroded the profitability of thrift institutions whose portfolios contain large numbers of fixed-rate mortgages made when rates were much lower. Unless interest rates decline sharply in the future, increasing numbers of these institutions will be forced to liquidate or to merge with stronger financial institutions, and the number of bankruptcies is certain to increase.

It is undeniable that the decrease in new residential construction and in house sales has hurt construction workers, real estate brokers, developers, and mortgage lenders. At the same time, it is important to keep in mind that the U.S. economy in early 1982 was experiencing the deepest and longest recession since the end of World War II, and that the plight of the auto, steel, and several other industries matches that of housing. Virtually any combination of economic recovery and lower interest rates would benefit the housing sector. Nonetheless, it is unlikely that the levels of new construction, rates of appreciation of house prices, and the

23. Ibid., p. iv.

24. "The Great Housing Collapse," *Newsweek*, 29 Mar. 1982, pp. 61-62.

volume of sales during the 1980s can equal those of the 1970s and that the housing sector, like many others, may have to shrink somewhat. In addition to being exceedingly costly, several of the proposed measures to stimulate new construction and home sales could make it even more difficult for the housing sector to make the adjustments that will be required during the 1980s.

LESSONS FOR POLICY

Each of the housing crises that have allegedly occurred in the past decade has entailed errors in either analysis or policy or some combination of the two. For example, while the extent of abandonment and its causes is still not well understood, it is likely that high levels of subsidized new construction during the first part of the decade contributed to its intensity, and that cash subsidies to low-income households would have helped maintain the existing housing stock by allowing them to pay market rents.

As for the homeownership affordability crisis, rising house prices during the first part of the decade may in fact have created problems for some first-time homebuyers. The expectation that prices would continue to increase, in combination with the tax advantages of ownership, nonetheless induced record numbers of households to buy homes during the decade. As the decade proceeded, it became increasingly apparent that the early analyses of affordability had incorrectly calculated ownership costs, and that most households that owned in 1970 or bought during the last 10 years benefited enormously from the rapid increase in house prices. By 1980, however, rising real interest rates, increasing unemployment, lower inflation rates, and growing uncertainty about future property values caused the real cost of homeownership to rise sharply and the sales of both new and existing homes to fall.

The rental housing crisis was also the product of faulty analysis. All available data indicate that real rents fell during the period preceding the alleged crisis, and that the size and quality of rental housing improved significantly. It is equally clear that the decline in real rents was due at least in part to decreases in the demand for rental units. Declining vacancy rates, frequently cited as evidence of a worsening crisis, were accompanied by low levels of private new construction, which were in turn the result of high interest rates and market rents that were below the levels that would make such investments profitable. Rising rent-income ratios were largely a statistical artifact reflecting the shift of many high-income renters to homeownership and changes in the characteristics of the population of renter households.

The most common mistake made by those who believe that a rental housing crisis exists is to confuse the fact that many low-income households are unable to obtain standard housing without spending an excessively high fraction of their incomes on rent with proof of market failure. The problem for most of these households is poverty, not inadequate housing. While poverty, excess rent burden, and inadequate housing remain serious problems for millions of Americans, there is no evidence that the problems have become more serious. The belief that measures such as rent control or bans on condominium conversions will eliminate income and housing deficiencies of poor households is mistaken; if these policies benefit anyone, it is likely to be middle- and upper-income rather than low-income households.

The condominium conversion crisis is, of course, closely related to trends in both the owner and renter housing markets. High rates of conversions, the lag in market rents behind the general increase in prices, and the low rates of private rental housing starts have common origins. In the last decade, several factors—including high rates of inflation, rising marginal tax rates, and the favorable tax treatment of interest payments, property taxes, and imputed rents—have made homeownership more attractive to increasing numbers of renters. Their shift to the owner market has reduced the demand for rental housing, making it difficult for landlords to raise rents enough to keep pace with higher operating and capital costs. The decline in real rents, moreover, has reduced the value of rental properties, inducing landlords to convert to owner-occupied units. Record-high mortgage rates have now all but halted new rental housing construction.

In recent months, declining vacancy rates have been interpreted as a rental housing shortage and have added to the demands for rent control or for moratoria and bans on conversions. Such policies cannot eliminate the shortage—if one in fact exists—and could well exacerbate it. In growing metropolitan areas, a shortage in rental units can be eliminated only by a more rapid shift of renters to homeownership or by new construction; but new construction will not occur until market rents reach levels that justify private investment, or until the government provides subsidies that reduce the cost or increase the profitability of rental housing. The enactment of bans on condominium conversion, rent control, and similar measures can only worsen the problem, because potential investors are likely to demand a risk premium in the form of higher rents before they will commit themselves to new rental housing projects.

Because record-high interest rates have halted most conversion activity, the issue has become less burning recently. A decline in real interest rates, however, will almost certainly produce another spurt of conversions that will doubtless resurrect the controversy.

WHAT SHOULD WE DO?

President Nixon's National Housing Policy Review, President Reagan's Commission on Housing, and virtually every independent evaluation of America's housing problems and policies during the past two decades have reached virtually identical conclusions: that housing conditions have improved steadily in the postwar period, that the improvement largely reflects steady growth in per capita and household incomes, and that government programs have made at best a minor contribution to this improvement. As the fraction of households living in substandard housing has declined, moreover, the housing problems of low-income households have been more clearly identified as a matter of poverty. Finally, the studies all point out that middle- and high-income households receive the bulk of government subsidies for housing in the form of tax expenditures.

Previous studies of America's housing policy are also remarkably consistent in their evaluation of federal housing programs.[25] In particular, they uniformly conclude that these programs tend to be both inequitable and inefficient. The inequity arises from the fact that government programs provide subsidies to only a small fraction of eligible households; while recipients obtain very large subsidies, most households receive no assistance whatsoever. The inefficiency results from the heavy emphasis on new construction programs. It is at least twice as expensive to build new units to house low-income households as it is to assist poor households to rent existing units. Although the justification for new construction programs has often been the goal of shoring up the building industry, the available evidence suggests that most subsidized new construction displaces private building activity, and that government programs tend to increase rather than to reduce instability in the new industry.

Given their agreement about the nation's housing problems and the deficiencies of previous federal programs, it is not surprising that previous evaluations offer nearly identical recommendations. All urge a reduction in the extent of housing subsidies for middle- and high-income households, arguing that these programs are inefficient because they induce homeowners to consume more housing than they would otherwise. Recommended policy changes usually take the form of a cap on interest and property tax deductions, or a system of tax credits that would provide the same amount of subsidy to all homeowners. The current system of deductions, in contrast, benefits higher-income households more than lower-income ones.

While the arguments favoring these changes are quite persuasive, the chance of political acceptance is very limited, except in the context of a comprehensive restructuring of the tax code involving substantial decreases in marginal tax rates. Previous studies are also unanimous about the best approach to housing subsidies for low-income households. As the report of President Reagan's Commission on Housing concludes, "A housing payments program (HPP) for lower-income consumers is the most efficient way to help the largest number of poor families in their quest for a decent home."[26] Political reality led the commission to add, however, that "such a program may not be sufficient where there is a serious shortage of adequate apartments," and to recommend that the Community Development Block Grant (CDBG) program add a housing component that would make new construction an eligible activity.

Given the consistent findings of past evaluations of federal housing programs and policy and the uniformity of their recommendations, the persistence of errors in analysis and policy is remarkable. In too many instances, premature and partial analysis of incomplete

25. Henry J. Aaron, *Shelter and Subsidies: Who Benefits from Federal Housing Policies* (Washington, DC: Brookings Institution, 1972); *Housing in the Seventies; Report of the President's Commission.*

26. *Report of the President's Commission*, p. xxix.

data produces headlines that are never quite corrected by subsequent in-depth studies. In addition, federal housing policy, like every other kind, is strongly influenced by politically powerful interest groups. In the housing policy area, these groups generally believe their interests are advanced by high levels of new construction. Unfortunately, they appear to be unaware of, uninterested in, or simply do not believe the growing evidence that subsidized construction largely displaces private construction activity, resulting in small net additions to the housing stock. Similarly, tenant advocacy groups that continue to press for rent control, bans on condominium conversions, and other restrictions on private rental markets are not deterred by the findings of studies showing that condominium conversions provide large benefits to buyers, do no more than inconvenience most displaced tenants, and have very little net impact on the rental housing market.

Book Department

INTERNATIONAL RELATIONS AND POLITICS

ARMSTRONG, WILLIS C., LOUISE S. ARMSTRONG, and FRANCIS O. WILCOX, eds. *Canada and the United States: Dependence and Divergence.* Pp. xiii, 331. Cambridge, MA: Balinger. 1982. $25.00.

This edited volume is the product of a study undertaken by the Atlantic Council of the United States to determine the foreign policy implications for this nation of significant political, social, and economic changes taking place in contemporary Canada. It contains 10 separate essays covering such divergent topics as the future of Canadian federalism, environmental concerns north of the border, and the impact of American investment in Canada. Each of the contributing authors attempts to outline the character of a real or potential irritant in Canadian-U.S. relations and endeavors to provide some recommendations as to how these problem areas can best be handled to the satisfaction of the governments and peoples of both nations.

The overall objective of this volume appears to be to sensitize American policymakers and the general public to the "likely future trend of Canadian events" and to urge them to "consider where U.S. interests lie and what the United States can do to safeguard these interests" as such events unfold. This is not a particularly new goal. Others on both sides of the border have previously called for greater American concern for relations with the nation's "most important ally." Nonetheless, this volume does provide a clear and current exposition of American stakes in both the continued future of Canadian confederation and a harmonious North American neighborhood. The book carefully outlines for those new to the Canadian scene both the historical antecedents of contemporary change within the dominion and the roles Canadian domestic forces and American influence have played in reshaping the national consciousness and perspective. Each of the authors stresses the extent to which the United States is a visible participant in the course of Canadian national development and does not shy away from discussing the proper manner in which the American government and people should exert their influence in the future.

This American focus on the Canadian-American relationship is both a strength and weakness in the volume. While such a perspective does effectively communicate to an American audience the need for this nation to be more aware of its northern neighbor and to take appropriate actions to perpetuate good U.S.-Canadian relations, at times it also projects the inaccurate image that political, economic, and social change in Canada is subject to exclusive American control. Similarly, many of the authors, in presenting policy options for the United States in dealing with Canadian affairs, slip into the unfortunate habit of assuming that what is good for Americans is necessarily desired by Canadians. Both of these attitudes betray a certain imbalance in analysis of the full dimensions of this bilateral relationship and seem to contradict the volume's professed theme of mutual dependence and divergence.

As with most edited works, *Canada and the United States* contains both essays of superior quality and those with less insight. In the case of the former, the pieces by Annette Fox and Alfred Hero, Jr., on environmental issues and Quebec's impact on the United States, respectively, are worthy of special attention. Both deal with complicated and evolving topics in a current and straightforward manner that impresses upon the reader both the importance of such issues to future Canadian-U.S. relations and the need to develop new approaches in dealing with them. Other essays in this volume could benefit from their example.

On the whole, however, *Canada and the United States* represents a welcomed new addition to a very limited selection of studies on Canadian-U.S. relations. Its focus on current and future questions in the relationship should draw the attention of informed Americans to the need to enter into a new dialogue regarding what our policy toward Canada should be in both the short and long term. Such open discussion can only improve the status of our relationship with our neighbors to the north, for it is their frequent complaint that those of us south of the line regularly fail to acknowledge their existence or deal with them outside of the context of a limited caricature of the Canadian nation.

DOUGLAS C. NORD
University of Minnesota
Duluth

BARTON, JOHN H. *The Politics of Peace: An Evaluation of Arms Control.* Pp. ix, 257. Stanford, CA: Stanford University Press, 1981. $18.50.

John Barton presents a well-written survey of his own unevenly optimistic and pessimistic perspective on the role of arms control for moderating the risks of the international system.

The book begins with some general chapters on the sources and initiation of war, marred only, perhaps, by an interesting illustrative digression on the origins of the U.S. Civil War, an example many theorists might regard as somewhat atypical of the origins of international strife.

Barton then moves into a very realistic analysis of the role international law can play in moderating wars and arms races, reflecting the author's own legal training but also enough of a familiarity with international process to preclude any overrating of the role of law. The remainder of the book then amounts to a survey of the various half-steps which have been taken in international agreements on arms—basically a summary of how things stood just before President Reagan was elected. The change of tone brought in by the Reagan administration, with its initial emphasis on war-fighting scenarios and more acrimonious confrontation with the Russians, may have upset much of what we had previously concluded in the arms control area, but it is not really reflected in the book.

Barton makes good use of anecdotal and case material and generally offers a persuasive picture of what arms control might accomplish. His analysis, however, is a little less specific than some readers might desire, blurring the details of many of the issues he discusses, leaving the reader with a general message of "don't expect too much, don't stop trying."

While Barton's overall analysis is very well-informed, his conclusions by comparison thus seem somewhat weak and halfhearted. Barton does not claim that the success of arms control depends more on a change in human motivation than on detailed analysis of particular cases; by and large, in fact, he argues the reverse. Yet the book's tone is almost more in step with an emphasis on motivation than on analysis. The book thus may be of value as an introduction for the lay reader more than as an intellectual spur to the academic already working in the field.

GEORGE H. QUESTER
University of Maryland
College Park

BRUBAKER, EARL R. *Individual Values and Global Sharing.* Pp. vi, 146. New York: New York University Press, 1980. $17.50.

Accelerating recognition of global interdependence pushes the challenge of disarmament and world peace to the forefront of issues which attract the attention and energies of individuals throughout the world. With apparent great interest in order and justice, an obvious fundamental question is, How are these extraordinary global collective goods to be financed? Required payments and moral suasion for additional funds directed by the United Nations at member governments has been a strategy of developing failure, jeopardizing individual citizen demands for world order and peace. This small volume makes a modest contribution in analyzing the financial difficulties of the United Nations by proposing an intriguing complement to existing financial approaches.

Brubaker surveys the budgetary plight of U.N. peace-keeping activities and appraises traditional approaches to international cost sharing. This is followed by a particularly useful examination of alternative schemes to meet ongoing U.N. financial crises, including national taxes, voluntary contributions by government, taxes on transnational interactions, and payments by aggressors or beneficiaries.

The core of his analysis, however, is based in standard microeconomics of sharing, proposing individual voluntary contributions as a means for partially financing the global collective good of peace-keeping. The usual thrust of collective good financing analysis runs in the direction of taxation, but the free rider-forced rider tradeoff is troubling to Brubaker. He recognizes that rational individuals will understate their demands for a collective good, expecting a free ride on the contribution of others. He stands on a weak free rider hypothesis, however, agreeing that while socially optimal flows of voluntary payments will not be forthcoming, sufficient contributions may be made to add importantly to U.N. resources. He sees a possible innovating role for the United Nations as an entrepreneurial intermediary/agent in energizing sufficient individual contributions to make international peace-keeping a more viable prospect. The possible partial success of such efforts is apparent in the considerable voluntary contributions in cash and in kind to domestic public good activities, as well as in the record of such nongovernmental international organizations as the Red Cross, CARE, and in the International Council of Scientific Unions.

Brubaker does not naively argue that the whole of U.N. peace-keeping functions could be financed in this manner, for he emphasizes the preliminary, exploratory nature of his proposal. He does, however, view with strong disfavor the prohibition which currently exists with the United Nations in soliciting voluntary contributions from individual citizens for its work. The U.N. secretary general could utilize the United Way or Red Cross structures for solicitation avenues, with themes of fair shares and contributions on the basis of perceived benefits.

While these ideas may sound simpleminded to some hardheaded diplomats and social scientists, the relative failure of traditional modes of U.N. financing and the likely strong latent demand for peace by the world's citizens suggest that Brubaker's modest exploratory proposal is worth serious investigation.

HAROLD L. JOHNSON
Emory University
Atlanta
Georgia

ELAZAR, DANIEL J., ed. *Judea, Samaria, and Gaza: Views on the Present and Future*. Pp. 222. Washington, DC: American Enterprise Institute for Public Policy Research, 1982. No price.

One people's Judea, Samaria, and Gaza are part of another's Occupied Palestine. Therein lies the problem to which this volume is addressed. Can it be resolved? Peacefully? Daniel J. Elazar, who is perhaps best known for his work on federalism in the United States, argues that it can, but only if it is understood that "the system of fully sovereign states as developed in modern Europe is not appropriate for the Middle East" because politics there revolves around peoples, not lasting nation-states with fixed territorial boundaries. Indeed, he points out that "not a single boundary in the Middle East today is as much as a hundred years old." Moreover, "the peoples are so situated that homogeneous states have rarely if ever been attainable."

Palestine/Israel is no exception. Its strife, in Elazar's view, can be resolved only through a system of shared power that will draw two lessons from the period of Ottoman rule. First, there must be ethnic autonomy or home rule for all peoples in the area—the millet system. Second, these peoples must be protected by external powers with whom they have an affinity. In the case of Jews, the external power would be Israel; for the Palestinian Arabs, it would be Jordan, which is far more problematic. This is the principle of extraterritoriality or capitulations. How would an arrangement based on these two conditions function? Here Elazar is less specific. Certainly it would depend on a degree of cooperation not now present in the area. First, it would require that each of the people in Judea, Samaria, and Gaza/Occupied Palestine accept the right of the others to be there—which brings us back to the basic question of the legitimacy of the partition of Palestine by Israel and Jordan in the first place. It would also depend on the ability of Israel and Jordan to enforce law and impose order on dissident or extremist groups. And from a legalistic perspective, a system of laws relating to peoples rather than territory could result in such inequities as to be inherently unstable. Nevertheless, among a group of very poor alternatives, Elazar's approach may well offer the greatest hope for peace in the area.

The remainder of the book consists of a series of essays on the demography, hydrology, economy, sociology, politics, and law of Judea, Samaria, and Gaza/Occupied Palestine and Jordan that more or less support Elazar's conclusions. Although original and thought provoking, these are marred by pro-Israeli biases ranging from subtle to unrestrained. In fact, one gets the impression that the authors may not even be aware of how one-sided their approaches will appear to outsiders who do not share their mind-set, their language, and their mutually self-reinforced celebration of their right to be in the occupied territories. For instance, Elisha Efrat bemoans the barrier that the 600,000 Arabs living on the West Bank present to Jewish settlement—they will not leave and there are no absentee landlords to buy out. Moshe Drori refers to Israeli breaches of conventional international law as "precedents," which he seems to think can be set at the will and pleasure of an occupying power and nevertheless be considered legitimate and binding by the rest of the world. He also maintains that "no Arab inhabitants have been displaced by Jewish settlements," which is probably not true even in a technical sense; but in any event he fails to mention the displacement of Arabs by Jewish settlers. He also tells us that the presence of Israeli Jews in the area is not in violation of international law because it consisted of "voluntary movement of individuals." Subsequently, however, when it suits another purpose in his discussion, we are told that these Jewish "pioneers . . . were encouraged by Israel to settle in Judea and Samaria." This is indeed the creating of facts run amok.

Avraham Lavine is committed to the notion that a people whose land is occupied and who are subjugated by an occupying power can develop a high sense of self-esteem, self-confidence, independence, and political efficacy through improved social services and social work! He thinks increasing juvenile delinquency among Arabs in the occupied territories is due to improved social and economic conditions, and fails even to consider the impact of the occupation itself. Mordechai Nisan develops the argument that the Palestinians' fundamental problem is not that their country is occupied by Israel, but rather that it is ruled by the Hashemite government of Jordan, which was exported from Arabia as a result of British intrigue in the 1920s.

Sadly, Elazar himself does not escape this tendency. In order to rationalize shared Israeli-Jordanian rule over the occupied territories, he asserts that the Palestinians are a "public," but not yet a people. Sound familiar? Still, the book presents an interesting, refreshing, and original place to begin thinking new thoughts about the future of an old problem.

DAVID H. ROSENBLOOM
Syracuse University
Syracuse
New York

EVELAND, WILBUR CRANE. *Ropes of Sand: America's Failure in the Middle East.* Pp. 384. New York: W. W. Norton, 1980. $14.95.

Wilbur Crane Eveland has written a fascinating, exasperating, highly personal memoir copiously filled with names and places and dates. There is ample footnoting used to elucidate special points. However, there is no documentation of bibliography in the scholarly sense, and we are therefore required to take the accuracy of Eveland's memory at face value.

The fascination stems from the revelations; the exasperation I felt concerns the problematic need to accept some quite staggering assertions at face value.

Eveland's career began with military intelligence work in World War II. He remained in the Army and served in military attaché positions in the Middle East. He performed various missions for White House policy planners, and finally on behalf of the CIA without, however, becoming a career regular in that organization. Eventually he shifted to a career as petroleum and construction company consultant for Middle East projects.

Eveland's story concentrates on activities and involvements in Iraq, Syria, Lebanon, and Egypt. The major focus is on the Eisenhower years, and Eveland's best chapters concern Lebanon.

According to the author, American policy in the Middle East has lacked a clear vision and consistent implementation. During the Eisenhower-Dulles years the Middle East was viewed primarily in the light of a frantic anticommunism. Eveland believes that the direct Russian threat was exaggerated and that the focal point of attention should have been the instability of the local regimes. Attempts to bolster regimes through money, arms, and finally through clandestine CIA operations proved mostly dysfunctional, being ill-considered or ill-timed.

Eveland drops a few bombshells: in addition to the widely ascribed role of the CIA in the return to power of the Shah of Iran, he alleges that Gamel Abdel Nasser of Egypt was launched as a CIA protegee; later, the U.S. became disillusioned with him; in 1967 Eveland charges the United States set up Israel to bring down Nasser, while Mohamed Heikal, editor in chief of Egypt's leading newspaper, was to have worked with or for the CIA. All of this is a bit mind-boggling.

Several significant chapters deal with the ongoing Lebanon crisis. The politics of Lebanon are found wanting, even as Eveland expresses his obvious sympathy for the Lebanese people and his affection for two outstanding leaders: former President Camille Chamoun, and former U.N. representative Charles Malik. American effort at support came reluctantly and late. U.S. troop landings in 1958 were an effective military display, but the corollary political efforts failed to achieve the goal of stabilizing a friendly regime, which was subordinated to the search for anticommunist alliance and fear of Soviet confrontation.

Eveland makes some effective points in demonstrating the initial bombast and subsequent watering down of grandiose policies: especially the Eisenhower doctrine. He consistently denounces the covert activities of the CIA. These, he says, either failed or backfired and undermined that intelligence function of gathering sound information which Eveland thinks should have been the chief mission of the CIA.

In the early 1960s, American policy steadied on the side of Israel, and Eveland clearly thinks this the compounding of previous mistakes. He alleges the systematic use by Israel of American anticommunism to further her own position by assuming the mantle of a staunch anticommunist bastion. Why indict Israel for perceiving a communality of the interest, and why omit the relentless hostility to Israel of the Soviet Union and her satellites and camp followers?

Eveland's sympathy seems to lie with the Arab people, which cannot be faulted, especially since he has few illusions about Arab political systems. An equal empathy with the Israelis might have placed the events of the Middle East in a better perspective. This, in fact, appears to have been an essential flaw in U.S. Middle East policy which the author castigates so much: it was a policy made by an excessively homogeneous establishment whose ability to perceive local complexities was limited.

HANS E. SEGAL
Cleveland State University
Cleveland
Ohio

MARER, PAUL and EUGENIUSZ TABACZYNSKI, eds. *Polish-U.S. Industrial Cooperation in the 1980s.* Pp. xxix, 409. Bloomington: Indiana University Press, 1982. $25.00.

This book presents the results of two joint Polish-American seminars—the first held in Bloomington, Indiana in December 1978, the second in Warsaw, Poland in March 1979. These results are embodied in 12 essays by the participating Polish and American specialists.

Alas, so much has happened in Poland since 1978-79 that the editors could neither update their materials nor change their focus. They have therefore continued to operate within the framework they originally established in 1978—the best ways of deepening Polish-American cooperation, abstraction made of Poland's economic solvency and political stability—and they have prefaced all this with a somewhat awkwardly updated section entitled "Summary, Conclusions, Recommendations."

What was the original focus of the seminars? Participants focused in particular on the role of industrial cooperation (IC) between the U.S. and Polish industrial firms in the existing environments within which foreign firms must operate in both countries. Special attention was paid to a complex manufacturing venture between International Harvester and Bumar established for the manufacturing in Poland of crawler tractors designed and engineered by the American partner. This type of cooperative industrial venture, according to the editors, was supposed to represent the wave of the future: "While conventional trade will remain important in the 1980s, more complex forms—IC that is—may become increasingly significant in East-West commerce during the 1980s and 1990s."

Marer and Tabaczynski were aware—at least in the "Summary, Conclusions, Recommendations" section—of the deepening Polish crisis, of Poland's accumulating hard currency debts, of the disastrous long-run consequences of its leaders' development strategy, of the rigidities of its centralized management, of the deficiencies of its economic accounting, and so on. But all this, they stated, was alleged to be cured eventually by the "January 1981 Polish plan of economic reform which is very important for the improvement of the situation in Poland." As it is by now clear, not much has materialized of this "important plan," one of the innumerable and much-heralded "economic reforms" always glowingly announced and more or less silently aborted. As for the events in which the trade union Solidarity participated, they are glossed over in the same summary section, undoubtedly under the prodding of the Polish editor, with the innocuous phrase: "It is necessary, however, to add that the events in Poland since the summer of 1980 (workers' protest against management and the price system) have posed short-term problems to the development of IC with foreign partners."

One cannot blame Marer and Tabaczynski for having been caught short by the "events." The analysis of recent events is indeed a perilous exercise. But these events have nevertheless shown that the Polish system was in a far tighter bind than was surmised in the tranquil seminars of 1978-79. By now the IC and other forms of cooperation may be called into serious question: Poland is not only virtually bankrupt economically but is also extremely unstable politically. Editorial recommendations such as those included in this book seem strangely inappropriate today: "An important advantage of having a commercial base in Poland is its geographical location, which may facilitate export penetration by American firms of the other East European countries and may serve as a convenient production base for marketing in Western Europe."(!)

A last sad note: the publishers' flyer notes that "several Polish contributors [to this book] have held government and university positions; their status since December 13, 1981 is not known." Alas again.

The book preserves, however, a historical interest for all students of Eastern European affairs.

NICOLAS SPULBER
Indiana University
Bloomington

AFRICA, ASIA, AND LATIN AMERICA

America's Watch Committee and the American Civil Liberties Union, compilers. *Report on Human Rights in El Salvador*. Pp. xviii, 312. New York: Vintage Books, 1982. Paperbound, $3.95.

Out of the ashes of World War II emerged public international acknowledgment that "the inherent dignity and the equal and inalienable rights of all members of the human family is the foundation of freedom, justice and peace in the world." To achieve this dignity, freedom, and justice and, by extension, peace, nation-states pledged themselves to the goal of promoting universal respect for and observance of human rights. Though the realization of the goal has been elusive, the international community has come to recognize the common danger posed by disregard for and violations of human rights. *Report on Human Rights in El Salvador* is a chilling account of that danger.

The work is divided into three parts: Part I gives the socioeconomic sources—emphasizing malnutrition, poor housing, unemployment, inequitable distribution of income and land, and unsuccessful attempts at agrarian reforms, and so on—of the current civil war in El Salvador; Part II, encompassing nine of the book's thirteen chapters, focuses on the human rights situation in that country; and Part III, covering the last two chapters, highlights U.S. involvement.

Based on thoroughly documented case histories from victims, relatives of victims, witnesses, representatives from transnational organizations such as the International Commission of Jurists, Amnesty International, and the Inter-American Commission on Human Rights, the report adduces compelling evidence showing that the government of El Salvador is waging a campaign of terror against its own people. The terror includes arbitrary arrest and imprisonment, abolition of an independent judiciary, the closing down of newspapers and schools, the bombing of radio stations, torture, and murder.

If one should take murder and torture as examples, the latter human rights violation is not engaged in "mainly for the purpose of extracting information" but "to strike terror in the hearts of others." So victims are seized not in battle but at home and at their work places. And in the case of murder, teachers are gunned down before pupils, and fathers and brothers in front of relatives.

The book is important not only because by unmasking human rights violations it may help to awaken international opinion against the government concerned, but also, in a very concrete way, its case histories will help people to evaluate the conduct of governments and reinforce the view that how a state treats its citizens is of urgent concern to the international community. The work, though biased in favor of political and civil rights, shows how repeated patterns of violations in the area of social and economic rights lead to violations in the civil and political rights and invite threats to international peace.

The book should be read by all who are concerned about human rights, and especially those who seek to modify or change U.S. economic and military support for the existing regime.

WINSTON E. LANGLEY
University of Massachusetts
Boston

BALLARD, J. A., ed. *Policy-Making in a New State: Papua New Guinea 1972-77*. Pp. xx, 331. St. Lucia: University of Queensland Press, 1981. $32.50.

This book deals with changes in policies and policymakers in Papua New Guinea during the period from the election of the National Coalition in 1972 through the advent of self-government (December 1973) and independence (September 1975) up to the end of Michael Somare's first term as prime minister in 1977. Ten authors have written twelve papers describing and interpreting problems of policymaking in areas including the transfer of power from Australia, the role of the new cabinet, administrative reform, the economy, law, land issues and agriculture, rural development, and the establishment of provincial governments.

Most books on the winding down of colonialism and the formative years of political independence focus not on policymaking but on the struggle for independence and on the activities of mobilized nationalist movements. Such a book could hardly be written about Papua New Guinea, because there was no nationalist movement to speak of; the largest group in the country—the Highlanders—were not anxious for the colonial masters to leave; and by 1972 the Australians indicated their desire to set Papua New Guinea free. Indeed, in the early 1970s Papua New Guinea revealed a situation Kipling would have loved, with about 7000 extraordinarily well-paid expatriates—largely Australians, but including also American, British, East African, Canadian, Indian, and Pakistani carpetbaggers who had washed ashore or otherwise found employment—holding virtually every important public service position.

It is noteworthy—and unfortunate, but not surprising—that all ten contributors to this volume are expatriates—nine are Australians; Ballard is an American. The Papua New Guineans who might have contributed were otherwise occupied in the positions these expatriates once held. Most of the authors held senior posts in the colonial and transitional administration and accordingly were in ideal positions to write these essays. Significant also is that these are what might be called liberal expatriates—that is, individuals who placed Papua New Guinean fortunes above their own. None is what might be termed a radical, nor was there more than a small handful of indigenous radicals during this period. Thus one reads here about moderate policy outcomes devised by moderate policymakers. None of the policy here discussed hurt the Australians, the white planters, or others who acquired benefits during the colonial period. For a radical, neo-Marxist critique of these same years, one must see Amarshi, Good, and Mortimer, *Development and Dependency: The Political Economy of Papua New Guinea* (Melbourne: Oxford University Press, 1979).

These essays are very well-written, especially those of Ballard and Garnaut. Despite Ballard's largely successful effort to place the essays in the context of policymaking in new states, the contributions often focus on such idiosyncratic matters that they are unfortunately likely to attract the interest mainly of students of Papua New Guinea. One is struck by the fact that most of the names mentioned in the book are of expatriates, even after 1975. Although some localization took place during these years, it is apparent that expatriates, albeit more furtively now, are still a very significant element of Papua New Guinea's policymaking elite.

GEORGE H. GADBOIS, Jr.
University of Kentucky
Lexington

DANNS, GEORGE K. *Domination and Power in Guyana: A Study of the Police in a Third World Context.* Pp. xiv, 193. New Brunswick, NJ: Transaction Books, 1982. $29.95.

This is an unusual book. It is an extraordinarily lucid, candid, and yet balanced account of the development of police as the major focus of political power in a postcolonial state. Many social scientists who have researched authoritarian societies of the postcolonial world would like to have written such a book but have not for fear of alienating both liberal colleagues and the authoritarian regimes which exercise more or less control over further in-country research. Indeed, the account is so straightforward that Danns, who apparently continues to live and work in Guyana, seems no less than courageous.

The book is well organized. Each chapter prepares the reader for subsequent chapters, beginning with a statement of purpose and extending through a review of relevant literature; a comprehensive overview of police in Guyana society; chapters on politics and corruption, ethnic and industrial unrest, and police-military relationships; and a concluding chapter devoted mostly to domination and power in contemporary Guyana. British use of police to exploit their colonial subjects, American manipulation of industrial unrest and of the international economic and political setting, the unbridled pursuit of economic and political advantage by ethnic groups and labor unions, and the selfish machinations of mesmeratic leaders of Guyana in the postcolonial period are equally impaled on the pen of Professor Danns.

There are a number of interesting and useful theoretical distinctions, such as that between charismatic and mesmeratic leadership, throughout the book. But these are instances of theory in the service of excellent description, not the reverse. Differences between developed and developing societies with respect to the functions of police comprise a major but underdeveloped theoretical thrust of the book. These differences, discussed in terms of historical factors, might be more thoughtfully related to economic and demographic differences. Additionally, the author sketches an idealized model of progressive stages in the evolution of postcolonial societies in which police constitute a primary focus of power. This latter attempt to generalize details of the Guyanese experience to other societies appears to work best vis-à-vis postcolonial societies of the Caribbean area. Dann's attempts to develop theory are much less convincing than his analysis of the central place of the police in Guyanese bureaucracy and politics, perhaps because the means of discerning the various phases of historical evolution are not clearly stated.

The bibliography adequately accounts for the sources cited in the book but is not particularly valuable as a general guide to literature on police in postcolonial states. The index is minimal.

Overall, the book comprises an excellent case study worthy of consideration by those who would develop and test grand theory concerning the development of authoritarian societies in the postcolonial world.

RONALD PROVENCHER
Northern Illinois University
Dekalb

DUIKER, WILLIAM J. *The Communist Road to Power in Vietnam.* Pp. xvi, 393. Boulder, CO: Westview Press, 1981. $32.50.

This is an original and important study of the Communist movement in Vietnam. Written by a scholar who already has distinguished himself in his earlier Vietnamese publications, William J. Duiker presents new and original insights into the Communist struggle through his extensive and critical use of party documents, commentaries, and analyses. Unlike other studies of the subject, this book presents readers with a description of the roots of the movement and traces both its successes and setbacks against the writings of non-Marxist scholars who have relied on other information for their own works. Through discussion of Marxist theory and descriptions of events and important figures, the reader comes to know the men who made the revolution and the way they thought about it at various stages. In addition, Duiker's story is told against the changing background of Vietnam—under colonialism, during World War II, the war against France, and later against the United States—and world events which help the reader to appreciate the external influences as they intrude on local events.

This is not a study without controversy. Many would quarrel with Duiker's descriptions and analyses of the Communist movement in South Vietnam, both during and after World War II, his treatment of many turning points in the wars against the French and the Americans, and his analysis of the settlement in 1973. The Tet offensive is a case in point. Few would disagree that it was a turning point in the U.S. involvement in the Vietnam war. However, whether the South Vietnamese and the United States won it in the field and lost it in the political arena will not be resolved by reading this book. Duiker provides a dispassionate analysis of the event as seen from both Hanoi and the West. In doing so he draws on the writings of Vietnamese, Americans, and Western correspondents. While his conclusion seeks a middle ground between both sides—neither victory nor defeat—his real point is that the war must be seen as an event on a continuum which, from the perspective of the Communists, was to get the United States out of Vietnam and not necessarily to win in one bold stroke—although some in Hanoi thought a general rising of the population and a sweeping victory might be obtained—and thereby remove the only remaining obstacle to their ultimate victory. In developing this and other crucial events, Duiker draws on a wide range of sources and acknowledges that future publications may make his conclusions obsolete.

I found the treatment of the negotiations and final treaty between the United States and Vietnam the least satisfactory part of the book. For someone who scrupulously examined every document that bore on his narrative, Duiker fails to describe and analyze the treaty. Article 1, for instance, declares that the United States and all other countries "respect the independence, sovereignty, unity and territorial integrity of Vietnam as recognized by the 1954 Geneva Agreements on Vietnam." Since the United States, from 1965 on, declared that it was ready to negotiate anything but the independence of South Vietnam, surely this article of the treaty deserved discussion, since it acknowledges the consistent position of the North Vietnamese and denies that of the United States. Other aspects of the treaty, such as Article 21, obligate the United States to "contribute to healing the wounds of war and to postwar reconstruction of the Democratic Republic of Vietnam and throughout Indochina." It is to be hoped that Duiker will one day expand his final chapter on Vietnam after 1975 and go back to the treaty of 1973 and its impact on Vietnam and the United States, especially in light of the failure of both nations to abide honestly and fully by its terms.

Finally, it is my hope that the publisher will see fit to bring this important study to a wider audience through the issuance of a cheaper edition so that it can be used in university classrooms where Southeast Asia and American foreign relations are studied. It tells an important story and deserves to be read more widely.

JOSEF SILVERSTEIN

Rutgers University
New Brunswick
New Jersey

HUBER, THOMAS M. *The Revolutionary Origins of Modern Japan.* Pp. xi, 260. Stanford, CA: Stanford University Press, 1981. $19.50.

It has almost become conventional wisdom to view the Meiji Restoration of 1868 as a revolution from above. In this provocative and incisive historical analysis of the revolutionary origins of modern Japan Huber demurs persuasively.

This insightful book sheds new light on the history of the restoration movement in the Choshu domain, which in many ways became a catalyst of Japan's transformation to a modern state.

The Meiji Restoration, he contends, was the result of protracted class struggle of Japan's service intelligentsia of minor administrators, scholars, village officials, and priests, mainly recruited from among the lower-ranking samurai class, against ossified feudal institutions and persistent dominance of the higher-ranking nobility's power and influence.

Against historians who are reluctant to concede a causality between the sociopolitical disorder of the Bakumatsu period (1853-67) and institutional reforms instigated by the Meiji restorators after 1868, Huber points to a continuous commitment to structural reform by the service intelligentsia which in effect turned to rancorous polemics, agitation, and terrorist acts leading to civil war in Choshu, which finally toppled the vestiges of conservative power.

To advocates of the Western challenge thesis who interpret as basically imitative Japan's response of 1868, prompting a full-scale yet selective importation of modern, Western institutions, Huber responds that the Meiji Restoration was essentially an indigenous affair, and that the Western threat had been operationalized by "reformers to win broader approval for the basic structural changes they had long favored."

Methodologically, Huber has meshed careful historical study with well-documented elite analysis. Focusing on

Choshu's dissident service intelligentsia, he presents three vivid political portraits: Yoshida Shonin, the prolific leader, and two of his most prominent disciples, Kusaka Gensui and Takasugi Shinsaku. In this vein, the author ably chronicled the political struggles of Choshu's service intelligentsia against the domain's outmoded sociopolitical institutions during the Bakumatsu period.

Huber is at his best in analyzing the leading activists' social and educational background, their motives and course of action. Some of his assertions, however, are less convincing than others. Particularly his interpretation and bold elevation of Yoshida's thought to status of a blueprint for the Meiji reforms of the 1870s seems somewhat farfetched if not a retrospective prediction. Also, the narrative suffers from an exceeding degree of redundancy that should have been avoided to render this excellent historical study into more concise reading.

These shortcomings, nevertheless, should not distract from the basic value of this otherwise most stimulating work.

WALTER ARNOLD
Miami University
Oxford
Ohio

IBRAHIM, SAAD EDDIN. *The New Arab Social Order: A Study of the Social Impact of Oil Wealth.* Pp. xiv, 208. Boulder, CO: Westview Press, 1982. $18.00.

The oil embargo of 1973 and the subsequent escalation of prices by the Arab oil-producing countries, along with other OPEC members, made many Americans sharply and painfully aware of the power of these Arab states to influence their personal lives and, by extension, national policies toward the Middle East. But awareness has not been accompanied by any depth of understanding of how Arab society functions, and even less understanding of the direction it is taking as a result of the acceleration of oil-based capital inflow into the treasuries of Arab oil producers. This book represents a major contribution to the literature on Arab societal behavior.

The "new" Arab social order which is Professor Ibrahim's subject is still evolving in the 1980s, but already it can be seen to be a product of earlier orders, affected by the Arab experience of the two previous decades and with oil as the underlying factor. As Ibrahim notes, the new social order stems from a "silent" revolution—quite different from the loud revolutions that accompanied the struggles of various Arab states for independence from their colonial tutors. In the long run, he believes this revolution will have a far greater effect on the Arab future than revolutions with guns or Israeli military success over Arab armies. Guns can be muzzled, but the movement of Arab manpower and money across national borders is unstoppable and in time will contribute significantly to the reshaping of Arab society along lines not yet clear.

The author uses a method of presenting his findings which is unusual in a work that will certainly—and unfortunately—be classed as a scholarly study and hence have a limited readership. He gives us first six "images" of the Arab social person, each on symbolizing one aspect of structural change in Arab society. Three are positive: the newly mechanized Bedouin, the Saudi capitalist entrepreneur—"a master of subcontracting"—and the sponsor, *al-Kafil*, a figure who has emerged as a result of the stringent labor and migration laws developed in Arab oil-producing states to protect the small indigenous population. The other three are negative: the expatriate Egyptian peasant, the veiled female medical student, and the angry Muslim militant, all of whom represent the disadvantaged society that has continued to exist alongside the Arab privileged few and who seek to create a distinct Islamic cultural identity as a protest against the upwardly mobile, materialistic culture that they see as having been borrowed from non-Islamic sources.

Professor Ibrahim then proceeds to a detailed analysis of inter-Arab labor migration, which he estimates will reach 2.5 million by 1985. This migration is already generating vast changes both in the receiving countries—the oil producers—and the sending ones. Separate chapters are devoted to Egypt, one of the senders, and to Saudi Arabia, the major recipient, with 43 percent to 50 percent of its total labor force being expatriate Arab. He comments on the "myth" of Egyptian unwillingness, for millennia, to emigrate, with telling effect. Not only do Egyptians form one-third of the total Arab expatriate labor force, but the effect particularly on Egyptian universities of faculty transfers to other Arab countries has been devastating. An Egyptian professor seconded to Kuwait, for example, can earn twice as much in four years there as he would earn in a 30-year career in Egypt.

Professor Ibrahim provides an inter-Arab stratification scheme to define his new social order: the rich Arab states (five oil-producers), the well-to-do (four oil-producers plus Lebanon), the struggling middle (four states) and the poor Arab states (six). While one might quarrel with the inclusion of Lebanon presently as well-to-do and with Egypt as poor, in view of its highly developed infrastructure and skilled labor force, the scheme is essentially accurate.

Ibrahim is not optimistic about the future stability of the new order. Despite impressive growth rates, overall Arab growth has been uneven, with steep differentiations among member states of the Arab nation—which continues to be a condition devoutly to be wished for among 80-90 percent of the population. Arab dependence on foreign trade and products of the industrialized countries increasingly impedes both the development of political stability and internal socioeconomic development. Ruling elites maintain their authority by a variety of fictive measures, such as "crisis politics," single-party oppression, or "selling the dream" of a march to greatness under their leadership. With popular social discontent, Islamic militancy, and ethnic group consciousness all on the rise, there exists the very real possibility of an Iran-type movement uniting all Arab social classes to overthrow the existing elites. It is a disturbing prospect and one which should send policymakers scurrying to read books such as this one with great care, as they ponder the problem of shaping a viable Middle Eastern peace.

WILLIAM SPENCER

Micanopy
Florida

THORNTON, RICHARD C. *China, A Political History 1917-1980*. Pp. xvi, 518. Boulder, CO: Westview Press, 1982. $32.50. Paperbound, $15.00.

Professor Thornton of the Institute for Sino-Soviet Studies, George Washington University, has set forth how he believes the policies of the USSR and the United States of America affected political events in China. He has clearly demonstrated that the Chinese Communist Party was not a monolithic structure with Mao Tse-tung at its head. He has given a very detailed account of how frequently opponents were purged and supporters inserted in key posts, and how the Chinese People's Republic evolved from a decentralized, regionally focused state into a highly centralized polity. Fortunately for readers such as I, the Chinese names of the many leaders referred to are transliterated into English in the old Wade-Giles system; a change into the current method would have been too onerous a task.

From a fresh perspective, some new conclusions are drawn from well-known facts. When the Japanese invaders forced the reallocation of Kuomintang resources to meet the invasion, this forestalled the destruction of the Communist Movement. In 1946 Mao was in Yenan and did not lead a guerrilla force to victory in Manchuria, as was supposed. Although the Russians turned over to the Communists large numbers of artillery, tanks, and North Korean troops, they suffered a stunning defeat at

Ssupingchieh at the hands of the Nationalists. An American embargo against Chiang Kai-shek prevented him from continuing his offensive tactics, since he then had no assured sources of supply. The embargo was lifted shortly thereafter, but no further grant aid was forthcoming from the United States until November 1948. The common features of the Soviet and American Near Eastern strategies of the time were the creation of a strong Soviet position in Manchuria and the establishment of a coalition government for China. The United States was unwilling to risk a global war with the USSR, and China was lost to the Communists.

There was constant struggle within the Communist Party, and Mao Tse-tung very nearly lost his leadership of it in 1953 through a coalition of opponents. His 1959 Great Leap Forward, really undertaken to break free from Soviet controls, was an immense failure. The 1965 Cultural Revolution, begun so he could regain control of the party leadership, and the terrorization of the scholar class by the Red Guards through the use of Mao's little Red Book, "Thought of Mao Tse-tung," caused chaos. To indicate how Mao's power was further weakened, Lin Piao, who had been named his successor in the Chinese Constitution adopted in 1968 and who had been one of his strongest supporters, finally opposed his policies and is said to have tried to assassinate Mao; he fled China in a plane which crashed in Outer Mongolia. After Mao's death in 1976, Hua Kuo-feng, whom he had personally designated his successor, favored a normalization of relations with the United States and a rapid industrial modernization of China. However, he soon disappeared from the scene and was replaced by thrice-purged Teng Hsiao-p'ing, who took a pessimistic stand regarding China's ability to modernize by the end of the century and advocated keeping open the channels to Moscow, although he saw a positive value in the continued U.S. presence in Asia.

The book is so well printed that it actually invites one to read it, but if it is intended as a textbook, it is better fitted for graduate than undergraduate students of Chinese history. There are numerous notes, suggested readings, and a good index. It is a thoughtful book and should be read by all those seriously interested in Chinese events.

ALBERT E. KANE

Bethesda
Maryland

WALKER, THOMAS W. *Nicaragua: The Land of Sandino*. Pp. xvi, 137. Boulder, CO: Westview Press, 1981. $20.00. Paperbound, $10.95.

WEBER, HENRI. *Nicaragua: The Sandinist Revolution*. Revised, expanded edition of *Nicaragua: la revolution sandiniste*. Translated by Patrick Camiller. Pp. 154. London: New Left Books, 1981. $15.00. Paperbound, $5.95.

As the first volume of the "Nations of Contemporary Latin America" series edited by Ronald Schneider, Thomas W. Walker of Ohio University, author of *The Christian Democratic Movement in Nicaragua* (1970), and editor and contributor to *Nicaragua in Revolution* (1981), provides a scholarly inquiry into the history and demographic, economic, political, and sociological characteristics of the Nicaraguan people before and after the 1979 revolution.

Examined in the process are, first, the background, causal circumstances, development, and general characteristics of this insurrection—so different from the more common coups d'etat in Latin America that it constitutes, in fact, a social revolution; and then the early stages of the economic, political, and cultural reformulations that followed its more violent phase. Included were programs to improve the economic condition, literacy, health, and recreation of the less privileged classes; to sponsor a greater degree of equality between the sexes; and to foster "a new set of national values" via radio, television, press, and discussion groups.

Documented not only by way of published materials but also—and more importantly—personal observation and interviews during four visits to Nicaragua since the overthrow of Somoza, this volume also furnishes a virtually indispensable map, several photographs, and an annotated bibliography in English. A final chapter surveys the international relations of pre- and early postrevolutionary Nicaragua.

Weber travels a similar route, less extensive historically but perhaps more penetrating politically, and in greater detail. If we are to understand the point of view and behavior of many Europeans, and others, with reference to what is now occurring in the so-called Third World, a careful reading of this translation from the original French and particularly the latter portions in my judgment is imperative.

Rather perceptive, Weber is more interested than some observers in the precise character and functioning of the revolutionary process itself, or at least more determined to probe deeper into it. After sketching briefly the economic and political background of the Sandinista movement—which, with the aid of other forces, toppled the Somoza regime—he analyzes the development and character of this social movement; the successive phases of the revolution it helped sponsor; and, even more intensively, the economic, political, and cultural reorientation subsequently produced, its strategies, subterfuges, successes, and failures.

Also more sophisticated than some observers, Weber is aware that bureaucratization may develop during reconstruction to the point where it stifles democracy—and, in some instances, has already done so in Nicaragua, at least temporarily. But he believes—apparently as an article of faith, although some evidence is mobilized to support, and some to question, this anticipation—that revolutionary change in Nicaragua may be able to avoid certain adverse aspects of the Polish, Cuban, and Russian revolutions; preserve both political and cultural pluralism; rely less on force than on persuasion; and thus strengthen and deepen the democratic process.

The tone of Walker's account is aptly reflected in the dedication: "To the Proud and Indomitable People of Nicaragua, with Profound Respect and Love," a people with whom the author, by 1979, had "empathized for over a decade." No researcher can, in fact, be fully informative unless he or she does empathize—and sympathize—with his or her subjects of inquiry; yet this undoubted virtue must not lead to any loss of that special objectivity that can accrue to a "sociological stranger," in Georg Simmel's apt conception.

Both authors are reasonably free of this danger. But in each account objectivity does suffer at times, unfortunately, giving way occasionally to overstatement; Walker overlooks certain threats to political pluralism, as well as the tragic treatment of the Miskito Amerindians; and both authors, like many other well-intentioned persons, overlook the extensive development of the armed forces apparently far beyond local needs, plus certain worldwide geopolitical realities involved—unless these omissions are due, of course, to an early closing of the accounts, which necessarily lag behind even this May 1982 review.

The use of Marxist terminology by Weber throughout is acceptable insofar as these terms are employed descriptively or analytically, and not hortatorily or as mere clichés; do not reflect bias in observation and understanding; or do not force processes and institutions developed under a different set of circumstances in the Americas into rigid categories derived a century or more ago from an analysis—no matter how apt—of certain portions of European culture of that time.

Nevertheless, anyone desiring to be better informed regarding our economic and political frontyard will profit materially from each of these publications.

DONALD PIERSON

Leesburg
Florida

WIARDA, HOWARD J. and MICHAEL J. KRYZANEK. *The Dominican Republic: A Caribbean Crucible.* Pp. xv, 153. Boulder, CO: Westview Press, 1982. $18.50. Paperbound, $8.50.

This work is a recent addition to the Westview Press "Nations of Contemporary Latin America" series, monographic profiles of selected Latin American states including surveys of their culture, history, social structure, economies, and politics. While readers familiar with the Dominican Republic will find little new in this volume, Wiarda and Kryzanek have written a balanced, comprehensive introductory text on this resilient Caribbean nation.

The authors base their Dominican profile on various assumptions. The first is that the country has an importance in Latin American affairs disproportionate to its small size, population, and resources, because of its strategic location and because it has been a bellwether of political and social change in the region. In fact, the authors maintain that the Dominican Republic is a microcosm of the challenges facing Latin America today. By implication, therefore, examining the social tensions in the Dominican context will offer insights into the difficult process of change throughout the region.

A second assumption is that for the last two centuries, this island nation has been torn between the competing traditions of authoritarianism and liberal democracy. After carefully tracing the country's complex history during the nineteenth and twentieth centuries, paying special attention to the authoritarian Trujillo regime, Wiarda and Kryzanek note a significant third current emerging in the island's political culture. They argue that revolutionary socialism is a force in the contemporary Dominican ideological arena and that its explosive potential might grow if the island economy does not.

The authors' third assumption is that the Dominican Republic is politically and economically dependent on the United States and that the United States will intervene in Dominican affairs, as it did dramatically in 1965, when it perceives its interest threatened. Furthermore, the island's economic dependence on North Americans for capital, markets, and industrial technology is critical for any analysis of the Dominican potential for economic growth and development.

I have only one question about the authors' presentation. Wiarda and Kryzanek stress that in attempting to alter the terms of their economic dependence, Dominicans have created a unique development model including such industrial incentives as tax exemptions and free trade zones. Based on the brief discussion of the Dominican development calculus, however, it would seem that the program differs little from other development efforts now under way in the Caribbean. More material than is provided here is necessary to sustain the claim for the singularity of the Dominican formula.

One stylistic complaint is that the book has no footnotes. Presumably this absence reflects the choice of the series editor rather than the authors of this volume. Nevertheless, the lack of references is regrettable in this stimulating and crisply written profile of the Dominican development process.

SHERRIE L. BAVER

City College
City University of New York
New York

EUROPE

BARNES, DENIS and EILEEN REID. *Governments and Trade Unions: The British Experience 1964-79.* Pp. xiii, 240. Exeter, NH: Heinemann Educational Books, 1981. $37.50.

For anyone interested in the vital years of governmental and trade union collaboration—namely 1964-79—this volume by Sir Denis Barnes and Eileen Reid is invaluable. Both authors are connected with the Policy Studies Institute.

During the 1960s and 1970s, three British prime ministers were prevented by the industrial and political power of the trade unions from pursuing policies which the former declared to be essential to the national interest. All governments lost their elections which followed the defeat of their policies.

Both the Labour and Conservative governments, for example, attempted to recreate the partnership established with the trade unions during the 1939-45 war, and continued with the Atlee government. The two parties strove to assert government authority, to restrain the bargaining power of the unions by statutory income policies, and to reduce union power by legal means. None of these procedures proved successful.

The conclusion of this book is that any effort to establish an agreement with British unions is limited. Continuation of the existing relationship between governments and the trade union movement in times of high unemployment, high inflation, and low economic growth could have unpredictable political results.

In the November 1979 election, the government tried to convince the country that it intended to continue the war against inflation. Governmental policy was covered by a White Paper, *Winning the Battle Against Inflation* (Comd. 7293), issued in July 1978. This paper stressed the government's success in reducing the rate of inflation and indicated that there was "general agreement . . . on the economic objectives to be pursued for jobs, prices and output." Inflation was to be held below the current level of 8 percent; this meant that wage settlements should not rise above 5 percent.

The Trades Union Council rejected this policy by a large majority, urging instead that the labor movement emphasize free collective bargaining. The 5 percent level was considered too low, and it was destroyed by the unions in the next six months.

The authors outline the main features of the problems which must be faced:

1. Trade unions will continue to insist on free collective bargaining.
2. Unions will want changes in the law which will increase their membership and their bargaining power.
3. Unions will pursue their syndicalist aims, and seek to increase their industrial power in the public sector through the extension of public ownership of more public enterprises.
4. Unions will aim to use every means available to extend their political power.

Government's reaction to these union objectives will "depend on which party is in office, and the nature of the political relationship with unions." Conservative governments, as the present one, will strive to reduce trade union bargaining by legislation and to keep militant unionists under control.

Although the labor movement is not the only pressure group whose activities cause inflation, it is a mass group which exercises pressure on governments in full view of the public. The age-old view of labor considering itself the law, and stressing transformation of the system in which it functions, will not be successful if the Conservatives can regulate unions' activities by law. The authors feel that labor will not be controlled in the 1980s.

MARY E. MURPHY
California State University
Los Angeles

BEER, WILLIAM R. *The Unexpected Rebellion: Ethnic Activism in Contemporary France.* Pp. xxxii, 150. New York: New York University Press, 1980. $18.50.

William Beer has written "a sociological study of a social movement," specifically a study of contemporary ethnic activism in seven language-based regions of France: Alsace, French Flanders, Brittany, the French Basque Country, French Catalonia, Occitania, and Corsica. Beer defines ethnicity as a sense of identity and shared solidarity by a social group based on common descent, common language, and common cultural characteristics. He defines ethnic activism as a combination of ethnic regionalism which seeks redistribution of valued resources within the framework of the state, and ethnic nationalism which seeks a new political entity, either special status for a region or formation of a separate state. Besides these overtly political types of ethnic activism, there are folklore, literary, and linguistic organizations. All these types of activity are present in France today and are collectively called ethnic activism.

Ethnic activists can threaten the stability, effectiveness, and legitimacy of Western democratic governments because they are a single-issue pressure group refusing to play the pluralist democratic game. Class solidarity, economic interests, charismatic authority, or even religion cannot attract ethnic activists into permanent cooperation with those outside their own group. They resist efforts by political parties to federate them into broad coalitions. As a result, stable governing majorities can become difficult to maintain; government performance can decline; popular confidence in democratic government can recede; and a full-blown crisis in democratic government may occur, to which ethnic activism has contributed. Ethnicity has become a bigger problem in Western politics in recent years, and ethnic conflict particularly threatens the unity of new nations that have emerged since World War II.

Professor Beer has divided his study of ethnic activism into two parts. The first inquires into the historical origins of ethnic activism in France and discusses it as a problem for modern French society. The second discusses the general processes at work in the movement in the form of theoretically derived propositions and hypotheses based on empirical evidence—specifically, its basic components, the underlying conditions producing it, and the characteristics of its leadership. France was chosen for study because it is one of the oldest European nation-states, with a centuries-old tradition of political centralization and cultural monism.

Beer concludes that the current resurgence of ethnic activism has three major causes. The first is the decline in importance of the nation-state in industrial society, a result of the appearance of supranational economic units such as the European Economic Community (EEC) and military units such as the North Atlantic Treaty Organization (NATO). The centers of decision making are less frequently in the national capital and more often in remote cities such as Brussels or Washington; threats are no longer from neighbors but from global blocs; and a worldwide, interdependent economic system has developed, reducing the importance of national citizenship. French participation in these international systems has undermined the credibility of the nation as a viable unit. Second, the French government's efforts at decentralizing administrative procedures and emphasizing local responsibility for social and economic development has encouraged ethnicity in politics. The rapid industrialization and urbanization of France under De Gaulle, which modernized previously underdeveloped regions and spotlighted central prosperity and peripheral poverty, has created social strain and dissatisfaction that has also encouraged ethnic activism. The third major cause is the example provided by worldwide decolonization and the well-publicized efforts of national liberation movements in the Third World, especially in former French colonies. Beer believes that if long-standing regional and class inequalities can be reduced in France, then new principles of social and political affiliation could develop, and ethnic activism could become more of a force than it is today.

Beer is to be congratulated for tackling a contemporary problem of international scope, and for using a multidisciplinary approach. Much of what he suggests is thought-provoking and may, in fact, be true. But it is hard to accept on the basis of the evidence he has presented. His evidence often appears flimsy and inadequate to support the generalizations it is meant to undergird, and there is an occasional leap from evidence to conclusion which is difficult to follow. He relies almost exclusively on hard or quantitative evidence in discussing a movement which he describes as based on shared language and culture and having political goals. The book would have benefited from a more thorough discussion of all issues, using perhaps some "soft" or qualitative evidence to flesh out the bare bones; sometimes the book appears to be a skeletal outline of major topics rather than a full discussion.

Beer's discussion of the historical origins of ethnic activism is hurried and brief, a few pages for a country in which the tension between regionalism and centralized national government has been a major political issue for centuries dating from the Middle Ages. The current revival of ethnic activism in France might appear less serious if more were known about its historical background. The seven ethnic regions selected for study have widely different characteristics and traditions and should not be lumped together to the extent that the author has done. He defines Occitania as the Midi from Gascony to Languedoc, Provence, and the Dauphine. For French historians or students of modern French politics, that definition is meaningless—it is the whole south of France—and to lump Occitania with Alsace and Brittany in generalizing about ethnic activism compounds the problem. Not infrequently, Beer adds references to Quebec, although that province has not been part of France since the mideighteenth century. He paints boldly with wide strokes, and his canvas dazzles the eye and makes the head swim. His book is well written and thought-provoking, but it has too many evidential and procedural problems to convince the reader that ethnic activism is a serious political threat in contemporary France, and may be more so in the future.

SHARON KETTERING
Montgomery College
Rockville
Maryland

CROWTHER, M. A. *The Workhouse System 1834-1929: The History of an English Social Institution.* Pp. 305. Athens: University of Georgia Press, 1982. $24.00.

Crowther's work explores nearly every aspect of the workhouse system to 1929, after which it merged with the institutions associated with the welfare state. He discusses the organizational changes in its administration; the personnel involved; the discipline, routine, and other matters relating to internal functioning of workhouses; the types of people who entered them; and the relation of workhouses to the community. He backs his conclusions with a multiplicity of evidence including graphs, charts, and statistical analyses which emerged from data he fed into the computer. The result is an impressive work: a sound monograph on an important English institution.

Crowther offers the reader so much information that his work has several theses, not one. Indeed, the only unifying theme seems to be that from first to last the workhouse filled one of the purposes of its Utilitarian proponents: to carry such a social stigma that people would try mightily whenever possible to avoid entering it. Usually, from beginning to end, most workhouse occupants were the aged and infirm, even though the diet, in terms of nutrition, and the living conditions, in terms of sanitation, might be and often were better than those enjoyed by the laboring poor in their own domiciles. Workhouses tended to be so expensive, furthermore, that authorities usually preferred to offer outdoor relief rather than find space for the poor inside the institution. Crowther points out that as the practice of medicine became more professional, the infirmaries connected with the workhouse tended to become separate from them, to become hospitals run not by the workhouse master or matron but by doctors. Despite spasmodic efforts, however, neither the local authorities ultimately responsible for the institutions nor the personnel who directed their internal operations ever became professionals. Finally, as the author makes clear, he bases his generalizations on the best evidence available, but the reader should remember that conditions in each workhouse varied enormously. A workhouse in a rural area scarcely compared to one in London.

Crowther assumes—perhaps necessarily in this kind of work—the reader's familiarity with English history and English institutions, such as voluntary hospitals. People not well read in such matters will find the book heavy going. Crowther's work is sound administrative history, but not history for the general reader. But it offers a wealth of information which historians will have to consider carefully in future studies of the operation of the English Poor Laws.

FRANKLIN B. WICKWIRE
University of Massachusetts
Amherst

FRENCH, DAVID. *British Economic and Strategic Planning 1905-1915*. Pp. x, 191. Winchester, MA: Allen and Unwin, 1982. $25.00.

It has frequently been asserted that Britain's last Liberal government was unable to organize the home front adequately because it was so rigidly committed to laissez faire and free trade. In this important study, David French shows how limited is such an explanation of the policies pursued between 1905 and 1915. The starting point for the policies of the Asquith regime was not an economic ideology but the naval and military plans it hoped to implement. "Strategy" before 1914 meant the purely naval and military aspects of the war. The army wished to play a major role on the continent but did not have the troops to do so, or even the plans to raise them. The navy greatly overestimated Germany's vulnerability to a blockade. Both worked within a scheme that saw Britain's role as the economic provisioner of the powers ranged against Germany. To deprive the economy of manpower by trying to raise a large army, it was assumed, would be self-defeating. "Business as usual" was not some plot to protect the civilian economy for selfish purposes, but the sine qua non of Britain's role in the defeat of a German enemy.

Such considerations meant that the government failed to plan for the war that actually happened. No one dreamt that Lord Kitchener would feel compelled to raise a huge volunteer army in 1914-15 or that the civilian economy would have to be converted to war production to equip it or that a stalemate on the western front would consume unprecedented quantities of munitions. It was not laissez faire that made for the lack of a national plan in 1914, but rather the failure to understand how massive a civilian mobilization was required to support the armed services in a modern war. The New Armies created vast new problems for the British. They deprived industry, commerce, and agriculture of much of the manpower needed to carry on normal activities. They created a huge demand for food, equipment, and transport. They were a major factor in undermining the strategy of business as usual. If the relatively free play of market forces could not ensure the requirements of a mass army, then clearly much more direction was needed.

Abstract principles had little to do with policies adopted. The major lines of division were between advocates of different strategies. Lloyd George grasped the implications of the new military directions as Asquith did not. In a cabinet in which Runciman and McKenna wanted to continue with business as usual and Kitchener aggressively sponsored the concept of the "nation at arms," the chancellor of the exchequer became the leading advocate of the creation of a total war economy. The shell scandal provided the occasion for the collapse of Asquith's Liberal government. It did not cause it. If not totally imaginary, the shell shortage was exaggerated by Sir John French to excuse his faulty tactics on the western front. But the scandal brought the debate over the future development of the British economy to a head. It opened the way for Lloyd George to begin implementing his vision of a total war economy. *British Economic and Strategic Planning* is a stimulating piece of scholarship. Perhaps more to the point, it is a sound and persuasive one.

HENRY R. WINKLER
University of Cincinnati
Ohio

GATES, ELEANOR M. *The End of the Affair: The Collapse of the Anglo-French Alliance, 1939-40.* Pp. xviii, 630. Berkeley: University of California Press, 1981. $28.50.

Eleanor Gates's extraordinarily detailed narrative concentrates on eight dramatic weeks in the spring and summer of 1940. It begins with the German breakthrough of 10 May, which, as is well known, triggered the Strange Defeat and the Fall of the Third Republic. It ends with an account of the tragic and bloody—1297 French sailors were killed—and arguably unnecessary destruction of a large part of the French fleet at Mers-el-Kébir on 3 July. This action was carried out by Great Britain, theoretically still an ally of just-defeated France. The infant Vichy regime broke off diplomatic relations with England only five days later.

It is surely ironic that as of this writing the worst damage to the British fleet in the still unresolved conflict with Argentina over the Falkland Islands has been caused by French-built Exocet missiles launched from French-built Super Etendard fighters. Were Gates to have delayed completion of her book until 1982, she would doubtless have utilized these facts. They sustain her fundamental hypothesis that the Entente Cordiale between France and Britain (1904-40), and its resumption under a different guise in 1944, was not based on a fundamental identity of aim and spirit of the two principal Western European democracies. Rather, this alliance appears as a fairly brief episode in the histories of two very different polities, undertaken and then abandoned according to a relatively narrowly conceived national self-interest.

Since it is highly doubtful that any significant new archival material will be discovered at this late date, this massively documented and gracefully written study will remain definitive for a long time. Besides her thoroughness and style, Gates has a gift for psychological analysis. She takes the differing reports, usually apologias, by participants in the innumerable policy debates of May-June 1940 and reconstructs a coherent and persuasive account of what most probably happened during a time of confusion and catastrophe. Her analysis of individual leaders is on the whole balanced and fair, and her portrayals of Paul Reynaud and Winston Churchill are exceptionally judicious. Charles de Gaulle appears less frequently in her pages, as his principal role in history begins just at the moment her narrative concludes.

The major difficulty readers will encounter, especially in the early sections of this book, is chronological. In her effort to be complete, Gates will carry one theme—for example, the crisis over Dunkirk—through June 1940. Then she will backtrack and pick up another theme in a manner that is sometimes confusing. The patient reader will, however, gain many rewards, and the clarity and coherence of this work increase as the "end of the affair" approaches.

DAVID L. SCHALK
Vassar College
Poughkeepsie
New York

GRAHAM, LAWRENCE S. *Romania: A Developing Socialist State.* Pp. xviii, 136. Boulder, CO: Westview Press, 1982. $17.00.

Dramatic changes in the geographic area of one's scholarly endeavors are risky undertakings. It is, of course, possible to bring fresh insight, but a more common result is a stumble. The book under review demonstrates that the author has badly misstepped.

Professor Lawrence's imperfect knowledge of Romanian leaps out at the reader on almost every page. Like a pupil learning his lessons, he constantly gives the reader the Romanian translation of an English word: we are told that "Bulgarians" is *Bulgari*, "Transylvania" is *Transilvania*, "Bucovina" is *Bucovina*, "intellectuals" is *intelectuali*, and so on. It becomes wearisome, not to say embarrassing. The coinage of the term "conflictual" and other eccentricities inspire still more doubts.

Professor Lawrence does not know Romanian history. He does not realize that the Ceaușescu family is merely the modern counterpart of the old *boiars* in terms of its free-wheeling nepotism and ruthless exploitation of its stranglehold on power. He knows all too little about many important historical figures, some of whose names—Ana Pauker and Horia Sima—he regularly misspells. He tells us that "not much is known about the Antonescu government," which held power in World War II; he sees "no need for extensive documentation of the political, social, and economic changes carried out" in the period 1947-50; and when he cannot check the accuracy of some of his figures, he laments that "all that can be done is to call the reader's attention" to the problem.

There are some serious conceptual problems. Professor Lawrence includes the peasants in the working class—a formulation his hosts in Romania cannot have given him. He refers to a living Romanian Communist as "one of the party's more cosmopolitan members," apparently in ignorance of the fact that many Eastern European Communists did long stretches in the camps when someone pinned the label "cosmopolitan" on them. He calls the Romanian Communist Party "essentially a vanguard organization," leading one to wonder whether he knows just what Communist parties are. Finally, he attempts to sum up with this meaningless line: "The image projected is thus one of dynamism, of a regime always on the move and constantly engaged in employing the nation's economic and human resources to the fullest extent possible."

This is all very sad. Professor Lawrence is a sound scholar in his own field, Latin America. Somewhere on the way to the Balkans, he lost his bearings.

WOODFORD McCLELLAN
University of Virginia
Charlottesville

HAHN, WERNER G. *Postwar Soviet Politics: The Fall of Zhdanov and the Defeat of Moderation, 1946-1953*. Pp. 243. Ithaca, NY: Cornell University Press, 1982. $22.50.

Covering a period of more than 30 years (1946-77), Werner G. Hahn demonstrates the existence among Soviet political leaders and intellectuals of a continuing rivalry between dogmatists and independents. His chief concern is to elucidate the competition during the immediate postwar years.

Stalin's top deputy from mid-1946 to early 1948, Andrey Aleksandrovich Zhdanov, often has been depicted as a dogmatist, probably because the idea of the division of the world into two irreconcilable camps became official Soviet policy after mid-1947 and before mid-1948. In 1947 and 1948, however, three great debates were waged in the Soviet Union—one in philosophy, another in biology, and a third in economics. In the philosophy debates Zhdanov sided ultimately with the independent, usually younger, philosophers, backing their proposal to create a new journal, *Voprosy filosofii*. As his son Yuriy—later for several years husband of Stalin's daughter Svetlana—embraced the Western theories of genetics, he was identified with the opponents of Lysenkoism. He does not appear to have taken a stand in the debate between economists Ye. S. Varga and N. A. Voznesenskiy. Varga maintained that socialist elements had entered into the economies of the capitalist countries, as a result of which peaceful coexistence between capitalism and socialism may have been facilitated. Voznesenskiy and other Varga opponents countered with the idea that monopolies were so powerful in the capitalist states that their governments were incapable of acting in any manner but as their instruments. After a pretense at acknowledging his errors in March 1949, Varga managed to survive, thanks perhaps to Stalin's friendship. At almost the same moment Voznesenskiy was deprived of his functions, apparently in response to Stalin's own aspiration to the status of economic theoretician. Later in the year he was arrested; in 1950 he was executed. Voznesenskiy had long been Zhdanov's protégé. Zhdanov's fall from favor in mid-1948, shortly before his death, for being on the wrong side in the debates and for holding presumably friendly views toward Yugoslavia thus did not portend well for Voznesenskiy's future.

Defeated in 1949 in the struggle led by Stalin against cosmopolitanism and local nationalisms, the independent philosophers began to make a comeback even before Stalin's death in 1955. After Khrushchev's fall in October 1964, Lysenkoism faltered and, in the late 1960s, geneticist ideas prevailed. In 1973, the independents made another surge forward with the reappointment of anti-Lysenkoist B. M. Kedrov, one of the leaders in the philosophical debates of the late 1940s, as the chief editor of *Voprosy filosofii*. Between 1974 and early 1977, chief editor I. T. Frolov continued the independent tradition by holding to the view embraced—at one moment at least—by Brezhnev that détente in international relations will require elaboration of a sophisticated communist philosophy able to compete in the world struggle for minds.

An abundance of detail complicates Hahn's exposition. His general thesis nevertheless deserves attention.

TRAIAN STOIANOVICH

Rutgers University
New Brunswick
New Jersey

JANOS, ANDREW C. *The Politics of Backwardness in Hungary 1825-1945*. Pp. xxxvi, 370. Princeton: Princeton University Press, 1982. $27.50. Paperbound, $12.50.

The ideological framework of this impressive study is boldly presented in its title.

Why did Hungary, a country that shared much of the religious and institutional heritage of Western Europe, fail to replicate the social and political experiences of the latter in the nineteenth and early twentieth centuries? The answer, Janos argues, lies not with cultural idiosyncrasies or historical accident, but with the internal dynamics of the modern world system that stimulated aspirations not easily realizable within the confines of backward economies in peripheral nation-states.

Janos develops his theme by examining a century of Hungarian economic, social, and political history. During the period he covers, Hungary witnessed attempts to transplant liberal institutions from the West; the corruption of these institutions into a neocorporatist bureaucratic state; and, finally, the rise of diverse Left and Right radical movements as much in protest against this institutional corruption as against the prevailing global division of labor and economic inequality.

Revealing significant analogies between the Hungarian past and the plight of the countries of the Third World today, Janos's arguments are interesting not only to the specialist on Central-Eastern-Balkan politics but also to students of development, dependency, and center-periphery relations in the contemporary world.

Although Janos tells his story in masterful fashion, making an important contribution to the history of Central Europe, supporting it with an impressive bibliography that includes references to the Hungarian studies, I am somewhat surprised that no works by Eduard Beneš and Thomas G. Masaryk are included.

JOSEPH S. ROUCEK

Bridgeport
Connecticut

KNOTT, JACK H. *Managing the German Economy: Budgetary Politics in a Federal State*. Pp. xviii, 214. Lexington, MA: D. C. Heath, 1981. $22.95.

This study of the German economy holds that West German fiscal policy reflects the interaction of a composite of conflicting interests. Two conflict threads make up the policy fabric, threads "derived from the dichotomy between cognitive and political uncertainty contained in the political decision-making model." Knott, who teaches at Michigan State University, seeks to show how these conflict threads intertwine in the making and execution of policy.

In his descriptive background, Knott outlines sources of economic tradition in the Federal Republic which contribute to how economic problems are perceived and what governmental actions are considered legitimate and appropriate. He describes major economic issues facing the Federal Republic and relates these to partisan conflict, federal relations, and bureaucratic politics.

The main body of the book focuses on the application of formal economic analyses in a political organization setting during the planning of budget policy. "The hypothesis is that prediction uncertainties are distributed politically among the organizational actors." The analysis shifts from the central government to federal political relations, with discussions of joint budget and fiscal policy planning between the states and central government and explanation of the changing organizational interests of each side with varying economic conditions. Attention is also paid to intergovernmental grants in aid to manage the economy as well as demographic factors. An alternative political explanation is given for grant politics.

What Knott, a political scientist, attempts throughout the study is to seek a happy marriage between his own discipline and economics. Using this dual approach, he throws light on the practice of economic management in the Federal Republic and also offers some recommendations for accommodating budgetary, political, and economic goals.

The book is carefully planned; from 1974 to 1976, Knott conducted over 50 interviews with officials in the Finance and Economic Ministries, in the chancellor's office, and in the Bundestag. The organization is excellent, from the general to the particular. The lists of figures and tables are impressive. This is undoubtedly an important contribution to the understanding of the German economy.

At the same time, a note of caution should be added. There is a deplorable trend in the scholarly world to write in a manner understandable only to a limited number of professional peers. In the social sciences, historians, generally free of this fault, present clear-cut prose familiar to any reasonably intelligent reader. Such able historians as Carlton J.H. Hayes or Arthur M. Schlesinger, Jr., are noted for their clarity of expression.

This is unfortunately not true of the disciplines of economics and sociology, in which far too much attention is paid to what has been described as special lingo, jargon, tangled vocabulary, or even less graceful terms—writing that is wordy or involved. The more complex the writing, the more use of tortured nomenclature, the more prestige is to be expected inside the discipline. Note the confusing jargon of the Nobel prizewinners in economics, or the grandiloquent phraseology, understandable chiefly to himself, of the late Pitirim Alexandrovich Sorokin, professor of sociology at Harvard.

Admittedly, mathematics and the pure sciences such as physics and chemistry require a highly specialized nomenclature. But this is altogether unnecessary in the social sciences, where scholarly work should concentrate on clarity instead of a specialized jargon intelligible to only a few peers. Above all, much more attention should be paid to definitions and meaning so that readers will know exactly the nature of the analysis.

By no means should Professor Knott be held responsible for the linguistic demands of his discipline. His is a first-rate study on an important subject. But perhaps the day will come when such studies as this one will be published in two versions, one in specialized jargon and the other translated into basic English for the benefit of retarded intellectuals.

LOUIS L. SNYDER
City University of New York
New York

MYERS, HENRY A. *Medieval Kingship.* Pp. ix, 467. Chicago: Nelson-Hall, 1982. $25.95. Paperbound, $13.95.

Henry A. Myers, professor of political science and history at James Madison University, has written in cooperation with Universitätsprofessor Herwig Wolfram of the Institut für österreichische Geschichtsforschung at Vienna—Myers wrote the book while Wolfram suggested additions and revisions—a textbook-like treatment of medieval kingship; that is, a study of "both the rule of one person over a political unit, as at least its nominal head, and the art or science by which such a ruler governs well" during the Middle Ages. The authors "hope that the book will appeal at least to those of the general public who enjoy stories of kings and queens and that many medievalists will also find things in it which are new and of interest to them, particularly in the sections dealing with the early Middle Ages."

On the whole, the greater part of the book is presented on a rather elementary college textbook level; the base studies are Painter's *The Rise of Feudal Monarchies* (1951), Lyon's *Constitutional and Legal History of England* (1960), Petit-Dutaillis's *Feudal Monarchy in France and England* (English translation 1936), Zacour's *An Introduction to Medieval Institutions* (1969), and Hill's *Medieval Monarchy in Action* (1972). Scholarship in the French language is systematically ignored, but long irrelevant German language works a century and more old are not only included in the bibliography but even cited in the notes. However, important German studies by scholars such as Mitteis are not to be found in the bibliography, which includes 12 pages of secondary sources but only a dozen works written after 1970. On most topics, Myers and Wolfram ignore scholarship done during the past 20 to 30 years, and despite the "incomparable facilities for medievalists of the Institut für österreichische Geschichtsforschung," old and faulty editions of important sources are frequently cited and often quoted at length in Latin in the notes. Indeed, the 80 pages of notes could have been reduced substantially had the authors refrained from such quotation as is unlikely to appeal to "the general public who enjoy stories."

Concerning the early Middle Ages, those familiar with Wolfram's detailed treatment of early medieval titles and his somewhat idiosyncratic treatment of early medieval kingship will find his views presented in an appropriately simplified manner. However, the insistence that early medieval thinkers and especially those dealing with the Merovingians did not emphasize Old Testament kings as a model is completely wrong. The authors' efforts to press this contrary thesis leads them to fail to appreciate the Davidic allusion in Gregory's observations concerning Clovis: "God cast his enemies before him on the ground . . . for the reason that he walked with a righteous heart . . . and did what was pleasing to His eyes."

The treatment of thinkers such as John of Salisbury, Saint Thomas, and Marsiglio is satisfactory, but to consider Marsiglio and Sir John Fortescue as theorists of the "High Middle Ages" does serious injury to accepted notions of periodization. In addition, there are many errors of fact, such as considering Alfred the Great a tenth-century king. In addition to errors, there is much nonsense. For example, Myers and Wolfram seem struck by analogies between the early Middle Ages and early American history, and insist on calling the Frankish ax a tomahawk. More serious in this vein is their observation that Arbogast "successfully attacked some of the Franks, who had defeated the Roman General Bradfords (sic) of that time by skillful retreats and forest ambushes in which they decimated (sic) the Roman forces with a hail of poisoned arrows." It would appear that Myers and Wolfram are alluding to the British general Edward Braddock, who was killed in battle at Great Meadows, Pennsylvania, on 13 July 1755 by a combined force of French and Indians under Captain Beaujeu. One wonders if the medievalist authors were also struck by the fact that Braddock fought at Fontenoy in 1745. It would also seem that Myers and Wolfram lack a grasp of Roman history, at least insofar as it concerns the Roman military practice of decimation. Clearly the authors are victims of overspecified training, while the book is not.

BERNARD S. BACHRACH
University of Minnesota
Minneapolis

SMITH, ROBERT J. *The École Normale Supérieure and the Third Republic.* Pp. viii, 201. Albany: State University of New York Press, 1982. $39.00. Paperbound, $12.95.

In this well-written work, frequently cited in unpublished form, Smith examines Normale from various viewpoints—social, intellectual, and political, using comparisons with the other *grandes écoles*—and emerges with the best explanation available of the school's influential role in the Third Republic. Although most of its graduates pursued educational careers, Smith is interested in explaining the emergence of *normaliens*, such as Monod, Lavisse, Jaurès, and Herriot, who dominated French life from 1870 to 1914.

The predominant political orientation of the school was left-center. Smith attributes this fact to Normale's traditions: the use of small *conférences* where critical discussion was encouraged, the classicism of the curriculum, the competitive entrance examinations passed only by an intellectual elite, student folkways, and the influence of teachers and administrators such as Lucien Herr. Smith provides a short intellectual sketch of the most influential of these men.

The broad political consensus of the school broke down after World War I for several reasons: the reforms of 1904 which made the school less exclusive, disillusionment growing out of the war, and the growth of both the right and the left in France. Yet most of the *normalien* politicians remained on the left center as radicals or socialists. Both drew their ideas from similar rationalist and humanitarian foundations laid at Normale. All were humanists and democrats, according to Smith, and most preferred change by democratic means.

These men became politically influential because after 1870, France needed an ideological synthesis to support the new republican government and to smooth the cultural and psychological adjustment to industrialization and the new national culture. *Normaliens* were uniquely placed to articulate that ideology and to guide the educational reforms necessary to spread it to the masses. With new-found prestige, many entered careers in journalism or politics. The philosophy of the school emphasized individual freedom, which justified democratic politics as well as the importance of education and intellectuals. To their philosophic compatibility with the republic, the *Normaliens* added the mystique of the school and the myth—which Smith demonstrates was largely untrue—of their own moderate social origins; the school appeared truly democratic compared to the other *grandes ecoles.* Once given the example of men like Jaures, other *Normaliens* determined to pursue careers in politics and, aided by these factors plus a network based on school ties, they succeeded. Normale lost its privileged position after World War II, but not before it had contributed to establishing, as Smith describes, liberalism and republicanism as part of the national consciousness.

Some questions can be posed. Do classical studies normally contribute to liberalism, as Smith tends to assume? *Normaliens* did much to define the republic, but did Normale? Or could the political ideas of many of these men be found by reference to experiences prior to entering the school, as Smith indicates was true in a few individual cases? Is it wise to label the political traditions of an entire institution based on the ideas of a prominent minority—the deputies in parliament? How did the *normalien* political network function? Questions aside, however, Smith has provided a valuable study for an understanding of the republican leaders who emerged from the École Normale Supérieure and a fine example of educational history properly done.

JOHN M. BURNEY

Southwest Minnesota State University
Marshall
Minnesota

UNITED STATES

BALL, HOWARD, DALE KRANE, and THOMAS P. LAUTH. *Compromised Compliance: Implementation of the 1965 Voting Rights Act.* Pp. xv, 300. Westport, CT: Greenwood Press, 1982. $27.50.

Living in the midst of the politics of the present decade, the promises and actions of the Great Society seem long ago and far away. So much has changed in the intervening years that it is difficult to grasp the hopes and aspirations that characterized the Lyndon B. Johnson era. Yet most of the legislation of that period remains with us, and occasionally we are reminded of how it has led to the changed—if not great—society in which we live today.

One such piece of legislation that has so affected us is the Voting Rights Act (VRA) of 1965, the extension of which was hotly debated in 1982. *Compromised Compliance* is a well-researched and cogently written study of the VRA and its implementation in the years since its enactment. It is a timely volume, one that also serves as a fascinating case study in the implementation of major public policy.

Ball, Krane, and Lauth have focused their study of the ways in which the Department of Justice (DOJ), especially the Voting Section of the Civil Rights Division, attempted to implement what many—including the authors—think was radical legislation. Data used in the project included extensive interviews with DOJ personnel responsible for enforcing the VRA, as well as a wide variety of other political actors involved in the issue at the federal, state, and local levels.

The book's title partly reveals the hypothesis argued by its authors: as a result of a variety of political factors, compliance with the provision of the act was "compromised" throughout, resulting in something less than was originally intended. By focusing specifically on Section 5 of the VRA, which essentially required preclearance by federal officials for any changes in voting procedures sought by local authorities in certain voting districts, the authors show graphically how the meaning and intent of the original VRA was diluted in both interpretation and application.

Section 5 was designed to assure that progress made in broadening the base of political participation, through the extension of the franchise to specific minority populations through other sections on the act, not be reversed by new changes subsequently enacted by local authorities. In effect, if local authorities wished to change any provisions involving voting procedures, they were required to seek and receive permission to do so from the DOJ.

In their analysis of the implementation of Section 5, Ball, Krane, and Lauth have illustrated how the real world of politics can come crashing in on the legalistically well-turned and politically idealistic phrases of congressional action. Herein one finds the other half of the authors' argument: given the paramount importance of open and unfettered participation in political systems that purport to be democratic, "then the process of compromised compliance—whatever its virtues—is just not good enough." Clearly, Ball and his colleagues are disappointed at the system's failure to achieve the comprehensive goals envisioned by the VRA.

An important consideration that the authors treat throughout is the possible alternative route of "uncompromised compliance" that might have been pursued by the federal authorities. Their conclusion seems to be that this simply could never have been, given the complex of politics at the federal, state, and local levels and the interplay between concerned political actors and institutions.

The argument by the authors that despite being "compromised," the VRA was responsible for considerable improvement in the American democratic process is convincing; that the act was extended by the most recent Congress should, as well, have pleased them. Most significantly, their study is successful in explaining what a complicated and difficult procedure it is to realize certain policy goals, even when there is broad consensus on the values and the normative arrangements are in place for the implementation of the policy.

KENT MORRISON

University of Utah
Salt Lake City

BARANSON, JACK. *The Japanese Challenge to U.S. Industry.* Pp. xvi, 188. Lexington, MA: D. C. Heath, 1981. $19.95.

DESTLER, I. M. and HIDEO SATO. *Coping with U.S.-Japanese Economic Conflicts.* Pp. viii, 293. Lexington, MA: D. C. Heath, 1982. $24.95

Average American laypersons could be excused if they had an impression there is something cyclical about Japanese-American economic wrangles; I am not at all sure what Japanese laypersons should be excused for. Basically, these two books deal with this subject, although the case studies are different in both cases. The time period, generally, is the latter part of the seventies to the present. The case studies considered range from major to minor: from steel, automobiles, high technology, and color television to beef and oranges—for some reason the intensity of a particular conflict seemed to have little relationship to the relative importance of the commodity involved.

A number of important conclusions emerge from the two volumes which we and the Japanese will ignore in the future at the risk that some future conflict will easily escalate into the kind of major confrontation which neither country in any sense desires or can afford. One of the most important is that without in any way minimizing the economic components of a particular dispute, the more important element has always seemed to be the political aspect. Even taking into account the intrinsic impossibility of separating economics from politics, the political element has been the determining feature. And if it were possible to separate the economic from the political, the conflict would amount to little, since the economic objectives of both countries are basically complementary.

In a fundamental sense, much of the political problem comes from cultural misunderstanding. I find it interesting that in recent years there has been a proliferation of degree programs in major American universities that focus on doing business with the Japanese.

The Japanese have long complained that Americans keep getting into trouble because we do not know how to do business in Japan. The Japanese record in this respect is certainly superior to our own. Clearly we are beginning to take this disparity more seriously than we have in the past.

Both studies are quite explicit in trying to dispel a number of American myths about Japan. Japanese industry in a number of high-technology fields has clearly outstripped the United States, and there are areas where we probably can no longer do anything about it. There is virtually no evidence that Japanese industry competes unfairly. In contrast, American industry is less concerned with quality and more with appearance and size. American industry is also suffering from major cutbacks in research and development. It is not a reassuring picture; there is also an implication that American labor no longer has quite the same motivation, or work ethic, that it once did. On the other hand, Japan is acutely aware of the importance of the American market and prepared to go a long way to avoid antagonism. Certainly a vital part of the American genius is our technological and industrial ingenuity. We can compete if we so wish.

I think it is here, finally, that a rather different kind of warning is in order. While it is true that President Reagan's amiable, if uninformed, bluster about restoring American power is more silliness than anything else, what is true is that American society and the American economy are so strong, they can absorb an astonishing amount of punishment and survive, largely unscathed. No other society is in quite that position. It therefore behooves us to go more than halfway, to be more understanding than the next man. If we can learn to do this, with a strong leaven of humility, we could also find that much of the twenty-first century is also American.

JOHN F. MELBY
University of Guelph
Ontario
Canada

BECKER, SUSAN D. *The Origins of the Equal Rights Amendment: American Feminism Between the Wars.* Pp. ix, 300. Westport, CT: Greenwood Press, 1981. $27.50.

Susan D. Becker provides us with a timely and informative study of the origins of the Equal Rights Amendment (ERA). She analyzes the historically specific political and economic circumstances as well as the seemingly timeless ideological principles that aroused agitation for and opposition to the ERA in the 1920s and 1930s. During this period, it was distinct groups of feminists rather than feminists and antifeminists who confronted each other over the ERA. Having won the vote, suffragists focused their attention on achieving other forms of legal and economic equality but disagreed among themselves over the meaning of equality for women. The largest number emphasized inherent differences between women and men and sought specific legislation to safeguard what they saw as women's special needs—particularly in the workplace—even as they sought more equal access to economic and social arenas. A far smaller number, former militant suffragists and current members of the National Woman's Party (NWP), emphasized similarities between women and men and sought to abolish all legal distinctions based on gender, including protective labor legislation, through a federal amendment—the ERA.

Becker clarifies both sides of the debate between these two groups, assuming each one's genuine concern with the advancement of women. She also places their arguments within the context of a declining and then collapsing national and international economy. In addition, she introduces a number of issues around which all feminists rallied, such as jury service for women and equal job opportunities for married women. Becker challenges and extends existing literature on the postsuffrage debates in three areas. She argues that the trade union activists who supported protective legislation did not speak for all women workers, since several female labor leaders served on the NWP's industrial councils. She notes that the NWP was innovative in publicizing its efforts, thereby forcing its opponents to join in the use of radio debates and other mass media techniques. And she addresses the increasingly international dimensions of postsuffrage feminism and claims that the NWP served as the vanguard in forming Latin American and European alliances and in linking feminism to the fight against fascism.

These challenges shed new and favorable light on the NWP, light partially dimmed by Becker's evaluation of NWP leadership as elitist and their programs as narrowly legalistic and her description of the failures of those seeking internal democratization of the party. Becker too often seems to repeat rather than analyze the ambivalences that plagued her subjects on key issues, such as national versus international programs, elite versus grassroots control, and protective versus egalitarian philosophies. In reiterating these debates chapter after chapter, she limits her opportunities to expand the more innovative areas of her study. Yet her own ambivalences are genuine, emerging, it seems, from both complex historical condition and current feminist debates. Her introduction of these complex conditions and debates at the moment of the ERA's imminent defeat and her analysis of the ERA as one among many possible feminist strategies at the moment of its inception are crucial. Such an approach encourages us, as scholars, to use our skills to reassess rather than lament the feminist programs of the past and to use such analyses to illuminate current conditions and options.

NANCY A. HEWITT
University of South Florida
Tampa

BLANE, HOWARD T. and MORRIS E. CHAFETZ, eds. *Youth, Alcohol, and Social Policy*. Pp. xxvi, 424. New York: Plenum Press, 1979. $27.50.

We are reminded throughout this collection that alcoholism is not the only negative consequence of excessive alcohol consumption. Persons who would not be properly diagnosed as alcoholics experience difficulties on the job that may result in dismissal; become belligerent when intoxicated and damage relationships with family members and friends; and risk arrest and even death while under the influence of alcohol. These and other costs of excessive drinking recommend a thorough study of the phenomenon. Therefore, the Health Education Foundation is to be commended for organizing a national conference that produced the papers in this publication.

The collection is divided into four parts covering epidemiology, theory, public policy, and amelioration strategies. In each part, three articles essentially survey the literature on specific topics. For example, in the theoretical section, a developmental explanation anchored in findings on biological, psychological, and sociological variables is explored and recommended; studies of ecological variables, including climate, availability of raw materials, and distribution of outlets, are reviewed; and the influence of sex roles is examined in the literature and in data collected in 1975.

Some of the more striking statements are discouraging. We learn that government effectiveness in remedying problems is limited by political considerations. In addition, despite the development of a wide array of programs at colleges, "no reports have yet documented desired changes in alcohol related behaviors." More encouraging is the report that treatment programs in the Navy have produced cost-benefits over personnel replacement. Moreover, the wide variety of programs discussed suggests that researchers and practitioners retain hope.

The volume is a valuable source of ideas for research and control programs. It is also, unfortunately, short on originality and makes for tedious reading.

ROY L. AUSTIN
Pennsylvania State University
University Park

DINNERSTEIN, LEONARD. *America and the Survivors of the Holocaust.* Pp. xix, 409. New York: Columbia University Press, 1982. $19.95.

Leonard Dinnerstein's new book is a study, primarily, of the attitude of the American government in the years immediately following World War II toward Jewish survivors of the Holocaust. Marred somewhat by an unfortunate tendency to stray from the main theme, it is nonetheless a readable account of the efforts to gain admission to the United States of the people displaced by the war.

The end of World War II found many millions of displaced persons in Allied-occupied Europe. Many of them, particularly those from Eastern Europe who had records of collaboration, were not repatriable, and the problem of their resettlement was one of the more pressing problems the Truman administration had to face. Any eventual settlement of refugees in the United States would involve a high percentage of Jews, and feeling in the country ran high against immigration in general and Jewish immigration in particular. If statistical studies are any evidence, feeling against Jews was stronger in the mid-1940s than at any time in American history.

The fate of the Jewish refugees was even more precarious than that of the other displaced persons. Anti-Jewish sentiment in the American Army, which was in charge of the refugee camps in the occupied countries of Europe, was high. General Patton, *eminance grise* of the armored corps, writing in 1945 in his diary, remarked that others "believe that the displaced person is a human being, which he is not, and this applies particularly to the Jews who are lower than animals." Not surprisingly, under these circumstances, conditions for Jewish displaced persons were appalling. Jews were kept behind barbed wire, denied the right to leave the camps, and were generally fed and housed poorer than the surrounding German population. The situation did not begin to improve until Earl G. Harrison delivered his report to President Truman in August 1945.

The problem of possible large-scale settlement of Jews in the United States was an issue of enormous importance in the years following the war. Fear of competition in the job market, fear of Communism—with which the Jews, irrationally, were identified—and just plain fear led to broad opposition on the part of many congressmen and a very large part of the American public. Tied to this was the opposition, expressed by indifference, of the American Zionist organizations, who hoped that the promised land would be Petach Tichva, not Flatbush.

This study, whatever its merits otherwise, is flawed in several respects. It lacks focus, straying at times into the area of Arab-Jewish relations in Palestine and at others branching into a broad discussion of the displaced persons problem per se, rather than just the Jewish aspect of it. Additionally, it suffers from that common fault of Jewish historiography, that of seeing anti-Semitism as an abstract demonic force, a kind of metaphysical principle having position in space and time but no relation to the broader social structure. Finally, the book is so marred by stilted expression that those who value originality and vivacity in style might well be tempted to add as a subtitle "Quiet Days in Cliché." Even historical writing is bound by aesthetic considerations.

Nonetheless, these objections aside, it is a competent piece of research that fills an important gap in existing Jewish scholarship.

MURRAY SMITH
Verdun
Quebec

ETZOLD, THOMAS H. *Defense or Delusion? America's Military in the 1980s.* Pp.x, 259. New York: Harper & Row, 1982. $14.95.

This book will no doubt enjoy less exposure than it merits. Even when defense issues are concisely, straightforwardly presented, as they are here, they still demand hard thinking, and relatively few members of the lay public are willing to wrestle with the dilemmas they present. Let this review at least encourage as many as possible to read the book. As professor of strategy at the Naval War College, Thomas H. Etzold enjoys a superb vantage point from which to observe defense issues, and anyone from the intelligent nonspecialist to the expert will find something in *Defense or Delusion?* from which to profit. Etzold's is the best of the current crop of surveys of national security problems.

Etzold surveys the "military malaise" into which he believes the United States has fallen in terms of five categories of problems: the current environment of limited American power, continuing large responsibilities, and doubtful national will; the people who comprise or ought to comprise the military establishment; current weapons; nuclear issues; and issues of conventional war. He then offers prescriptions for "measured military renewal," ranging from the overall strategic issues to recommendations on such specifics as the M-1 tank and the MX missile.

While Etzold's style of exposition and argumentation is direct and in that sense simple, his ideas are by no means simple. An example is his approach to renewal of the draft. Though he surveys in detail the personnel problems of the armed forces and ignores none of the difficulties, he does not follow those analysts who see a cure-all in a return to conscription. At best, he argues, unless the United States were to undertake a drastic and unlikely expansion of its forces, the draft would add about 20,000 men per year to present strength. "Even if every single draftee were a mental giant and a high school graduate, a draft of that size would not transform the quality of a 2-million-man military." For so limited an improvement, the draft could scarcely be worth the turmoil it would engender. In any case, the principal personnel problem is not recruitment but retention, persuading skilled and intelligent people to remain. To deal with that problem, not the draft but a restructuring of incentives to continue in service is essential.

Etzold's skepticism about the draft is representative of his general distrust of the quick fix, of the notion that any of America's military problems are susceptible to repair swiftly, without complication, or by mere tinkering with existing arrangements. In every area, the problems run much too deep for quick fixes—as deep as the fact that a fundamental altering of the American economy has deprived us of heavy industry on the scale that made the United States the arsenal of democracy in World War II.

Given the depth of the problems and his rejection of patchwork solutions, Etzold might have probed a good deal farther into some of the most fundamental issues than he does—such as whether a continuous large-scale military commitment to NATO is compatible with the improved ability to conduct small-scale missions analogous to the Iranian hostage rescue, on which he places great emphasis. Perhaps Etzold will address such still deeper problems in the future. Meanwhile, he has conducted a first-rate tour of the current military horizon.

RUSSELL F. WEIGLEY
Temple University
Philadelphia

GILBERT, JAMES. *Another Chance: Postwar America, 1945-1968.* Pp. x, 307. Philadelphia, PA: Temple University Press, 1982. $17.95.

Another Chance enhances Professor Gilbert's reputation as an able scholar. Those who are familiar with his *Designing the Industrial State* and *Work Without Salvation* are aware of Gilbert's ability to interpret facets of the modern scene.

His new book deals with the complex forces that profoundly changed American life after World War II. Every area of the culture was affected: economic, political, social, religious, and military. All institutions within the cultural areas changed—some more than others, of course. The economic area had to cope with women in industry, new and improved technological discoveries, the increasing popularity of unionism of labor, the growth of suburbs, and the trek of millions of blacks from the South to the cities of the North and West. All of these significant changes are treated in such a way as to show their interrelationships in the evolving politics of the country.

Although the American victory in the war was complete, it was soon evident that the victory was flawed. Sharp disagreements between the Soviet Union and the United States quickly led to the cold war. This strained relationship was still evident at the end of the period (1968) treated in this book.

Certainly, as the author shows, our traditional policy of no entangling alliances was replaced by a series of regional military arrangements. These changes required new international fiscal institutions and new commercial relationships. All of these conditions encouraged the internationalization of American corporations and eventually led to their merging into huge multinational conglomerates.

Not only were international institutions altered, but the most intimate domestic institution, the family, was changed. The traditional American family of two or three generations living under one roof was no longer the universally accepted pattern. Grandparents lived alone or in some type of senior citizens home or community. People lived longer; more of them became calorie conscious and visited clinics or private physicians for regular physical check-ups.

A new age in world history was ushered in when atomic bombs were dropped on Hiroshima and Nagasaki. Gilbert makes very clear that never again would warfare or military preparedness be the same.

This well-written book should enjoy wide reading among students of recent American history.

GEORGE C. OSBORN

Gainesville
Florida

GOLDSTEIN, ABRAHAM S. *The Passive Judiciary: Prosecutional Discretion and the Guilty Plea.* Pp. xi, 104. Baton Rouge: Louisiana State University Press, 1981. $12.95.

The concept of discretion in the criminal justice process has long enjoyed the appreciation of practitioners and the attention of scholars. Both the practice of discretion and regard for the concept of discretion have a long history. Negotiating and bargaining in the justice system are not new; at least some of the forms of discretion have been officially approved; and discretion has been well researched. Nevertheless, there exists little if any consensus on the precise contours of the concept of discretion, on causes for increases or decreases in the exercise of discretion, on the currencies of exchange between and among those criminal justice participants who play at the game of discretion, or on the functions discretion performs or on the benefits discretion produces. In short, we have little agreement on what discretion really is or on whether its effects are, in the general case, deleterious, salutary, or merely benign.

Now we have Abraham Goldstein's book on discretion, and one which adopts a helpful new approach. Noting that most criticisms of the judiciary have emphasized its taking control of matters properly left to other branches—that is, the imperial judiciary argument—Goldstein criticizes judges for not asserting sufficient control over the criminal justice system generally and over the power of the public prosecutor particularly. How can it be, he asks, that the judge is so imperial elsewhere in his assertion of judicial control over executive power but curiously passive in relation to the prosecutor's discretion and to the plea arrangements made by the prosecutor? Why should this extraordinary latitude to charge, reduce charges, confer immunity, and dismiss exist? He concludes that it should not and that it need not.

Goldstein offers, essentially, two prescriptions: (1) given their authority over guilty pleas, judges should develop a "common law" of prosecutorial discretion; and (2) judges should assign a formal role to the victims of crime. Prosecutors may ask courts to accept a guilty plea or to reduce or dismiss charges for many different reasons. Their requests may be based on evidentiary grounds or on the desire to obtain the defendant's cooperation to facilitate another prosecution, or on the desire to lighten a heavy caseload, or on an attempt to gain a procedural advantage, and so on. The effective administration of justice requires that the judge inquire routinely to determine whether similar defendants have been afforded the same opportunities as the defendant in the instant case. The judge must ascertain whether guilty pleas and dismissals reflect a policy of discriminatory prosecution or some other form of unequal treatment. Thus, the prosecutor must be required to explain his reasons for, say, accepting a guilty plea in a class of case which is normally not prosecuted, or for not pressing forward in a class of case that is regularly prosecuted. The larger issues of policy governing the prosecutor's behavior would emerge if such inquiries were made regularly by the courts. Goldstein concedes that legislatures may not individualize justice enough, but if not, the remedy lies with the courts in sentencing, not with the prosecutor's manipulation of the charge.

Finally, Goldstein suggests that the victims should play a major role in the system, consulting with prosecutors after arrest, interviewing with probation officers before sentencing, participating in decisions on dismissals, charge reductions, guilty pleas, and sentencing. This would force the prosecutor to justify decisions to proceed with actions inconsistent with the victim's account—which might include the argument that the public interest is different from the victim's. And it would provide the judge with a party who has a genuine interest in correcting the version of the case reflected by the prosecutor's arrangements.

Mr. Goldstein, former dean of Yale Law School, delivered these lectures—later prepared for publication in this book—in 1977 as the Edward Douglass White Lectures at Louisiana State University. The scholarship which supports them is sound; the arguments presented are persuasive.

WILLIAM C. LOUTHAN

Ohio Wesleyan University
Delaware

GOVE, SAMUEL K. and LOUIS H. MASOTTI, eds. *After Daley: Chicago Politics in Transition.* Pp. xvii, 244. Urbana: University of Illinois Press, 1982. Paperbound, $7.95.

It is fair to posit that no city in the United States has spawned more volumes on its local politics and political life than Chicago. The local Democratic machine and the legendary mayor Richard J. Daley have been the subjects of numerous popular and academic accounts. The most recent of these renderings, *After Daley: Chicago Politics in Transition,* as advanced by the coeditors Louis H. Masotti and Samuel K. Gove, attempts to "gain [an] insight into the emergence of Chicago's new political era by examining the later years of the Daley regime, the Bilandic interregnum, and the volatile initial period of the Jane Byrne administration. " It is an attempt which is only partially successful.

In addition to the brief overview written by Masotti and Gove, the volume consists of 10 papers authored, for the most part, by well-known political scientists. As is true of any anthology, the quality of these papers varies considerably. Scholars of local politics should take particular note of Kathleen A. Kemp's and Robert L. Lineberry's contribution, which provides a good overview of the Chicago Democratic machine and goes on nicely to classify the various wards into the categories of controlled, deliverable, independent, and renegade; Michael Preston's discourse, which underscores the growing independence of the black vote; William J. Grimshaw's highly perceptive piece, in which he concurs with Preston's analysis of the increasing unreliability of the black vote and also notes that public employee unions—especially those which represent the transit workers, firefighters, and teachers—are entertaining a more independent and militant posture; and Kenneth R. Mladenka's contribution, which concludes that the nature of service delivery in Chicago is more a function of technical rational criteria than the result of machine politics.

The remaining papers in this volume can be read with a varying degree of profit. Joseph Zikmund provides a useful, matter-of-fact account of ethnic voting behavior in the Daley-Bilandic-Byrne era in which he underscores the usual machine reliability of voters of Polish descent. In a somewhat less than probing contribution, Joanne Belenchia concludes that Latinos have not been much of a factor in Chicago politics. Donald H. Haider makes the obvious point that Chicago needs to develop a comprehensive capital plan. Lawrence N. Hansen, in a somewhat tedious piece, notes the growing importance of the "up-for-grabs" suburban vote. My impression is that while offering a useful account of the Daley influence in Springfield, Gove fails to share with the reader all of his perceptions concerning the present-day relationship between the Chicago machine and the larger Illinois political system. In his concluding piece, Milton Rakove asserts that Jane Byrne has to some degree dismantled the old order but has not yet completely fashioned a new political regime.

So what can one conclude about the present-day nature and immediate future of machine politics in Chicago? In sum, the volume offers no definitive thematic conclusion, other than to suggest that politics in Chicago has become and will increasingly be more pluralistic in character. Any reader who is seeking a more concrete appraisal will have to wait until another jury returns its findings.

NELSON WIKSTROM
Virginia Commonwealth University
Richmond

HARRIS, WILLIAM H. *The Harder We Run: Black Workers Since the Civil War*. Pp. ix, 259. New York: Oxford University Press, 1982. $17.95. Paperbound, $4.95.

"As the 1970's ended, future prospects for most black workers were about as bleak as they had been when Lincoln signed the Emancipation Proclamation." This statement by William Harris may be unsupportable, but he has vividly shown that too little has been done to "limit the impact of race on employment and income." While trade unionism, the civil rights movement, and government efforts have substantially increased the number of blacks in high status positions, the black masses remain overrepresented on unemployment rolls and low-paying jobs.

Harris pessimistically sees little possibility of change for the better. Past discrimination has so burdened black workers, Harris contends, that equal opportunity is not equality at all. Harris has no patience with those who claim that preferential treatment of blacks is reverse discrimination. Some type of "class-based remedy" is essential, in his view, to enhance the black workers' position. At the same time, the country seems unprepared to "accept the special disability that centuries of racism have placed on black workers." Despite its pessimistic tenor, the book is not completely depressing. Harris details the triumphs as well as the tragedies, the magnificent courage of those who struggled successfully to rise as well as the despair of those who gave up.

The Harder We Run traces black workers from emancipation to the present. Chapters one to three cover, with notable gaps, the period to 1925. Chapters four and five treat the Brotherhood of Sleeping Car Porters, the Great Depression, and World War II. The final chapters concentrate on the 1960s and 1970s. Harris is especially effective in tracing the rise of trade unionism and the movement of blacks from the agricultural South to the industrial North.

Not surprisingly, Harris's study suffers from some of the unavoidable shortcomings of brief overviews—too selective in topics and limited in original research. It is not a comprehensive treatment of black workers in the United States. Nevertheless, it is a welcome addition to the literature of black and labor history. This highly readable monograph will be an exciting introduction to the novice and an engaging refresher for the professional. Above all, *The Harder We Run* is a sobering, necessary reminder of the importance of race in the impoverishment of black America.

JOE. M. RICHARDSON
Florida State University
Tallahassee

HOUSE, PETER W. *The Art of Public Policy Analysis: The Arena of Regulations and Resources.* Pp. 296. Beverly Hills, CA: Sage Publications, 1982. $25.00. Paperbound, $12.50.

Peter House explores the symbiotic relationship between professionals and politicians and concludes that the analyst is not the power behind the throne. In rapid succession, he challenges certain basic assumptions. Some problems cannot be converted to mathematical equations or computer programs. Models that appeal to technicians may be irrelevant to higher officials. Theoretical methodologies are often ill-suited to the realities of governance. Policy analysts rarely find sufficient time and resources to engage in comprehensive forms of rational decision making. Principals may not possess the interest or expertise to benefit from sophisticated briefings. In addition, those who hold the reins of power may bring into office preconceived values, ideologies, and obligations which negate the choices offered by policy analysts.

At present there is no policy science, only structured opinions with which no one can prove himself correct. The chasm separating ideal analysis from practicable procedures seems insurmountable. Frequently the distance between staff and the ultimate authority appears equally great. House describes how insulated bureaucracies establish their own rules away from visible policy arenas. Many agencies operate through inertia. "It is only when the situation is unique, when there is a crisis or a politically derived desire to change the status quo, that there is any need for a decisionmaker at all." Surprisingly, he overlooks the annual budgetary ritual in formulating his list of circumstances which induce policy change.

This study makes a genuine contribution by tracing the manner in which issues affect one another. Specialists bring differing agendas to decision makers. As director of Environmental Assessments for the U.S. Department of Energy, House demonstrates how competing concerns interact within government. He draws on current problems facing federal officials in formulating standards for clean air, hazardous waste disposal, electric utility boilers, and commercialization of energy. Policymakers encounter troublesome tradeoffs involving the three E's—energy, economics, and the environment. Each has its own constituencies, organizations, advocates, critics, and overseers. Multiple agencies and congressional committees promulgate policy. Many of these fields require plural permits and approvals from different levels of government. Unless coordination occurs, nobody is in a position to reconcile conflicting interests.

The author sees some light at the end of the tunnel. As an alternative to conflict, he endorses a cooperative mode in which all parties would accept combined, mutually advantageous goals to further the national interest. But who would enforce togetherness? His suggestion is that a White House-level "Court of Appeals" settle interagency, cross-policy disputes. House seeks a centralized solution involving expansion of the analytic capabilities of Office of Management and Budget or the Domestic Council. To some extent, he seems unaware of the countervailing movement toward decentralized decision making which is inherent in the New Federalism. In advancing the concept of comprehensive impact statements on a national and regional basis, he indicates that "these issues beg to be addressed." However, under White House and congressional delegations of block grant powers to states and localities, evaluations and decisions are already being made by subnational governments. Unfortunately, the message has not yet reached every segment of the federal bureaucracy.

What is House's prescription for invigorating the public policy process? In the short run, he offers some helpful—though obvious—home remedies, such as reaching out to those who have experience, brainstorming with experts in various disciplines, using persuasion and/or pressure as the need arises, and relying on horse sense. In the long run, he places greatest trust in sophisticated analytic techniques, albeit acknowledging that flaws must be weeded out and information made more complete. He suggests intensified instruction in policy analysis and the institutionalization of policy shops in the public sector. Staff members must be grounded in the techniques of planning, problem solving, management, communication, political sensitivity, teamwork, and implementation. Trainees must be prepared for the real world. To achieve consensus, they must be conditioned to accept concessions and incremental changes. He endorses a policy information system to permit complex cost-benefit analyses through the availability of a valid and reliable data base. His preference is for a Policy Analysis Screening System (PASS) which would provide the modern Othello and Iago with computerized storage capability and instantaneous access to accurate, updated information, documents, and developments in interrelated policy areas.

The reader will be impressed by House's candid, reasonable, and modest expectations. He concedes that there are "areas which we simply don't understand very well, and that all the formalism in the world can't cure this deficiency. . . . Unless we can really validate models and their data bases, there is no real basis for a decisionmaker to choose an analytic solution over his own judgment." For the forseeable future, the author comes to the conclusion that the best we can expect is a compromise in which "practical experience and common sense" are comingled with "formal analytic techniques."

LEONARD P. STAVISKY
Columbia University
New York

ISSERMAN, MAURICE. *Which Side Were You On? The American Communist Party During the Second World War.* Pp. xvii, 305. Middletown, CT: Wesleyan University Press, 1982. $19.95.

The glib answer to the question Maurice Isserman poses in the title of his thought-provoking and informative book is "several." Starting out as an advocate of collective security to check fascist aggression, the American Communist Party abruptly jumped on the isolationist bandwagon in 1939. Two years later, just as suddenly, it screamed for American intervention in World War II, and after Pearl Harbor, the Communist Party's patriotic fervor was second to none. However, this flagwaving sentiment did not survive the war's end and quickly shifted into a strident denunciation of American imperialism. Reflecting the vicissitudes of Soviet diplomacy, the twists and turns in the Communist line badly damaged the credibility of the party as a genuine representative of homespun radicalism and encouraged a general perception of it as a compliant agent of a foreign power. This popular image, carefully nurtured by the FBI and anti-Communist liberals, fostered a hysterical backlash of postwar political repression that culminated in the McCarthyite Red Scare.

Isserman does not let the American Communist Party off lightly for its shortcomings. He denounces it for perpetuating an authoritarian hierarchy that stifled critical reexamination of outworn doctrines and for toeing the Moscow line against its own best interests in promoting social change in the United States. However, Isserman does not sympathize with the cold war historians of the 1950s who viewed the Communist Party as a Soviet Frankenstein. Instead, he "belongs to a new generation of historians, with roots in the student movement of the 1960s, depicting the party as, at certain times and places, flexible, imaginative, principled, rooted in neighborhoods and workplace, and enjoying genuine popular support." Nevertheless, Isserman also departs from some of his New Left counterparts who glorify selected features of Communist history they regard as upholding the correct revolutionary posture.

In walking the fine line between orthodoxy and revisionism, Isserman only partially succeeds in proving his thesis. He sees the Communist Party under the wartime leadership of Earl Browder as passing through a transitional stage, away from the Kremlin and Stalinism and toward the adoption of a flexible brand of democratic socialism better suited to the realities of the American political economy. "Far from a single-minded conspiracy," Isserman writes, "Communist party policies were sometimes determined by the outcome of a behind-the-scenes struggle of groups with conflicting interest." Using the Browder papers, written memoirs, and oral interviews, the book does depict something short of the monolithic decision-making process usually associated with Communist Party affairs. Yet Isserman's point is weakened by the evidence he so relentlessly displays. During the period under discussion, no reorientation of the party's position took place without Moscow's stamp of approval; not until 1956 did American leaders exercise a measure of independence, and only then in response to Khrushchev's stunning anti-Stalinist speech to the Twentieth Party Congress. Seeking to sweep away the Stalinist debris, a younger generation of Communists tried to Americanize the party, drawing on their experiences during the coalitionist days of the Popular Front and Grand Alliance. Despite some success, they were too late, and since 1956 the party has wielded little influence on the left.

This book dispels any illusions about the vitality of the Communist Party after 1945 or its threat to national security. Already handicapped by internal conflicts, the Communist Party was an easy target of repression. Isserman also shows that the party did not corner the market on self-delusion. In a span of four years, American officials and the mass media converted Ruthless Joe Stalin into Uncle Joe and back again according to the dictates of U.S. foreign policy. A book that ventures into the mysteries of hackneyed factional disputes might have become a crashing bore; however, Isserman's sharp prose and critical engagement rescue it from suffering this pitfall. Those interested in a glimpse of the tormented world of American Communism owe the author a special debt of gratitude.

STEVEN F. LAWSON
University of South Florida
Tampa

JACKSON, BRIAN. *The Black Flag: A Look Back at the Strange Case of Nicola Sacco and Bartolomeo Vanzetti.* Pp. xiv, 208. Boston: Routledge & Kegan Paul, 1981. $12.95.

"Our words—our lives—our pain—nothing. The taking of our lives . . . —all. That last moment belongs to us—that agony is our triumph." These are Bartolomeo Vanzetti's last words. They are also the last words of Brian Jackson's study, and he employs them to remind us that his primary concern is with martyrs—individuals who "by the moment and manner of their dying, pulled the future towards them." According to Jackson, the effects of such individuals on "our moral, intellectual, and political landscape" is an issue quite different from "the question of guilt or innocence." Indeed, he argues, all that we can be certain of now is that Sacco and Vanzetti "were guilty . . . of a cultural crime. They were foreign, working class, armed and anarchist. . . . In the end it was for this that the state executed them."

Regrettably, Jackson's self-conscious concern with the cultural sources and resonance of the case is only fragmentarily reflected in the book he has written. The bulk of the study retraces the crime, rehashes well-worn arguments—despite the availability of new evidence—and repeats a half-century of inconclusive speculations. In a chatty tone, Jackson invites the reader to participate in the evaluation of evidence which creates a certain sympathetic bond with his readership. It does not, however, contribute to—indeed, it inhibits—a coherent cultural analysis of the myriad ethnic, class, and political issues that lent (and lend) the Sacco-Vanzetti case its potency over time. As so many who have preceded him, Jackson seems unable to analyze Sacco and Vanzetti's cultural crime until he has reached a final verdict on their legalistic guilt. It is a dilemma for many liberal sympathizers who seek to employ the defense of radicals as a vehicle for reforming, but not revolutionizing, the American legal system. Jackson recognizes that "as radical spirits Sacco and Vanzetti were in the end silenced by the prosecution, but on the way they were muffled by the defence." It is thus particularly unfortunate that Jackson himself continues to mute their radicalism and its multiple, often contradictory, cultural meanings.

Still, Jackson does suggest several points to be considered in such an analysis. He notes that Sacco and Vanzetti's early defenders excised antichurch and class war rhetoric from the pair's writings and that later analysts devoted only "a handful of pages" to the political philosophy—anarchism—the two men expounded. He also sees the importance of investigating the cultural milieu from which Sacco and Vanzetti emerged—Italian, working class, Catholic, and politicized—and of distinguishing defenders from this milieu from the philanthropic women, Communist Party organizers, trade unionists, and male intellectuals who also provided support. These aspects of Jackson's study may encourage a new, rather than just another, study of the Sacco-Vanzetti case which takes as its starting rather than ending point Vanzetti's last claim—"that agony is our triumph."

NANCY A. HEWITT
University of South Florida
Tampa

KNEESE, ALLEN V. and F. LEE BROWN. *The Southwest Under Stress: National Resource Development in a Regional Setting.* Pp. xv, 268. Baltimore, MD: Johns Hopkins University Press, 1981. $30.00. Paperbound, $9.50.

Published by Resources for the Future, "this volume is a capstone report" on the 1973-78 Southwest Region Under Stress Project. More than 40 senior scholars participated. A bibliography lists 145 books and articles published under the project's auspices. The hardcover volume is handsomely printed, bound, and illustrated. Two major features of the analysis are the large amount of data presented on water supply, air quality, recreation, and economic effects of energy-related development and the various case studies reported on. The Stress Project is a significant contribution to our understanding of the conflict between development and environment. The authors have done an outstanding job of consolidating and presenting the essential issues and findings of the project.

By Southwest, the project means the Upper Colorado River Basin in the "Four Corners" states of Arizona, Colorado, New Mexico, and Utah. This area is the setting for a classic conflict between development and environment. The basin is a principal repository of energy and mineral resources. There is also a general movement of population to this part of the Sunbelt. The Southwest, so attractive to both industry and population, is ecologically and culturally very fragile. It is characterized by great scenic beauty, aridity, and increasingly severe smog due to poor ventilation and frequent inversions. Indians, rural Hispanics, and rural Mormons are gripped by extreme poverty.

The report is divided into four major sections. In Part I, the principal features of the Southwest Region are profiled and the central issues are delineated. Part II examines the problem of water supply; Part III, air quality and recreational resources. The last section analyzes who will benefit from economic development of the region. The report concludes that water scarcity is due largely to legal overappropriation that can be corrected by institutional changes. Air quality and recreational resources are more serious problems. The large capital-intensive projects for energy exploitation may have only a modest continuing stimulation effect on the regional economy and hence on poverty groups. This forecast is especially pertinent to Indian reservations which own much of the water and resources. Most of the capital and labor will be imported; most of the benefits will be exported. Sucl. projects produce only a temporary boomtown phenomenon and exploitation of nonrenewable resources, leaving little permanent economic base. The report heavily emphasizes the potential uses of various tax devices as methods for creating pollution markets or capturing regionally the benefits from energy development for national use.

DUANE WINDSOR

Rice University
Houston
Texas

LABUNSKI, RICHARD E. *The First Amendment Under Siege: The Politics of Broadcast Regulation.* Pp. x, 184. Westport, CT: Greenwood Press, 1981. $27.50.

Labunski has both extensive training as a political scientist with work in that field and experience in broadcast journalism. This dual background is reflected in this book, for he brings both scholarship and fluent writing ability to his task.

Labunski begins his argument with the observation that there is a distinct difference between the treatment by the federal government of print media and broadcast media. Essentially, the crux of his argument is that except for the laws of libel, print media are unregulated, while broadcast media are extensively controlled. This is not quite true. The Post Office does have rules about what can be sent through the mail, and print media must conform in order to get lower mailing rates. There are also rules about the mailing of pornography, which today are very wide, but also today cable TV shows movies that differ little from mailable material.

Labunski concentrates his argument on four regulatory policies:

—the requirement for "Equal Opportunity"—that is, the requirement that the station allow a political figure to air his or her views; political opponents must get equal time;

—the "Fairness Doctrine," which requires that stations must devote a reasonable amount of programming to public issues of importance, and, in doing so, the program must show both sides of an issue;
—the "Personal Attack" rules, according to which if the station attacks a person's character, it must provide that person with a transcript of the attack and allow him or her equal time to respond; and
—the similar "Editorial" rules, according to which if the station takes a slant on an issue in an editorial, equal time must be allowed for the airing of opposing views.

In none of these four areas are the print media subject to the same sort of regulation as is the broadcast media.

Labunski takes a historical approach to the subject by devoting several chapters to a chronological discussion of the development of broadcast regulation. He then discusses the political environment of the Federal Communications Commission (FCC), the public interest and access, and, finally, the future of broadcasting regulations. In all of these subjects except the last, Labunski does an excellent job of briefly and clearly summarizing the subject. The book is under 200 pages long, so much detail is omitted. The last chapter is the weakest, for it essentially discusses only the provisions of H.R. 13015 and its failure to pass Congress.

The appendix of the book poses a "System Model" of the FCC. Purists may not agree that it is a true model, for some hold that a model must not only specify the important factors in a problem but also indicate how the factors interrelate. Labunski's model fails in this latter task and is really a checklist of factors to consider in evaluating the FCC. Most of these factors are discussed at one point or another in the body of the book, but it would have been very interesting to see Labunski try to apply his model in a rigorous way to the information set forth in the text. This might be difficult, for the body of his work has little quantitative data, while the model calls for much statistical data. Perhaps Labunski will gather these data and use them with his model in some future work.

O. ZELLER ROBERTSON, Jr.
Saginaw Valley State College
University Center
Michigan

LEVINE, ADELINE GORDON. *Love Canal: Science, Politics, and People.* Pp. xv, 263. Lexington, MA: D. C. Heath, 1982. $24.95.

Levine's volume is a case study of the environmental and human tragedy that occurred in the Love Canal area of Niagara Falls. At Love Canal, the indiscriminate use of synthetic products by the Hooker Company, a subsidiary of the Occidental Petroleum Corporation, led to toxic chemical leachates spreading from a chemical waste disposal site into a residential area of Niagara Falls. In August 1978, the State of New York acknowledged that an "imminent peril to the health of the general public" existed in the area. Levine's work begins at the point when the State of New York recommended that families with pregnant women and children under two years of age "temporarily move from the site as soon as possible."

The book is an outgrowth of a field research seminar—which eventually resulted in dozens of interviews with affected families and other key state task force personnel—three years of field notes, and several thousand newspaper reports. The volume chronicles the efforts of area residents to get the governmental assistance needed to escape their poisoned environment. It exposes to the reader how so-called experts were ultimately viewed with skepticism and how the residents developed organizational skills to deal with their problems. Ultimately the U.S. Congress passed legislation allowing the president to spend up to $20 million to relocate the 500 affected families. By the summer of 1981 this goal had been established. What had not been established, of course, was a way for the affected families to assess the amount of chemical contaminants stored in their bodies and the dangers not only to themselves but to the next generation. What makes this situation even more odious are the results of a recent study by the Environmental Protection Agency, which estimates that only 10 percent of the hazardous wastes produced in the United States are being disposed of safely and properly. The sad fact of the matter is that apparently we do not even know how many potential Love Canals there are.

Professor Levine has produced a scholarly work on a timely and important problem. She has drawn attention to a policy area which needs to be spotlighted. The potential enormity of the problem is such that further scholarly efforts in this area are warranted if other disasters are to be prevented. This volume is a sound first step in that direction.

JOHN S. ROBEY
East Texas State University
Commerce

MARTIN, JOHN FREDERICK. *Civil Rights and the Crisis of Liberalism: The Democratic Party, 1945-1976*. Pp. xvi, 301. Boulder, CO: Westview Press, 1979. $20.00.

Two stories are woven together in this volume: first, the flowering of liberalism in the Democratic Party in the first half of the 1960s, and its decline thereafter; second, for perspective, the course of liberal ideology from the time of the American Revolution and its relation to questions of race. The book can be read profitably in toto or simply as a first-rate account of the personalities, factional tensions, compromises, and travails of modern Democratic politics.

Traditional liberal ambivalence about governmental power was jarred by a succession of activist presidents and candidates in this century. Franklin Roosevelt put the government to work on the problems of the economy and the poor and reduced the fear of power in liberals. Truman, Martin stresses, took the bolder and more controversial step of asking that the government use its coercive powers to attack racial discrimination. Kennedy and Johnson in their time pushed well ahead on both fronts.

But the New Frontier and the Great Society were the work of a relative few who, it turned out, never had full public support for their policies of government power and racial equality and soon left the great majority behind. The liberal coalition began to fall apart. Busing, affirmative action, the War on Poverty, and other programs drew fire not only from their natural enemies, the conservatives, but from the minorities and the disadvantaged the programs were intended to benefit. Both asserted the right to rule their own affairs, abetted by the liberal politicians themselves, for whom power was something by right to be widely shared.

Then came the McGovern-Fraser reforms of Democratic presidential nominating procedures, which resulted in the exclusion of many party regulars who had worked for liberal causes over the years. The Vietnam war completed the dissolution—according to Martin, the self-destruction—of liberalism in the Democratic Party. The war alienated young people and the working class, once important elements of the liberal coalition, and with Watergate revived all the old concerns about the corruptibility of power. The legacy of this period is the politics of grassroots movements and special-interest organizations.

The book makes good use of primary sources, is engagingly written, and is both spirited and evenhanded—thoughtful retrospection for readers of all persuasions.

ROBERT J. SICKELS
University of New Mexico
Albuquerque

McCORMICK, RICHARD P. *The Presidential Game: The Origins of American Presidential Politics.* Pp. 279. New York: Oxford University Press, 1982. $19.95.

"Paradoxically," Richard P. McCormick observes at the outset of his important and thoroughly fascinating study, "a nation that has made a fetish of constitutionalism has lacked a constitutionally sanctioned method for selecting its most important official." McCormick, a distinguished political historian, goes on to trace the development of the presidential selection process during the first half-century of the republic. With admirable clarity he explains how and why successive generations of Americans so drastically altered the rules governing presidential selection that by the 1840s the process was not only different from, but contradictory to, that envisioned by the founding fathers.

When the founding fathers wrote the Constitution, they sought to ensure that only the most talented and virtuous men the republic had to offer could attain the presidency. They further sought to insulate the chief executive from undue popular influence, from intrigues, and above all from factions and political parties, which they viewed as unmitigated evils. To achieve those ends, they designed an elaborate plan for presidential selection, including an electoral college and a runoff election in the House of Representatives. But as McCormick observes, as early as the first presidential election in 1789 it became apparent "that their scheme was so defective as to be unworkable." As a result, succeeding generations simply modified old rules and improvised new ones.

According to McCormick, between 1789 and 1844 there were four successive versions of the presidential selection game: the "hazardous game," played by rival factions organized around Thomas Jefferson and Alexander Hamilton; the "Virginia game," introduced by the Jeffersonians to ensure their dominance of the presidency; the "game of faction," which pitted the followers of Andrew Jackson against their opponents; and finally, the "party game." Each of these games had its own set of rules and each departed from the constitutional model. The most significant departure of all was the party game, which emerged between 1832 and 1844 and which, as McCormick notes in his epilogue, lasted until after World War II. With its political parties, nominating conventions, and traditional campaigns, none of which had constitutional sanction, the party game represented a repudiation of the ideals of the founding fathers.

The disparity between constitutional theory and political reality, McCormick makes clear, deeply troubled thoughtful Americans. Even at the height of the party game, they had a nagging suspicion that this was not the way the game should be played. And even though they allowed political parties to dominate presidential politics, they viewed the party system with distrust. Yet despite their misgivings, Americans found themselves unable to agree on an alternative.

In recent years, the weakening of the party system, coupled with Vietnam and Watergate, has intensified the debate over the presidential selection system. Anyone wishing to explore the historical dimensions of this debate would do well to read McCormick's thoughtful and provocative study.

PATRICK J. MANEY

Tulane University
New Orleans
Louisiana

MORELAND, LAURENCE W., TOD A. BAKER, and ROBERT P. STEED, eds. *Contemporary Southern Political Attitudes and Behavior: Studies and Essays.* Pp. xviii, 296. New York: Praeger, 1982. $29.95.

In this year, when at least two major works have appeared commemorating the fiftieth anniversary of the publication of *I'll Take My Stand,* it is noteworthy that the book under review should be published. Not just one more book about the South, this is a major event in that it extends our knowledge of what is changing and what remains the same in the region. Brought together are a series of papers presented at the second Citadel Symposium on Southern Politics (1980). Both aggregate and survey data are used, as well as in-depth interviews, in an attempt to bring theoretical explanation to a variety of facts concerning political life in the contemporary South. Perhaps the great strength of this book rests on the self-conscious task many of the contributors undertook of evaluating selected propositions derived from V. O. Key's classic, now over 30 years old, *Southern Politics* (1949). Titles of the three parts into which the 14 studies and essays are divided are suggestive of the thrust of these collected papers: Ideology in Southern Politics; Perspectives on Southern Party Politics; and Linkages Between the Mass Public and Public Officials. Each is preceded by a concise editorial introduction, and the three parts are followed by a helpful and insightful general conclusion.

Key had emphasized how the South differed. A measure of what remains of that distinctiveness might be determined in part by the nature of the ideological and issue concerns held by residents in the region. The four articles of Part I consider the extent to which the South has been assimilated into the national culture, social, and political patterns of the nation—there is some indication that it may in fact be the other way around. The six articles comprising Part II examine contemporary party systems to ascertain whether the larger societal changes since World War II have brought the region fully into the national political system. Part III traces relationships between culture and politics, the relation between rulers and ruled. Four articles question the extent to which the democratic model operates in the linkage between government officials and the electorate.

While heavily statistical in analysis—78 entries are found in the List of Tables—these articles do not put the reader off. Most show mastery of multivariate analysis techniques. End notes are full of relevant citations from theoretical literature. The editors and sponsors of the conference leading to this book are to be complimented. It is well worth reading, as seldom does the reader find so much to stimulate interests. This book compares favorably with other contributions such as those of W. Havard (1972), Bartley and Graham (1975), and Bass and DeVries (1976). In some instances the selections presented here excel, if not in providing overall perspective, then in carefully derived data on which to consider an answer to the question, Whither the South?

PERRY H. HOWARD

Louisiana State University
Baton Rouge

PETROCIK, JOHN R. *Party Coalitions: Realignments and the Decline of the New Deal Party System.* Pp. 215. Chicago: University of Chicago Press, 1981. $20.00.

John Petrocik argues that the American party system has undergone a major realignment over the past 10 or 15 years. In a somewhat narrow but crucial definition, he proposes that "a realignment occurs when the measurable party bias of identifiable segments of the population changes in such a way that the social group profile of the parties—the party coalitions—is altered." This definition does not require a change in the aggregate levels of party support, nor does it demand the emergence of a new party or the demise of the Republican or Democratic Parties. The thesis of this book, based on this definition, is that the party system has undergone a major realignment over the past two decades. Petrocik argues that the contours of this realignment are not as gross as many might have expected, and this fact has led scholars to overlook it. Exploration of the argument demands that a distinction be drawn between critical and noncritical realignments. A critical realignment changes the balance of strength between the parties, whereas a noncritical realignment is one in which the strength of the parties is relatively stable. The recent noncritical realignment explored by Petrocik fits within his definition of being less dramatic and not involving a major shift in electoral strength or the demise of a major party.

The heart of Petrocik's argument that a realignment has been under way is that several traditional sources of Democratic and Republican voting strength are shifting allegiance, and that the groups changing the most are those that were instrumental in building the winning pluralities in the 1964, 1968, 1972, and 1976 presidential elections. Using a large body of longitudinal data, Petrocik identifies 15 party coalition groups that have undergone change in party preference over the past two decades. Only four of them, containing 34 percent of the population, have not changed their partisanship to some extent. Six groups, constituting 48 percent of the population, have become somewhat more Democratic and five groups representing 18 percent of the population have become less Democratic. Particular attention is given to demonstrating the changes that have occurred in the South, resulting from the courtship of white southerners by the Republicans as well as their abandonment of the Democratic Party. Furthermore, his data suggest that contrary to popular belief, most of the decline in Democratic support has come from changes in the party identification of native southerners, not from migration to the South by northerners.

Petrocik concludes that additional change will likely be a secular process and will result from the emergence of an agenda of issues that can galvanize voters and office-seekers. He does not see any current issue possessing the potential to do that and does not venture any guesses that appear to have the weight of evidence behind them.

This book will provoke considerable discussion, and the thesis will almost certainly be challenged by many of those currently caught up in the realignment debate. The noncritical realignment postulated by Petrocik does not fit neatly within any of the prevailing theories but represents an interesting and important analysis of party coalition and realignment theories. Although not a very long book, it is replete with useful figures, charts, and tables used to buttress Petrocik's arguments.

ROBERT J. HUCKSHORN
Florida Atlantic University
Boca Raton

ROZIER, JOHN. *Black Boss: Political Revolution in a Georgia County.* Pp. x, 220. Athens: University of Georgia Press, 1982. $15.95.

In 1966 John McCown, black and broke, carrying two 38s "just for white people" drove into sleepy Hancock County, Georgia, in a broken-down old Chrysler. Within a few years he controlled the previously white-dominated county. However, the black majority was beginning to demand its rights. It was a propitious time for the arrival of a bright, aggressive, fearless leader. McCown was quickly elected to the city commission and within five years dictated as completely and perhaps as unfairly as any previous white political boss.

McCown might have remained a minor figure in county politics, except that he became executive director of the Georgia Council on Human Relations. "A situation unique in American political history developed, as McCown built a small empire atop a growing base of government and foundation funds through the council." Most of the fund ended up in Hancock County. His personality, courage, and sense of theater enabled him to get millions of dollars from the United States government and foundations.

While McCown secured millions for the county, the money apparently aided primarily the few who worked for him. Mismanagement, shoddy recordkeeping, and corruption resulted in the failure of most projects. After eight years and millions of dollars, the county was still poor, but John McCown was not. During his era welfare cases increased 673 percent and unemployment 20 percent. McCown himself owned 525 acres of farmland, was building a house that would cost $60,000, and owned several pieces of commercial property and his own airplane. Poverty program officials feared that McCown was "becoming a black emperor, not different from a benevolent white plantation owner, except he is black."

McCown died in a plane crash in 1976 just before he was to be indicted. The full story of whether he was corrupt or simply careless with other people's money probably will never be known. One friend said part of what seemed to be stealing was his regular income. His salary was $50,000 per year, a phenomenal sum for Hancock County.

One thing, however, is clear. McCown gave blacks power and new self-respect. Unfortunately, he used the same methods racist whites had used for years: violence, intimidation, appeal to racial prejudice, exclusion from office because of race, threats, a countywide surveillance system, and questionable election practices. As a black minister said: "If it was wrong then [when the whites did it], it is wrong now."

Black Boss is fascinating and informative reading, a reminder that "good and evil" dwell in all races. It dramatically shows, in Rozier's words, that "in the . . . tumult of the 1960's, the headlines were made in Watts and Washington, in Birmingham and Selma. Without much notice, a revolution was going on in the old rural Belt, in counties like Hancock in Georgia and Greene in Alabama."

JOE M. RICHARDSON
Florida State University
Tallahassee

RUBIN, RICHARD L. *Press, Party, and Presidency*. Pp. 246. New York: W. W. Norton, 1982. $18.95.

This book attempts to answer two basic questions of interest to everyone concerned with American politics: first, how major changes in mass communications have influenced the people's choice in presidential elections; and second, how, in turn, the actions of the successful candidate, once in office, have been influenced by relentless media coverage and the new election environment.

These questions are answered in the painstaking academic manner of a candidate for a Ph.D. degree at an Ivy League university, although the author already has received his Ph.D. from Columbia University. The book is written in high academese. Strunk and White would never have sanctioned the long, convoluted sentences. The book is studded with footnotes, a tempting list of references for an interested reader to build into a library of his or her own.

Rubin studiously explores the history of the mass media in this country: press, radio, and TV. He presents a striking picture of Theodore Roosevelt's introduction of the creation of newsmaking into the presidency, and of the actions of Woodrow Wilson and Franklin Delano Roosevelt in using news creation to further their policies. Moreover, Rubin attempts to outline the changes TV has wrought in the whole political process.

Chapter headings give an indication of the abstract academic viewpoint the author has of reality: "Refragmenting the National Arena," "The Politics of Reorganization," and "The New Electoral Circuitry" are typical. The book avoids and evades some major realities, restricting itself to academic discussion.

For instance, there is no extended discussion of the important place scientific polling occupies in the American political system. Elmo, George Gallup and Louis Harris are not even mentioned.

Nor is there any reference to the new breed of political consultants who play so vital a role in the political process; or to the proven successful engineering of consent, which applies the findings of the social sciences to social goals, applying strategies and tactics of leadership to the political process—I used such approaches as far back as the Coolidge administration. And public relations and its practice, that played so important a role in the last administrations, is unmentioned too.

EDWARD L. BERNAYS
Cambridge
Massachusetts

SOMMERS, PAUL M., ed. *Welfare Reform in America: Perspectives and Prospects.* Pp. viii, 254. Boston: Kluwer-Nijoff, 1982. $29.00.

Welfare Reform in America is the second of a series of books stemming from the annual Middlebury College Conference on Economic Issues. It contains 12 articles that examine past and present American welfare efforts and consider the prospects of various welfare reforms which might be attempted. Obviously these are no small tasks, given the reality that while nearly no one is happy with the welfare system change is difficult because one man's problem is another's virtue.

Paul J. Lampman's lead article, "Goals and Purposes of Social Welfare Expenditures," reviews distributional goals of social welfare expenditures that are widely accepted but on which there is disagreement about the priorities: offsetting income loss, helping people buy essentials, reducing income poverty, and sharing the tax burden fairly. William P. Albrecht's "Welfare Reform: An Idea Whose Time Has Come and Gone" is perhaps the most interesting and readable article. Albrecht cogently argues that the shortcomings of the welfare system are sometimes more apparent than real; that despite its shortcomings, it is relatively good; and in any event, reform of the welfare system is not possible because it is politically impossible. We have reached an equilibrium which pleases no one; but that equilibrium will permit only marginal changes that hardly can be termed reform.

Three articles—by Sheldon Danziger and Robert Plotnick, G. William Hoagland, and Morton Paglin—clearly illustrate how different viewpoints on the effectiveness of welfare programs depend on how poverty is defined and measured. Food stamps, unemployment insurance, and the Aid to Families with Dependent Children-Unemployed Fathers Program are examined in separate articles.

The final four articles address possible next steps in the evolution of welfare in America. A useful article is a concise account of the evolution of an integrated approach to jobs and cash assistance over the past 45 years, penned by Larry L. Orr and Felicity Skidmore. Other articles speculate on why demand-side policies have replaced education-training and income transfer policies; the magnitude of welfare policy impact; and policy implications that stem from various negative income tax-public service employment schemes.

In his introduction, Sommers states that this book seeks to fill the need for a book of readings for an undergraduate or public policy school course on poverty and welfare issues. *Welfare Reform in America* fills this gap admirably.

GEORGE R. SHARWELL
University of South Carolina
Columbia

TOBER, JAMES A. *Who Owns the Wildlife? The Political Economy of Conservation in Nineteenth-Century America.* Pp. xiii, 330. Westport, CT: Greenwood Press, 1981. $27.50.

ALLIN, CRAIG W. *The Politics of Wilderness Preservation.* Contributions in Political Science, No. 64. Pp. 304. Westport, CT: Greenwood Press, 1982. $27.50.

James Tober, a research affiliate in the Program on Non-Profit Organizations of the Institution for Social and Policy Studies at Yale University, relates the gradual growth of the state's role in the regulation of wildlife as a study in the intricacies of the public policy process. He identifies the three major interest groups that have traditionally vied for access to wildlife:

sportsmen, market hunters, and landowners. Since game, birds, and fish do not recognize property lines, states assumed ownership and thus began the basis of their regulatory authority. Americans reacted against English precedents where landowners owned the wildlife on their estate in an exclusive manner. Even with state ownership, up to 1850 property owners were exempt from hunting seasons and could hunt for food any time they wished. By 1900, shorter hunting seasons became the rule and protection of game became more restrictive.

The total lack of federal regulation in the nineteenth century was disastrous in two specific instances. The first was the virtual elimination of the national buffalo herd, since nobody wanted them except Indians; and second was the extinction of the passenger pigeon by allowing its hardwood nesting forests to be completely cut down.

Tober's conclusion calls for increased state and federal regulation as well as international agreements to prevent the extinction of any more species.

Craig Allin, chairman of the Political Science Department of Cornell College in Mt. Vernon, Iowa, has expertly discussed the origins and background of the Wilderness Act of 1964. From the arrival of Columbus to 1890, he states, was a 400-year period of exploitation when Western civilization confronted the American wilderness. In the subsequent 90 years, the Outdoor Recreation Resources Review Commission identified only 64 extant wilderness tracts comprising 28 million acres in 19 states. Thus from the original 100 percent wilderness, only one percent remains. By a long and prolonged effort, ecologists, conservationists, and preservationists achieved passage of the Wilderness Act of 1964. This act creates a statutory wilderness of 9.1 million acres and protects it in its primitive state.

The opposition interests were the mining and lumber companies, ranchers wanting grazing land, and water engineers—mainly from California and Colorado—who want to build dams. The National Reclamation Association also opposed the Wilderness Act, not wanting to lose possible land for agriculture. The result was an interesting interplay of conflicting lobbies and ultimate compromise. The ideal of preservation had to be balanced with the economic realities of contemporary society.

The U.S. Forest Service now has the responsibility for wilderness management. It must preserve wildlife, forests, rivers, and fish while at the same time giving consideration to scenic trails and campsites. The Endangered Species Act of 1969 further enhanced its ability to preserve wildlife as well as the wilderness.

The two books are complementary in illustrating the trend away from laissez faire toward governmental management in the two areas discussed. Both books are well researched and make valuable contributions to a field of resource management, an area that becomes more critical every day of our national life.

FREDERICK H. SCHAPSMEIER
University of Wisconsin
Oshkosh

WILLIAMSON, JOHN B., LINDA EVANS, and LAWRENCE A. POWELL. *The Politics of Aging: Power and Policy.* Pp. xi, 331. Springfield, IL: Charles C Thomas. No price.

The Politics of Aging is a study of political gerontology and as such is an analysis of the power of older people as a group and individually and how this power is used to influence societal conditions. This topic is of increasing interest, since 11 percent of our population is now over 65 years of age and in 50 years it is projected that 18 percent of the population will be over 65.

The position of the elderly is traced historically, and Williamson and Evans note that with more stable, agriculturally based societies which had predictable food supplies, the position of the elderly in society improved. Surplus wealth and a culture which valued the meaning of the past enhanced the influence of the elderly, as did the advent of private property and the accumulation of assets. The elderly often controlled belief systems, information, and knowledge of rituals, and once in power, they often manipulated taboos to serve their own interests. In this manner, social power replaced physical power and vital information was kept secret, which further increased the status of the older guardians. In more recent times, the influence of the elderly peaked just prior to the Revolutionary War, since old people were seen, in the Calvinist perspective, as chosen by God. Industrial capitalism and urbanization contributed to a decrease in the influence of the elderly, but in the 1960s the emergence of power and influence could be seen in legislation, action groups, and national committees. It should be noted that in all discussions of increased influence of older people, women and poor older people were still powerless.

Williamson and Evans question modernization theory's explanation for the status of the elderly due to questionable methodological assumptions and selective reading of historical accounts. While the work of modernization theorists is critiqued, qualifications and specifications are noted which the authors believe increase the viability of the power of the theory to explain historical shifts in the relative power of the aged. A discussion of "Senior Power" seeks to combine "interest group pluralism" and "social movement perspectives" to explain and understand advances in the power of the elderly in this century. The result is a "coalition formation" approach which explains why policy gains for the elderly generally occur in conjunction with gains of other interest groups such as the poor, labor, and minorities.

The historical development of old age policy in the United States based on social principles in existence during three periods is examined. Familial power is analyzed using resource theory. As parental resources decline with increasing age, resources of offspring generally increase, thus increasing their relative power. The position of an extensive social control network which severely restrains the elderly is elaborated. Social Security, labeling, medicalization, and decarceration are all control mechanisms which devalue the aged and promote dependence. Gerontologists are identified as agents of social control by prolonging the identification of the elderly as a separate problem group, which results in increased dependency. Williamson and Evans believe that gerontologists have been remiss in exposing agents of social control and the beneficiaries of control. The final chapter analyzes political prospects for the future and the impact of the aged as a political force.

LES LEANNE HOYT CROFT
Wichita State University
Kansas

SOCIOLOGY

CASTEL, ROBERT, FRANCOISE CASTEL, and ANNE LOVELL. *The Psychiatric Society.* Translated by Arthur Goldhammer. Pp. xxiii, 358. New York: Columbia University Press, 1982. $24.95.

This is an unusual book, dealing with the U.S. psychiatric establishment, written by two French scholars, one a psychiatrist, the other a sociologist, in collaboration with an American psychiatrist. One reason for engaging in the study was that the United States is the most advanced nation in psychiatry, where every category of deviance and normality has its treatment modality.

Castel, Castel, and Lovell's objective is to explain what is taking place in American psychiatry and to warn against what might happen in Europe. They also seek to understand the logic of the process whereby human beings can be transformed into "targets of manipulative technologies" in today's industrial societies.

The work provides a review of nineteenth-century developments in mental health treatment, with more recent trends, including the 1950s movement to treat patients in community mental hygiene centers. The dream that comprehensive mental health services would be available for all persons in a community has not materialized in the last two decades. The authors see the discharge of seriously disturbed patients as being motivated by the need to reduce public spending and to increase private profits. Deinstitutionalization and collective care have been shown to be myths.

Working out of the three main centers of New York, Boston, and San Francisco, two of the authors spent more than a year in this country, with many interviews and access to records. Their bibliographic notes extend to 30 pages. The Castels's collaboration with Anne Lovell, an American experienced in mental hospital and prison reform, is reminiscent of Thomas and Znaniecki's fruitful cooperation on *The Polish Peasant* six decades ago. *The Psychiatric Society* is a highly objective and comprehensive survey of the U.S. mental health establishment, dealing with its larger role in the society, its relations with government and the private sector, the political forces that affect it and its norms, and issues regarding the future of the movement. A pertinent question concerns the relationship between psychiatry and social control mechanisms involving the power structure.

A chapter entitled "The Psychiatrization of Difference" shows how the treatment of delinquency, drug addiction, and alcoholism has been influenced by psychiatric approaches. Alternatives to psychiatry have met opposition combined with official strategies to embrace these alternatives.

This work merits, and will doubtless receive, recognition as a significant and provocative contribution to psychiatry in its larger social role.

JOHN E. OWEN

Arizona State University
Tempe

DRUCKMAN, DANIEL, RICHARD M. ROZELLE, and JAMES C. BAXTER. *Nonverbal Communication: Survey, Theory, and Research*. Pp. 264. Beverly Hills, CA: Sage Publications, 1982. $20.00. Paperbound, $9.95.

As Druckman, Rozelle, and Baxter tell us in their concluding remarks, the understanding of nonverbal behavior has a long history and is "one of psychology's oldest problems." The authors list Darwin and 1872 as their earliest date, but I trace this back to classical Greek mime and tragedy, at least.

The principal assumption of this interesting study is that "behavior derives its meaning from the broader context in which it is displayed." Therefore a great deal more than verbal speech goes into the actual communication between two persons, or more, on a private or more complex level of society as a whole, including its global relationships. The latter is a major focus of this particular investigation of nonverbal communication, as indicated early on in this quotation from Milburn:

> To function well together the superpowers need to be able to predict accurately the perceptions and responses of one another and, as a second-order perception, to understand that the messages that they as threat sources emit are thoroughly understood (p. 15).

Yet by the end, this study's conclusions carry a qualifier that suggests the superpowers may not be able to function too well, if that functioning is dependent on accurate prediction of nonverbal behavior: "Nonverbal behavior is clearly an area of human conduct sufficiently volitional to qualify as problematic to predict."

Another element of great significance, in relation to international politics and nonverbal communication, is variance in cultural factors. This important ingredient in the determination of meaning in communication between different national leaders and representatives receives a mere mention, without any exploration or careful treatment.

The main discussion of this book concerns five functions associated with nonverbal behaviors, as the authors perceive them: "to indicate prearticulated feelings, to provide clues to information-processing activities, to serve as emphases in persuasive appeals, to facilitate deception or holding back information, and to convey subtle messages." In general, the various studies documented and data provided have to do with "impression management" and not specifically with meaning in communication. Since the authors do manifest this interest and have turned to Goffman as a key resource, the whole subject of acting in relation to nonverbal communication and action should be a major part of the discussion; but it is not. I recommend in particular a study like Michael Goldmann's *The Actor's Freedom*.

At best, *Nonverbal Communication* alerts us to the more subtle ramifications of facial expressions, gestures, and so on, in daily communication involving tense, complex, and intricate social situations. This study points out, for example, that deception at least half the time in documented research is perceived as either honest or only evasive communication. But in other ways, the conclusions of this study belabor the obvious, as in the following: "Thus, whether or not an ambassador is successful in being deceptive, evasive, or honest may depend on the proper execution of nonverbal and verbal behaviors during an interview." Druckman, Rozelle, and Baxter are capable of giving their readers conclusions with more sophistication.

KAREN HERMASSI
University of California
Berkeley

HALEM, LYNNE CAROL. *Divorce Reform: Changing Legal and Social Perspectives*. Pp. xii, 340. New York: Free Press, 1980. $17.95.

In *Divorce Reform* we find one of the most comprehensive and historically insightful works to date. As Halem observes, a pervasive sense of impending disaster and a concern over the breakdown of the family have been evident since the time Christ said, "What therefore God has joined together, let not man put asunder." Throughout our history, divorce has been viewed as a pathological event which threatens one of our major institutions, the family, as well as the social fabric and order of the entire society. Perceptional definitions of divorce have determined societal views, all of which are negative and contain as a major consideration the notion of fault, the idea that a defect exists for which someone or something is to blame.

Halem traces the placing of blame through three important stages: moral, social, and psychopathological. When the divorce problem was attributed to morality, blame was placed on sinners, the problem was answered by punishment, and the legal reaction was an attempt to control divorce and its predecessor, marriage. The moral concept of the cause and effect of divorce was related to a functionalist view of the world. For society to be kept in balance and to continue to survive, individuals should be expected to suffer to benefit the common good.

The transition to viewing divorce as a social problem witnessed a shift in blame away from the individual and to social and economic factors such as industrialization, urbanization, and feminism. Individuals were increasingly seen as innocent victims and the role of the legal system was made to be that of a paternalistic guardian who would defend a victimized populace. Trial marriage and marriage contracts were proposed as measures to lower the divorce rate.

The psychopathological conception of divorce was micro in nature, returning culpability to the individual. Change, too large an undertaking for an entire society, was the responsibility of the divorcee, who was a maladjusted neurotic as a result of transitions in society. Psychotherapeutic treatment was seen as the solution and Freudian psychoanalysis was the avenue provided to help the misfits of divorce endure their individual turmoil. The legal system was expected to act as a therapeutic agent, a healer who administers treatment. A problem resulted, however, because the law relies on external sanctions to control behavior, whereas psychiatry stresses internal motivation for behavioral changes and the former is not considered effective treatment.

Legal changes in the area of divorce came not only from changes in attitudes, social and economic conditions, and input from the behavioral sciences, but also from an overburdened court system. Change was not always positive, as was the case during the period when theories of the social and behavioral sciences were reinterpreted as fact. While legal policies and practices changed with each ideological transformation, the idea that divorce was pathological and that remediation was possible remained as underlying tenets. The first significant modification in divorce codes in the twentieth century came with the advent of no-fault laws. Although no-fault laws failed to cause a decline in divorce rates or realistically address issues of divorce-related adjudication, there have been many positive consequences. Halem notes that the advent of no-fault divorce exposed legal abuses and inequities and made an attempt at redress, introduced new concepts of egalitarianism, brought law in theory closer to law in practice, and called attention to a very real need for reform, thereby serving as an impetus for change.

Halem's coverage of over 350 years of social, psychological, historical, and legal perceptions of divorce and the implications for reform is beyond the scope of any single extant work.

LES LEANNE HOYT CROFT
Wichita State University
Kansas

KEPLER, M. OLIVER. *Medical Stewardship: Fulfilling the Hippocratic Legacy.* Pp. xviii, 280. Westport, CT: Greenwood Press, 1981. $29.95.

Kepler's book is not that of an academic ethicist arguing over shades of meaning, but that of a medical practitioner who is deeply concerned by the marketplace mentality which has eroded the service and stewardship posture he believes should characterize the medical profession. A professor of family medicine at the Eastern Virginia Medical School, Kepler first delves into the philosophical and religious underpinnings of the meaning of medical stewardship. He then goes on to find great discrepancies between current medical practices and the legacy of service and responsibility contained in the Hippocratic tradition.

In the two initial chapters, Kepler traces the development of medical ethics from its Greek, Roman, Christian, and Arabic origins up to the American Medical Association's 1980 revision of its Code of Ethics. Eight appendices contain different codes of ethics and elaborations on patient's rights. He also looks at the meaning of the professional person as it has developed over time. In the two-page third chapter he defines the concept of medical stewardship by an analogy of a wheel with four spokes. At the hub of the wheel is the key idea—agape or philia, love which the medical profession, both as individuals and as complex organizations, should radiate to the world through the four spokes of responsibility, competence, discipline, and service.

In the next ten chapters Kepler uses these four cardinal principles flowing from the spirit of philia to expose what he considers wrong in U.S. medical education, organization of care, and the delivery of medical care. In doing so Kepler goes beyond the ethics of the doctor-patient relationship of focusing on such things as pulling the plug, although he does that too. But most important, he develops a social ethic of what individual doctors and organizations of doctors owe to the public welfare in terms of disciplining errant doctors, educating for humanitarian competence, organizing and financing care better to control abuses and excessive costs, and providing equal accessibility to medical care. He looks at responsible human experimentation, drug prescribing, relations among medical personnel, and many other topics.

While the book is occasionally deficient in citation, it should be required reading for all medical education students. The situation ethics of Kepler is fairminded and grounded in the religious tradition of service and stewardship and the professional tradition of competence and discipline. It is a wide-ranging and up-to-date book that appeals to the highest standards to elevate medicine beyond many of its current self-serving practices. This book reflects the wisdom and experience of a humane doctor that would provide an excellent stimulus to both doctors and patients if we are to reform thoughtfully our whole medical enterprise.

DUANE STROMAN

Juniata College
Huntingdon
Pennsylvania

LICATA, SALVATORE J. and ROBERT P. PETERSEN, eds. *Historical Perspectives on Homosexuality*. Pp. 235. New York: Hayworth Press/Stein and Day, 1981. $14.95.

This work publishes the Fall/Winter issue of the *Journal of Homosexuality*. Twelve well-written articles constitute a useful introduction to the complex subject of homosexuality in modern Western history. As Licata and Petersen suggest in their introduction, these articles reject simplistic perspectives that examine the history of homosexuality merely as a matter of deviance, illustrious homosexual individuals, or external victims.

As would be expected, definition proves to be a central issue in all the articles. Many questions cannot be escaped in any study of homosexuality. Is homosexuality only an invention of recent law and psychology? Is homosexuality, as K. J. Dover suggests in his *Greek Homosexuality*, not merely what is antithetical to the heterosexual, but a subdivision of the "quasi-sexual (or pseudo-sexual)"? How many types of homosexuality are there—male, female, child, a matter of identity or behavior, necessity, sale, or cultural choice and style? Who defines homosexuality at any given time, in any given culture—church, law, science, society, class, or literate and political homosexuals themselves?

In "Conceptions of Homosexuality and Sodomy in Western Europe," Arthur Gilbert finds the sources of the West's negative definition of homosexuality not only in its Judeo-Christian theological inheritance but in "Western civilization's association of the anus with evil, the devil, and bestiality." In "Sodomy and Heresy in Early Modern Switzerland," E. W. Monter suggests that Protestant and Catholic interest in homosexuality's perversity originated in times of crisis and was fed by orthodoxy's tendency to associate homosexuality with heresy and witchcraft.

Naturally the growing political societies and the law of early modern societies defined what was deviant. In "The Myth of Lesbian Impunity, Capital Laws from 1270 to 1791," Louis Crompton argues that "lesbian acts were regarded as legally equivalent to acts of male sodomy and were, like them, punishable by the death penalty." In "Ho Hum, Another Work of the Devil: Buggery and Sodomy in Early Stuart England," B. R. Burg challenges the proposition that law was intensely interested in trying acts of homosexuality, which were lumped with those of bestiality and homosexual child molestation under the heading "buggery."

The history of one encounter with the law is found in Brigitte Eriksson's translation "A Lesbian Execution in Germany, 1721." Catherina Margartheta Linck, after several serious bouts of religious enthusiasm and perpetual wanderings and military service disguised as a male, married and repeatedly sodomized her bride with a home-made leather penis. She was brought to trial. The trial was truly pathetic. It was a mixture of a bride's naivete, Catherina's sincere repentance, as well as a lot of early eighteenth-century moral theology, Saxon law, and psychological theories. Catherine Margartheta was sentenced to "death by the sword, in accordance with the gravity of her crimes."

What Michel Foucault said in general about sexuality's definition in modern history proved to be true about homosexuality in particular. Homosexuality lost much of its older religious and legal trappings in the eighteenth century—at least in the upper echelons of society—and it received new definitions under the inspiration of doctrines of earthly happiness, individualism, and privacy. Homosexuality was given new definitions in the nineteenth century. In his "Inverts, Perverts, and Mary-Annes: Male Prostitution and the Regulation of Homosexuality in England in the Nineteenth and Early Twentieth Centuries," Jeffrey Weeks shows "the ways in which the social and legal context dictated the close relationship between the homosexual subcultures and the cash nexus represented by the prostitution relationship," which itself was differentiated by sex, age, and class.

Unlike the progressive definition of homosexuality discussed in Hubert Kennedy's "The 'Third Sex' Theory of Karl Heinrich Ulrichs," not all redefinitions of homosexuality were enlightened. Science, medicine, sociology, and psychology, of course, can furnish the definitions for new inquisitions. Two articles on the Nazi treatment of homosexuals—Erwin Haeberl's "'Stigmata of Degeneration': Prisoner Markings in Nazi Concentration Camps" and Rudiger Lautmann's "The Pink Triangle: The Persecution of Homosexual Males in Concentration Camps in Nazi Germany"—reveal how the cruelest ideas of racism, in the hands of the state, can lead to systematic destruction of the unwanted.

However, pessimism generated by Nazi and other victimizations of homosexuals should not obscure the expanded rights, increased tolerance, and self-acceptance won by large sectors of the lesbian and gay communities in the Western world in this century. Salvatore Licata traces the stages of this advance in the United States in his "Homosexual Rights Movements in the United States."

This volume, with its annotated bibliography and book reviews, successfully meets its goal of suggesting how rich and fascinating is the field of homosexual history that awaits study. The question of sources is still to be solved, especially if we are to understand the practices, expressions, and judgments of homosexuality among Europe's rural masses and their urban counterpart. No doubt one popular approach to homosexuality will survey it as one pseudosexuality among many, explaining the various human, bodily, economic, social, cultural, and private functions it served.

JOSEPH A. AMATO
Southwest State University
Marshall
Minnesota

SHERMAN, MICHAEL and GORDON HAWKINS. *Imprisonment in America: Choosing the Future.* Pp. xi, 146. Chicago: University of Chicago Press, 1982. $15.00.

This book is an eminently rational appraisal of the serious position in which we find ourselves in the use of prison as punishment. Unlike many forecasters in social science, Sherman and Hawkins are well informed of the past—which is just as well in the field of corrections—and are clear that numbers, no matter how they are packaged, will not tell the future at all. Rather, a careful accounting of past mistakes and why they occurred, the authors suggest, will place us in a better position, not so much to tell the future but, they hope, to choose our future.

This is indeed an optimistic approach to the problem of prisons, the history of which, Sherman and Hawkins also realize, gives very little grounds for optimism. They recount how most, perhaps all, attempts at reforms in the past have failed, possibly in the worst way of all in bringing about conditions that were in many respects worse than those that the reformers were trying to correct. They report that despite a great deal of money spent on research, prisons cannot be shown to deter, either generally or specifically, nor do they have any consistent relationship with the crime rate. The only reasonable defense of prisons, they conclude, is that of incapacitation, even though they recognize that there are problems involved in predicting future behavior of offenders. However, they argue convincingly that these problems are outweighed by other moral considerations.

There is also an excellent chapter explaining the slippery notion of overcrowding and the variable nature of the notion of capacity of prisons. This chapter alone is worth the price of the book—a reasonable one for a hardcover these days.

The most important idea Sherman and Hawkins try to convey is that in the minds of the American public—and perhaps penologists—punishment has been equated with prison, and that people are unable to accept any other form of punishment such as probation, work release, and community service as alternatives to prison because they do not see them as punishments. Here, Sherman and Hawkins have almost, but not quite, made an important breakthrough in thinking about criminal punishment, but it seems they could not quite bring themselves to follow the logic of their position through to its conclusion. The main reason for this, I think, is that they tried to do a very difficult balancing act, by appealing both to those whom they thought of as liberals on the one hand and to those whom they regarded as conservative on the other. But in criminal justice, when one views policies in retrospect, it is notoriously difficult to figure out which side is which. The result is that the authors lose their way.

Their solution, in the long run, is that we should reduce the numbers in prison by imprisoning only violent offenders. Fair enough. But what punishments should be given the rest? Sherman and Hawkins advocate the usual well-worn punishments of work release, restitution—what about those who are indigent: would they get prison instead?—and the rest, not attending to the well-known drawbacks of each of these punishments. Nor do they recognize that these punishments may not be seen as punishments by the public, not because the public has equated punishment with prison, but simply because such programs are not punitive enough in and of themselves. Sherman and Hawkins then go on to compound their predicament by recommending, quite forcefully, that violent first offenders should be given stiff prison terms. So we have the ultimate self-defeating paradox: in their attempt to eliminate the equation of prison with punishments, they actually advocate more prison.

It is perhaps symptomatic of the preoccupation with prison as punishment that the authors wrote a book about prisons, when what they should have done, if they were serious about searching for alternatives to prison, was to have written a book about other punishments—all kinds of punishments—in search of those that could match prisons in seriousness. Until we face up to this task, prisons will continue to dominate in our society as the only serious punishment available to criminal justice.

However, in spite of this difficulty with the central theoretical thrust of the book, it is well worth reading. It is concise and clearly written. It issues a challenge to penologists and other policymakers in the field of corrections, claiming that there is a vacuum in the making of policy right now, and, agreeing with Romilly's advice to Bentham, that the public cares very little for crime or punishment. The authors argue that for those who do care, the opportunity to affect policy is always available.

While some might argue—I among them—that precisely because policymakers in corrections have not taken into account public feeling about crime and punishments, many of their reforms have failed, Sherman and Hawkins do issue an important challenge. Though they say their proposals are "modest," if adopted, they would have very serious effects. For example, if prison terms were strictly handed down for violent first offenders, my guess is that the already high proportion of minorities in prison would drastically increase. The crisis of criminal punishment does not call for modest proposals, for these will merely continue in slightly different form, the muck of the past.

Instead, the time is right for a clean break; a radical proposal that will turn past practices of criminal punishment on their heads. When will it come?

GRAEME R. NEWMAN
State University of New York
Albany

SIPES, RICHARD GREY. *Population Growth, Society, and Culture: An Inventory of Cross-Culturally Tested Causal Hypotheses.* Pp. vii, 126. New Haven, CT: Human Relations Area Files, 1980. $12.00. Paperbound, $6.00.

Little is really known about human fertility behavior, and much of what is thought to be known is not so. These are the conclusions of Sipes's empirical investigation of the relationship between the population growth rate in developing nations and 362 socio-cultural items said at one time or another to be involved in the relationship.

Some of the findings are commonplaces: the population growth rate will decrease as the value of children to parents decreases, as the need for a male or female heir for religious rituals decreases, as sex seen as recreation rather than procreation increases, as equality between sexes in sex regulations increases, and as women's freedom of movement increases.

Any "we already know it all" confidence is lost, however, when Sipes shows that these are among only 15 hypotheses strongly supported by the data in their originally predicted direction. On the other hand, 26 hypotheses turned out to be strongly supported, but in the opposite direction from that hypothesized. The more than 300 remaining hypotheses faded into unimportance because of weak support, no apparent effect, no significant evidence, or small sample size.

Sipes's orientation is that there is a so-called world population explosion, that the societies contributing most to it are the nonindustrialized ones which have experienced a reduction in mortality as a result of exposure to modern medicine and other technology, and that these societies are most in need of population control. Of these, the sample of 20 selected for his study were the Chagga, Comilla, Dusun, Dyak, Ganda, Iban, Kalinga, Kikuyu, Lugbara, Nayar, Panajachel, Papago, Samoan, Sotho, Swazi, Telugu, Tepotzlán, Toda, Tzintzuntzan, and Zuñi.

Although Sipes is intellectually committed to the hologeistic method, he is careful in pointing out the limitations of his data: area-limited because there are no societies represented from South America, and type-limited because only nonindustrialized sedentary societies are used. Tepoztlán and Tzintzuntzan, two of the 20 societies in his sample, he came to believe had erroneous population growth rate values assigned and hence some tabulations are based on only the remaining 18 societies. There is a problem with the map on page 32 which shows the geographic distribution of the sample societies. It includes the Hopi, who are not among his 20, and omits the Kikuyu who are.

Social scientists are the readers for whom Sipes intended this report of his ambitious and important project. The dissertation-like structure of his slender book—introduction, method, data collection, test results, conclusion—may discourage potential readers. Sipes's extensive explanation and defense of his methodology, along with an account of his experiences in data-gathering—

experiences apparently new to Sipes but familiar to demographers—add to the academic tone of the presentation.

A supplement, three times the length of this volume, is being published separately. It contains the coding protocol, trait codings, and data on the 12 quality control tests.

FREDERICK B. LINDSTROM
Arizona State University
Tempe

TURNER, BRYAN S. *For Weber: Essays on the Sociology of Fate*. Pp. x, 408. Boston: Routledge & Kegan Paul, 1981. $30.00.

Sociologists have long tended to treat Marx and Weber as having established profoundly discrepant foundations for social analysis. Whether Weber has been seen as having devised his own schemas in deliberate opposition to historical materialism or as having developed them with minimal reference to Marx, almost all scholars—whether Weberian, Marxian, or otherwise—have agreed that Weberian sociology is deeply at odds with Marxian sociology over many basic theoretical issues. Indeed, the line between Marxian and Weberian thought has at times been treated as the primary axis of differentiation in the formation of sociological thought.

Bryan Turner's wide-ranging collection of essays develops a revisionist challenge to this common view. Writing from within the camp of British neo-Marxism, Turner argues that Weber's theoretical ideas are essential for carrying forward the Marxian analysis of modern social conditions. Turner's Weber is one whose typological schemas add precision and variety to Marx's conception of structure, whose analysis of prebendalism in Oriental societies complements Marx's treatment of the Asiatic mode of production, whose discussions of theodicy, class bases of religious and ideological ethics, the routinization of charisma, and the secularization of modern culture provide new insight into matters of superstructure, and whose indictments of the emerging twentieth-century civilization made him the "Jeremiah of modern capitalism." For Turner, the neo-Marxists who have resisted the use of Weber's insights have been fated to reenact various facets of his intellectual role, but usually with less vision and clarity of analysis.

Turner's scholarship is serious, catholic in scope, and diverse in its modalities. His essays include critiques of the ways in which Weber's work has been regarded in French structural Marxism and in the Frankfurt School; general interpretation of Weber's sociology of religion; explications of Weber's treatment of the dynamic tensions between feudal and prebendal elements of premodern structures of authority; a consideration of the ways in which Weber's comparative studies drew on the Orientalist scholarship of the nineteenth century; and critical examination of recent research on the rise of early capitalism and the transformation into late capitalism. In passing, many specific matters are discussed with impressive insight, such as the religious coloring of the ethic Florence Nightingale developed as a foundation for secular nursing, the articulations of economic and political factors in the traditional structuring of Iranian society, the Orientalism of the standard scholarship on which Weber depended, and some limitations of A. G. Frank's views on underdevelopment in the non-Western world.

On some other matters, Turner, despite his thoughtfulness, seems to go astray. He is certainly right to underline Weber's emphasis on the class and status interests conditioning all religious beliefs, but not to overlook the respects in which class and status relations are themselves shaped by the institutional workings of religious ethics. Thus in trying to counter a standard emphasis on the prominence of religious ideals in Weber's thought, Turner falls into the position of not being able to account deeply for the differences in practical and ethical situations of Brahmins,

Mandarins, Islamic prebendalists, Puritan capitalists, and so on. In explicating the Orientalism taken over by Weber from prior scholarship, he neglects the decisive break Weber made by treating Indian, Chinese, and Islamic civilizations as fully independent cases—as different from one another as from the West—rather than simply as variant manifestations of an Asiatic form of society. An interesting discussion of the problem of English common law for Weber's theory of capitalist development overlooks the strongest solution—namely, that Weber failed to grasp the formal rationality grounded in the procedures of common law, a rationality that played a positive role in English development and a still greater role in American development.

The effort to redefine the relations between Marxian and Weberian scholarship in a new spirit of cooperation is as commendable as it is overdue. Turner is to be thanked for the boldness of his revisionism in this regard. Those of us who view the revision from outside neo-Marxism will want to be on guard, however, against pressures to simplify Weberian theory to assure its fit with Marxian theory. Turner places great stress, especially for Asian societies, on the respects in which Weber's sociology of authority is an essential complement to Marx's analysis of modes of production. It is not a bad insight. If emphasized inordinately, though, it will tear apart the rich texture of theory that Weber used to interrelate the principal independent, irreducible dimensions of social life.

VICTOR LIDZ
University of Pennsylvania
Philadelphia

ZIMRING, FRANKLIN. *The Changing Legal World of Adolescence*. Pp. xvi, 208. New York: Free Press, 1982. $14.95.

In 160 cogent pages, this book contends that adolescence, the period between childhood and adulthood, should cease to exist in the law as though it were completed entirely on a single birthday. Instead, Zimring would legislate it as a sequence of phases, each bounded by changes in various rights, responsibilities, or entitlements at different ages. For some matters, change would also require satisfactory performance on tests of competence, notably driving. Following these pages and not tightly linked to them is a 41-page appendix, called "An Introduction to Legal Reasoning," that consists of excerpts from a 1977 U.S. Supreme Court case, Carey, Governor of New York, et al. v. Population Services et al. In it, the justices, with some dissent, declared unconstitutional a New York law that prohibited, among other things, sale or distribution of contraceptives to minors under age 16.

With a steady stream of apt examples, quotations, and epigrammatic phrases, Zimring argues elegantly the case for guiding policy by the goal of "doing less harm." This benefits-minus-costs standard readily justifies laws outlawing sexual intercourse, exposure to pornography, and cosmetic or dental surgery without parental consent to 12-year-olds, but permits their receiving contraceptives or treatment for venereal disease without their parents being informed. His "jurisprudence of semi-autonomy" would give adolescents "a learning permit" to practice many adult roles with some restrictions and perhaps without being held fully responsible for their mistakes, before becoming fully grown up legally.

That his principles are often not easily applied, Zimring illustrates well by a chapter on strategies to discourage smoking by teenagers. It concludes that a smoking lounge should be banned in junior high schools, probably also in high schools, but certainly not in universities. He points out that many of his specific recommendations are already established by custom, statute, or court decision but contends that their analysis by his perspectives will help to resolve the many other continually emerging controversies in the future legal world of adolescence.

This book is remarkably comprehensive in summarizing pertinent law, history, and sociology but surprisingly neglectful of the most prominent controversies today in the author's specialty of criminal law, such as when a juvenile lawbreaker should be processed in the adult criminal courts, and when juvenile court records should be available to adult courts. Nevertheless, he lays a strong foundation for addressing these and many other questions, notably by such tenets as "Whenever state or parental regulation is harming more than helping, policy should probably be changed," but "The civil right not to be gratuitously harmed is one we owe to all children of all ages."

DANIEL GLASER
University of Southern California
Los Angeles

ECONOMICS

BOSWORTH, BARRY P. and ROBERT Z. LAWRENCE. *Commodity Prices and the New Inflation.* Pp. xiii, 215. Washington, DC: Brookings Institution, 1982. $24.95. Paperbound, $9.95.

"When the international price of sugar goes up, the price of candy goes up, but when the sugar price falls, candy prices don't. That's how commodity price fluctuations bring about inflation." Right? No. Wrong—or in any case irrelevant—according to Bosworth and Lawrence.

In modern industrial economies, wages and the prices of many finished goods tend to be sluggish. In these fixed-price markets, much of the short-run response to external changes is through variations in output and employment levels. When commodity prices rise sharply, policymakers face a dilemma. If they opt for tight monetary and fiscal policies to prevent the general price level from rising as a result of the commodity price rise, the result is likely to be falling employment and output in the rigid-price sectors of the economy. President Ford quickly abandoned his Whip Inflation Now (WIN) program for this reason. On the other hand, if loose monetary and fiscal policies are chosen, the economy is subject to unexpected inflation, which has its own costs, particularly since this transitory surge in inflation may become embedded in the economy through the wage-price spiral.

Bosworth and Lawrence suggest that the large fluctuations in commodity prices in the 1970s became major sources of instability for the economy as a whole in the manner described above. Their solution to the dilemma is to attack the problem at the source: use microeconomic policies to stabilize commodity prices.

While their arguments are generally plausible, there remains a major methodological weakness in their approach to the problem: the commodity markets are not explicitly linked to a well-defined macroeconomic model of the economy. This is not an easy task, but in the absence of such a link, their specific results become suspect. This becomes most apparent in their analysis of the contribution of commodity price increases to inflation (Chapter 3), as the authors themselves seem to indicate (see the last part of the footnote on page 45).

Bosworth and Lawrence's solution is elegant but difficult to implement, which they recognize. My analysis of UNCTAD's proposal to stabilize the prices of primary commodities found that large amounts of capital and stocks are needed for successful stabilization (Mathur, Ph.D. dissertation, MIT, 1980).

These difficulties suggest that in the long run the appropriate policy prescription is to go to the true source of the problem: the fact that so many markets in today's economies are fixed-price instead of flexible-price. How to transform fixed-price markets into flexible-price markets would clearly require at least another book, but it is surprising that Bosworth and Lawrence failed to mention this possibility.

In spite of these weaknesses, this book is a major contribution to our understanding of the effects of commodity prices on inflation. Further, the book is refreshingly free of jargon.

SUBODH C. MATHUR
American University
Washington, DC

CARRON, ANDREW S. *The Plight of the Thrift Institutions.* Pp. x, 96. Washington, DC: Brookings Institution, 1982. $10.95. Paperbound, $4.95.

In 1981 there were 4613 savings and loan associations, 463 mutual savings banks, and 21,915 credit unions in the United States. According to Andrew Carron, between 609 and 1076 of the savings and loan associations could soon find themselves in an untenable position, unable to break even without drastic cost-cutting, good fortune, or government aid. A much smaller share of mutual savings banks will find themselves in this situation, while credit unions do not appear to face such serious difficulties.

How the savings and loan associations and mutual savings banks reached this situation of distress is the subject of Andrew Carron's monograph. The lesson appears to be that when regulations are truly constraining, serious problems result; when regulations are relatively unimportant, economic activity can proceed without dislocation.

The Federal Reserve Board regulates the maximum rates that commercial banks and thrift institutions—savings and loan associations, mutual savings banks, and credit unions—may pay on deposits. Until the late 1970s, these rate ceilings were generally competitive with market interest rates. In addition, the return on assets, mainly mortgages, was well above the cost of funds. After 1977 this relationship no longer held. Further, the rapid growth of new unregulated money market mutual funds contributed to a net outflow of funds from savings and loan associations and mutual savings banks. Unfortunately, these thrift institutions were unable to adjust their assets, mainly mortgage loans outstanding, as quickly as their cost of raising funds. They were locked into fixed-rate mortgages bearing yields consistent with market rates of the past, rates much lower than the current cost of raising funds.

The basic problem, then, is one of a maturity imbalance—between assets and liabilities—for financial intermediaries. Current policies are designed to address this problem, such as the elimination of deposit interest rate ceilings, variable rate mortgages, mergers, and changes in the types of loans that may be extended by thrift institutions.

Carron outlines the web of government regulations that has constrained the thrift industry. He provides a clear analysis of why these policies have created the current plight of the thrift institutions. He makes use of data from the Federal Home Loan Bank Board to analyze approximately 4000 savings and loan associations, and data from the Federal Deposit Insurance Corporation to analyze approximately 320 mutual savings banks. The empirical model estimated with these data is used to forecast the income statements and balance sheets of thrifts under a variety of assumptions about the future of interest rates, and deposit-rate ceilings. This model yields the estimates of numbers of institutions in distress noted above.

Having examined the historical context and prospects for the near future, Carron turns to a careful examination of the policy alternatives. He examines various forms of direct assistance, as well as changes in regulatory policy. The analysis is clear and the book well worth reading. The reader is left with a serious question unanswered, however. In the present context, is there a role for such a segmented financial market? In other words, what are the social costs and benefits of maintaining a separate sector of the financial markets whose major focus is residential financing?

GERALD S. GOLDSTEIN
Northwestern University
Evanston
Illinois

DE SAINT PHALLE, THIBAUT. *Trade, Inflation and the Dollar*. Pp. 418. New York: Oxford University Press, 1981. $24.95.

At the end of World War II, the United States emerged as the world's preeminent power, politically and economically. Thirty years later, the United States can no longer claim to be the best in everything. The Europeans and Japanese have built up tremendous economic power, and the Soviet Union is a major challenger in the military-diplomatic arena. The decade of the 1970s brought us many sudden and often traumatic changes that have made us recognize our position in an altered international environment. As we enter the decade of the 1980s, the painful task of devising new approaches to the problems that plague us is under way. This book, by a former director of the Export-Import Bank, is a useful guide to an understanding of our economic difficulties, especially in the international front.

The book begins with a summary of the basic balance of payments concepts. The chronic deficit suffered by the United States in its balance of payments in recent years is due to the changing nature of international trade and finance, especially the role played by energy trade, a topic de Saint Phalle discusses in Chapter 3. The United States gradually reduced its domestic production and turned into a net importer, adding to the strain in balance of payments. Such a turn of events is partly attributed to "inconsistent, unproductive, and costly" governmental regulations in energy matters. In order to reduce the pressure on the balance of payments, as well as to ensure long-term energy security, de Saint Phalle advocates a policy of stimulating domestic production and reducing imports. He carefully examines the various energy policy options and discusses the problems in developing oil, natural gas, and coal. The setback suffered by the nuclear industry, however, is not examined in depth. He sees the problem in the nuclear power industry as one of "national attitude," leading to a "grievously damaged" position for the U.S. nuclear trade. The reason seems to be his perception of competition with the Europeans in nuclear technology. De Saint Phalle argues that if the United States lags behind, the Europeans will catch up, taking away this market. Supporting continued funding for the Clinch River breeder project, he makes the argument that if we do not do it, the French would and "the United States could well end up importing breeders from France," as though that would be an act of national disgrace. At this time, due to dramatic political changes, all countries are examining the viability of the nuclear option, and a final verdict may not be in for quite some time.

In Chapter 4, the various phases through which the world monetary system went are traced. The gold standard, the postwar IMF system established in 1944 with the inspiration of J. M. Keynes, its breakdown in the late 1960s, attempts to revive it in the 1970s, the European version of the IMF system called the "European Monetary System," and the currently prevalent dirty float or managed currency system are discussed with an eye for detail as well as balance. De Saint Phalle sees the problem suffered by the international monetary system as basically due to the U.S. overexpansion of money supply which kept feeding dollars into the unwary international financial system. It was inevitable, therefore, that the value of the dollar collapsed, along with the IMF system, which was based on the ability of the dollar to maintain its credibility as the key currency. Worldwide inflation is also partly attributable to this dollar proliferation. De Saint Phalle's solution reflects the monetarist diagnosis: curb the growth of money. "The decision to shrink world monetary expansion," he writes, "starting with the U.S. dollar has, sooner or later, to be made." Failure to institute such a control, he warns, is likely to lead to "total collapse" of the capitalist system. One way to avoid collapse is to replace the dollar with a new "currency that is not subject to control" by any one nation. De Saint Phalle, however, has no specific suggestion as to how to bring that about, except to say: "Maximum cooperation in international money matters. . . . comes from mutual dependence, with shared responsibility, shared risk-taking, and shared benefits." It is not clear what form the cooperation is supposed to take. He is perhaps referring to the existing international economic-financial bureaucratic organizations. These institutions, like the IMF, World Bank, Inter-American Development Bank, and so on, are discussed in Chapter 6, mostly in an approving fashion. They do provide a framework within which cooperation can take place.

Cooperation is the underlying theme of the book. On East-West trade, trade with the People's Republic of China, the North-South dialogue, trade with the Third World countries and Marxist regimes, de Saint Phalle's approach is cooperation rather than confrontation. On the clamor over the controversial North-South issues, he advocates bringing in "practical businessmen with international experience" to ensure a cooperative approach—a worthwhile suggestion indeed, although the Third World representatives may not be very receptive to the idea in view of the highly political nature of the debate at this time.

One threat to cooperative international trade relation is the rising tide of protectionism. De Saint Phalle is forthright in his criticism of this economic dimension of nationalism. Arguing against governmental interference in free trade, he appeals to American "tenacity" and "long-range self-interest" to resist protectionism and maintain international competitiveness. He makes it clear that he is not in favor of using economic tools, like the embargo, to gain international political ends.

Clearly, de Saint Phalle takes what is known as the liberal international businessman's position. He does make a good case for it. Avoiding polemics, he takes a pragmatic posture toward the economic challenges that lie ahead. Policymakers and businessmen will find many useful insights in this book that may prove helpful in charting their strategy for the future.

K. V. NAGARAJAN
Susquehanna University
Selinsgrove
Pennsylvania

MACAROV, DAVID. *Worker Productivity: Myths and Reality*. Pp. 224. Beverly Hills, CA: Sage Publications, 1982. $20.00. Paperbound, $9.95.

This book concludes that money is the most effective work motivator. That takes three pages. The bulk of the book is an iconoclastic review of the history of productivity research.

First it underlines the importance of work in Western values, the pervasiveness of the work ethic. Second, it traces the historical shift of interest in productivity from reducing labor to increasing output. Third, it reviews the contribution of three successive approaches to increasing productivity: the scientific management school—Taylorism and all that; the human relations school, including the studies of Frederick Herzberg and others distinguishing between satisfactions and dissatisfactions from work; and finally, the structuralist school, combining scientific management and human relations approaches.

Macarov's critique of many decades of research is devastating. He shows that the Hawthorne experiments, from which the human relations school derives, were badly, if not fatally, flawed. The Herzberg-type studies demonstrating a disjunction between sources of work satisfaction and work dissatisfaction assume but do not establish a relation between either and productivity. Reviewing the job redesign movement aimed at job enlargement and enrichment which stands Taylorism on its head, Macarov recognizes that many workers do not want more responsibility or more complex and challenging tasks. It, too, is founded on the fallacy that work satisfaction translates into higher productivity.

Macarov reports on his study of an Israeli kibbutz, where monetary incentives can be ignored, and finds confirmation of the disjunction between sources of work satisfaction and dissatisfaction. But he finds no relation between them and work behavior, or between human relations at work and under- or overworking.

He finds a relation between work satisfaction and productivity only in service industries, not in goods-producing industries. But he discovers no persuasive evidence of the directionality of causation.

At this point, the book, heretofore tightly structured, careens in diverse directions. Having failed to find adequate explanations for productivity differences in any of the schools reviewed, Macarov points out that workers bring different predispositions to work and hence will respond differently to the same situation and will behave differently whatever management may do. He suggests work personalities as possible explanations of behavior, and sketches possible determinants thereof: age, education, birth order, religion, class, child care patterns. This terrain, though much traveled, remains poorly mapped. Continuing the search for work motivations, he informs us in the penultimate chapter that money is the most important of them all.

In counterpoint, we are told that it does not matter much that we do not understand the springs of labor productivity because it is not that important—labor contributes only 10-25 percent of the increase in productivity anyway. This historical perspective is no consolation to the typical business decision maker for whom labor is the most important cost. Worker productivity itself is no longer terribly important because we are headed pell-mell toward a workless society run by automata. A casual look at trends in labor force participation rates should dispel this perennial mirage. Concern with productivity is but a reflection of an obsolescent work ethic which itself is only a myth. Whatever their attitudes toward work in the abstract, most workers in practice dislike their work, want more leisure, and would choose to work less at less pay. This belittling of productivity is based on dubious inferences, if not on dubious evidence. But it should not detract from the genuine merits of the book, which is an interesting and far-ranging survey of what we thought we knew about worker productivity, whose most valuable conclusion is that we still have much to learn.

CHARLES T. STEWART
George Washington University
Washington, DC

SCHAFER, ROBERT and HELEN F. LADD. *Discrimination in Mortgage Lending.* Pp. ix, 407. Cambridge: MIT Press, 1982. $40.00.

The principle that mortgage lenders should not discriminate on grounds of race, sex, religion, or age is now embodied in law. This book tests for mortgage lending discrimination in California and New York. Schafer and Ladd conclude that mortgage lenders do not discriminate on the basis of sex or age but do on race.

State-of-the-art econometric techniques—which can in theory detect discrimination—are used and results are meticulously reported. This does not mean that the study is flawless. Quite the contrary. The technique is very much dependent on the available data.

To detect discrimination, Schafer and Ladd regress mortgage lending decisions to accept or reject an application—and the terms granted—against borrower characteristics, including proscribed ones, as well as property and neighborhood characteristics. The critical failure is the lack of adequate data on neighborhood characteristics. These are important because they determine whether the owner-occupant has an incentive to maintain property or whether neighborhood deterioration makes such investment unwise. If so, the lender is at risk of property value decline due to neighborhood decline, as well as to deterioration in the property itself, if default occurs. And default is more likely when property value declines, since the owner's equity is diminished perhaps to zero. Thus the lender rightly resists granting loans in declining areas.

Unfortunately for their results' validity, Schafer and Ladd provide inadequate measures of neighborhood conditions. The variables used are often insignificant and/or have the wrong signs. The finding of racial discrimination may very well be spurious, since race of borrower is correlated with neighborhood condition.

The book's purview is narrow. The authors do not discuss issues such as why irrational discrimination would persist in competitive profit-oriented markets. Nor do they consider the effect of their proposed solution: penalizing institutions found guilty of discrimination with the use of regression techniques and limited neighborhood data. The need for lending institutions to accept risky loans or to defend themselves against false charges of discrimination will burden central-city lending institutions more than those in the suburbs. Since capital is mobile, these are the institutions which are likely to close or simply not grow. As a result, already scarce and expensive mortgage credit will become even more scarce and expensive for the urban poor whom such sanctions are designed to aid.

SUSAN M. WACHTER
University of Pennsylvania
Philadelphia

WHYNES, DAVID K. and ROGER A. BOWLES. *The Economic Theory of the State.* Pp. xv, 236. New York: St. Martin's Press, 1981. $27.50.

David K. Whynes and Roger A. Bowles attempt to generate insights on the development of the state by applying economic models to political behavior. The formation and growth of the state—an association of individuals conforming to social rules laid down and enforced by a social decision maker with a monopoly of power within a defined territory—are explored by considering individual action—"the constrained optimisation of an objective function"—and collective action—using the "theory of the firm"—under conditions of uncertainty—using game theory. Assuming that a major objective of the system is "to generate a stream of consumption benefits" to individuals over time under conditions of scarcity, the specification of private and public property rights enables cooperative and thereby efficient interaction to predominate. The state settles disputes about specification, sets relations where bargaining costs are prohibitive, and enforces obligations to prevent cheating.

After a discussion of collective decision-making systems, the principal dynamic for state development—political response to market failure—is analyzed. Problems of monopoly, public goods, externalities, and uncertainty prompt nonmarket processes to emerge. Understanding these relations in economic terms enhances analysis of structural and operational matters: separation of powers, bureaucratic accountability, federalism, and international affairs.

This book is uneven; clear exposition is mixed with digression and confusing presentation. This is essentially a matter of analytic style and organization for which the conventions of the economics literature bear principal responsibility. Development of the central theoretical argument is not sustained; rather, conceptual tools are demonstrated to have a catalogue of interesting uses. The internal footnoting system provides more characters than a Russian novel;

each citation includes in the text a synopsis of the full model and distracts attention from the basic analysis. While sometimes technically sophisticated, the book often treats political, scientific, and philosophical models too simplistically and often seems content to show that good economic analysis can reinvent the wheel. Indeed, there is recurring defensiveness over comparisons with philosophical analysis—characterizing the state of nature as a philosopher's fairytale and explaining a "lack of clear conclusions" by economics' reluctance to imitate philosophers and "feed in some strong value judgements."

Several fascinating problems are raised: separation of powers, accountability and discretion, modes of international association, and biological determinants of human behavior—altruism or selfishness. Unfortunately, the attempt to develop a comprehensive economic theory of the state has generated a serious opportunity cost: depth has been sacrificed.

JAMES E. LENNERTZ

Lafayette College
Easton
Pennsylvania

OTHER BOOKS

ADELMAN, JONATHAN R., ed. *Communist Armies in Politics.* Pp. xi, 225. Boulder, CO: Westview Press, 1982. $22.00.

ASHBY, ERIC and MARY ANDERSON. *The Politics of Clean Air.* Pp. viii, 178. New York: Clarendon Press, Oxford University Press, 1981. $34.50.

BAILEY, VICTOR, ed. *Policing and Punishment in Nineteenth Century Britain.* Pp. 248. New Brunswick, NJ: Rutgers University Press, 1981. $23.00.

BALAAM, DAVID N. and MICHAEL J. CAREY, eds. *Food Politics: The Regional Conflict.* Pp. ix, 246. Totowa, NJ: Allanheld Osmun and Co., 1981. $29.75.

BAY, EDNA G., ed. *Women and Work in Africa.* Pp. xiv, 310. Boulder, CO: Westview Press, 1982. $18.50.

BERGER, ARTHUR ASA. *Media Analysis Techniques.* Pp. 160. Beverly Hills, CA: Sage Publications, 1982. $15.00. Paperbound, $7.95.

BERKI, R. N. *On Political Realism.* Pp. vi, 282. London, England: J. M. Dent & Sons, 1981. $27.50.

BEST, GARY DEAN. *To Free a People: American Jewish Leaders and the Jewish Problem in Eastern Europe, 1890-1914.* Pp. xi, 240. Westport, CT: Greenwood Press, 1982. $27.50.

BLAIR, PHILIP M. *Federalism and Judicial Review in West Germany.* Pp xiii, 332. New York: Clarendon Press, Oxford University Press, 1981. $65.00.

BLAND, LARRY I., ed. *The Papers of George Catlett Marshall, Vol. 1.* Pp. xxx, 742. Baltimore, MD: Johns Hopkins University Press, 1981. $30.00.

BONOSKY, PHILLIP. *Are Our Moscow Reporters Giving Us the Facts About the USSR?* Pp. 262. Moscow, Russia: Progress Publishers, 1981. Distributed by Imported Publications, Chicago. $7.00.

BORUS, MICHAEL E., C. GREGORY BUNTZ, and WILLIAM R. TAXH. *Evaluating the Impact of Health Programs: A Primer.* Pp. xv, 147. Cambridge, MA: MIT Press, 1982. $20.00. Paperbound, $9.95

BULMER, MARTIN. *The Uses of Social Research: Social Investigation in Public Policy-Making.* Pp. xiv, 184. Winchester, MA: Allen & Unwin, 1982. $28.50. Paperbound, $12.50.

BURKHAUSER, RICHARD V. and KAREN C. HOLDEN, eds. *A Challenge to Social Security: The Changing Roles of Women and Men in American Society.* Pp. xxii, 272. New York: Academic Press, 1982. $27.50.

BURTON, ORVILLE VERNON and ROBERT C. McMATH, JR., eds. *Class, Conflict, and Consensus: Antebellum Southern Community Studies.* Pp. xxvi, 308. Westport, CT: Greenwood Press, 1982. $29.95.

CAIDEN, GERALD E. and HEINRICH SIEDENTOPF, eds. *Strategies for Administration Reform.* Pp. xv, 246. Lexington, MA: Lexington Books, D. C. Heath, 1982. $26.95.

CARLTON, DAVID and CARLO SCHAERF, eds. *The Hazards of the International Energy Crisis.* Pp. xviii, 206. New York: St. Martin's Press, 1982. $22.50.

CARSON, W. G. *The Other Price of Britain's Oil: Safety and Control in the North Sea.* Pp. xi, 320. New Brunswick, NJ: Rutgers University Press, 1982. $24.00.

CHAPMAN, RICHARD A. and J. R. GREENAWAY. *The Dynamics of Administrative Reform.* Pp. 249. London, England: Croom Helm, 1980. $37.50.

CLAWSON, ROBERT W. and LAWRENCE S. KAPLAN, eds. *The Warsaw Pact: Political Purpose and Military Means.* Pp. xxv, 297. Wilmington, DE: Scholarly Resources, 1982. $19.95. Paperbound, $9.95.

COOPER, TERRY L. *The Responsible Administrator: An Approach to Ethics for the Administrative Role.* Pp. viii, 175. Port Washington, NY: Kennikat Press, 1982. $17.50.

CORTNER, RICHARD C. *The Bureaucracy in Court: Commentaries and Case Studies in Administrative Law.*

Pp. vii, 220. Port Washington, NY: Kennikat Press, 1982. $25.00.

COWLING, KEITH. *Monopoly Capitalism.* Pp. 200. New York: Halsted Press, 1982. $25.95.

DAHMUS, JOSEPH. *Seven Medieval Historians.* Pp. xvi, 323. Chicago, IL: Nelson-Hall, 1982. $20.95.

DAVIES, NORMAN. *God's Playground: A History of Poland in Two Volumes. Vol. 1.* Pp. xxxiii, 605. New York: Columbia University Press, 1982. $60.00 set; $35.00 ea.

DAVIES, NORMAN. *God's Playground: A History of Poland in Two Volumes. Vol. II.* Pp. xxvii, 725. New York: Columbia University Press, 1982. $60.00 set; $35.00 ea.

DENKTASH, RAUF. *The Cyprus Triangle.* Pp. 222. Winchester, MA: K. Rustem & Bro. and George Allen & Unwin, 1982. $17.95.

DOCKES, PIERRE. *Medieval Slavery and Liberation.* Pp. vii, 291. Chicago, IL: University of Chicago Press, 1982. $27.00.

DONINI, ANTONIO O. and JOSEPH A. NOVACK, eds. *Origins and Growth of Sociological Theory: Readings on the History of Sociology.* Pp. 195. Chicago, IL: Nelson-Hall, 1982. $19.95. Paperbound, $9.95.

DUNCAN, COLIN. *Low Pay—Its Causes, and the Post-War Trade Union Response.* Pp. xv, 159. New York: John Wiley & Sons, 1981. $41.95.

EELLS, ROBERT and BARTELL NYBERG. *Lonely Walk: The Life of Senator Mark Hatfield.* Pp. 201. Portland, OR: Multnomah Press, 1979. $8.95.

EGAN, CLIFFORD L. and ALEXANDER W. KNOTT, eds. *Essays in Twentieth Century American Diplomatic History Dedicated to Professor Daniel M. Smith.* Pp. xii, 225. Washington, DC: University Press of America, 1982. $20.75. Paperbound, $10.50.

FAINSTEIN, NORMAN I. and SUSAN S. FAINSTEIN, eds. *Urban Policy Under Capitalism.* UAAR, Vol. 22. Pp. 303. Beverly Hills, CA: Sage Publications, 1982. $22.50. Paperbound, $9.95.

FESHARAKI, FEREIDUN et al. *Critical Energy Issues in Asia and the Pacific: The Next Twenty Years.* Pp. xvi, 314. Boulder, CO: Westview Press, 1982. $23.00.

FEUER, LEWIS S. *Einstein and the Generations of Science, Second Edition.* Pp. xlvii, 374. New Brunswick, NJ: Transaction Books, 1982. $12.95.

FISHKIN, JAMES S. *The Limits of Obligation.* Pp. viii, 184. New Haven, CT: Yale University Press, 1982. $18.50.

FITZSIMMONS, STEPHEN J. and ABBY J. FREEDMAN. *Rural Community Development.* Pp. xvi, 524. Cambridge, MA: Abt Books, 1981. $28.00.

FONER, PHILIP S. and SALLY M. MILLER, eds. *Kate Richards O'Hare: Selected Writings and Speeches.* Pp. 363. Baton Rouge, LA: Louisiana State University Press, 1982. $35.00. Paperbound, $9.95.

FRANKLIN, JOHN HOPE and AUGUST MEIER, eds. *Black Leaders of the Twentieth Century.* Pp. xi, 372. Urbana, IL: University of Illinois Press, 1982. $19.95.

FRIEDMAN, EDWARD, ed. *Ascent and Decline in the World System.* Pp. 303. Beverly Hills, CA: Sage Publications, 1982. $25.00. Paperbound, $12.50.

GALNOOR, ITZHAK. *Steering the Polity: Communication and Politics in Israel.* Pp. xii, 411. Beverly Hills, CA: Sage Publications, 1982. $25.00.

GALPERIN, GEORGI. *Ethiopia: Population, Resources, Economy.* Translated by J. Shapiro. Pp. 286. Moscow, Russia: Progress Publishers, 1982. Distributed by Imported Publications, Chicago. $7.00.

GANSLER, JACQUES S. *The Defense Industry.* Pp. 346. Cambridge, MA: MIT Press, 1982. Paperbound, $9.95.

GEORGE, PETER. *The Emergence of Industrial America: Strategic Factors in American Economic Growth Since 1870.* Pp. xii, 242. Albany, NY: State University of New York Press, 1982. $33.50. Paperbound, $10.95.

GERGEN, KENNETH J., MARTIN S. GREENBERG, and RICHARD H. WILLIS. *Social Exchange: Advances in Theory and Research.* Pp. xviii, 306. New York: Plenum Press, 1980. No price.

GERMINO, DANTE. *Political Philosophy and the Open Society.* Pp. 190. Baton Rouge, LA: Louisiana State University Press, 1982. No price.

GIDDENS, ANTHONY and DAVID HELD, eds. *Classes, Power, and Conflict: Classical and Contemporary Debates.* Pp. x, 646. Berkeley, CA: University of California Press, 1982. $42.50. Paperbound, $14.95.

GLASSBERG, ANDREW D. *Representation and Urban Community.* Pp. ix, 232. New York: Crane, Russak & Company, 1981. $19.50.

GOLDSTEIN, JOEL K. *The Modern American Vice Presidency: The Transformation of a Political Institution.* Pp. xii, 409. Princeton, NJ: Princeton University Press, 1982. $28.00.

GOODWIN, BARBARA. *Using Political Ideas.* Pp. 294. New York: John Wiley & Sons, 1982. $48.95.

GREELEY, ANDREW M. *Catholic High Schools and Minority Students.* Pp. x, 117. New Brunswick, NJ: Transaction Books, 1982. $14.95.

GREENBAUM, HOWARD H. and RAYMOND L. FALCIONE, et al. *Organizational Communication, Vol. 7.* Pp. 400. Beverly Hills, CA: Sage Publications, 1982. $30.00. Paperbound, $15.00.

GRIBBIN, JOHN. *Future Worlds.* Pp. 224. New York: Plenum Press, 1981. $14.95.

GRUEN, GEORGE E. et al. *The Palestinians in Perspective: Implications for Mideast Peace and U.S. Policy.* Pp. vii, 109. New York: Institute of Human Relations Press, 1982. No price.

GUREVITCH, MICHAEL et al., eds. *Culture, Society and the Media.* Pp. 317. New York: Methuen, 1982. $25.00. Paperbound, $11.95.

HAMMOND, THOMAS, ed. *Witnesses to the Origins of the Cold War.* Pp. 328. Seattle, WA: University of Washington Press, 1982. $22.50.

HAWLEY, AMOS H. and SARA MILLS MAZIE, eds. *Nonmetropolitan America in Transition.* Pp. xvii, 833. Chapel Hill, NC: University of North Carolina Press, 1981. $27.50.

HEATH, JAMES. *Torture and English Law: An Administrative and Legal History from the Plantagenets to the Stuarts.* Pp. xviii, 324. Westport, CT: Greenwood Press, 1982. $35.00.

HEILBRON, J. L. *Elements of Early Modern Physics.* Pp. xii, 301. Berkeley, CA: University of California Press, 1982. $30.00. Paperbound, $10.95.

HERSTEIN, SHEILA R. and NAOMI C. ROBBINS, eds. *United States of America: Vol. #16 in the World Bibliographical Series.* Pp. xii, 307. Santa Barbara, CA: CLIO Press, 1982. $45.00.

HIGGINS, JOAN. *States of Welfare: A Comparative Analysis of Social Policy.* Pp. vi, 193. New York: St. Martin's Press, 1981. $25.00.

HIMMELSTRAND, ULF et al. *Beyond Welfare Capitalism: Issues, Actors and Forces in Societal Change.* Pp. xviii, 370. Exeter, NH: Heinemann Educational Books, 1981. $55.00.

HIPPCHEN, LEONARD J., ed. *Holistic Approaches to Offender Rehabilitation.* Pp. xvi, 487. Springfield, IL: Charles C Thomas, 1982. No price.

HIRSZOWICZ, MARIA. *The Bureaucratic Leviathan: A Study in the Sociology of Communism.* Pp. x, 208, New York: New York University Press, 1980. $27.50.

HOGWOOD, BRIAN W. and MICHAEL KEATING, eds. *Regional Government in England.* Pp. x, 277. New York: Oxford University Press, 1982. $44.00.

HOLSWORTH, ROBERT D. *Public Interest Liberalism and the Crisis of Affluence.* Pp. 158. Boston, MA: G. K. Hall, 1980. $17.50.

HOPKINS, TERENCE K. and IMMANUEL WALLERSTEIN. *World-Systems Analysis: Theory and Methodology, Vol. I.* Pp. 200. Beverly Hills, CA: Sage Publications, 1982. $20.00. Paperbound, $9.95.

HOUSE, PETER W. and WILBUR A. STEGER. *Modern Federalism: An Analytic Approach.* Pp. xvi, 301. Lexington, MA: D. C. Heath and Company, 1982. $29.95.

JACKSON, CARL T. *The Oriental Religions and American Thought: Nineteenth-Century Explorations.* Pp. xii, 302. Westport, CT: Greenwood Press, 1981. $27.50.

KERKVLIET, BENEDICT J. *The Huk Rebellion: A Study of Peasant Revolt in the Philippines.* Pp. xvii, 305. Berkeley, CA: University of California Press, 1982. Paperbound. No price.

LAQUEUR, WALTER, ed. *The Second World War: Essays in Military and Political History.* Pp. 407. Beverly Hills, CA: Sage Publications, 1982. *No price.*

LEE, EVERETT S. and HAROLD F. GOLDSMITH, eds. *Population Estimates: Methods for Small Area Analysis.* Pp. 248. Beverly Hills, CA: Sage Publications, 1982. $22.50.

LEWIS, I. M. *A Pastoral Democracy: A Study of Pastoralism and Politics Among the Northern Somali and the Horn of Africa.* Pp. xxi, 320. New York: Africana Publishing Company, 1982. $32.50.

LIEBMAN, LANCE. *Ethnic Relations in America.* Pp. vii, 179. Englewood Cliffs, NJ; Prentice-Hall, 1982. $13.95. Paperbound, $5.95.

LLOYD, PETER. *A Third World Proletariat?* Pp. 139. Winchester, MA: George Allen & Unwin, 1982. $19.50. Paperbound, $6.95.

LOWY, MICHAEL. *The Politics of Combined and Uneven Development. The Theory of Permanent Revolution.* Pp. 242. London, England: Verso Editions and NLB, 1982. $19.95. Paperbound, $8.50.

McQUOWN, NORMAN A. *Language, Culture, and Education: Essays by Norman A. McQuown.* Pp. xiv, 239. Stanford, CA: Stanford University Press, 1982. $17.50.

MEDVEDEV, F. and G. KIELIKOV. *Human Rights and Freedoms in the USSR.* Translated by L. Lezhneva. Pp. 256. Moscow, Russia: Progress Publishers, 1981. Distributed by Imported Publications, Chicago. $4.00.

MELDAU, ELKE C. *Benefit Incidence: Public Health Expenditures and Income Distribution: A Case Study of Columbia.* Pp. 224. North Quincy, MA: Christopher Publishing House, 1980. $9.75.

MITCHELL, DANIEL J. B. *Unions, Wages, and Inflation.* Pp. xii, 290. Washington, DC: Brookings Institution, 1980. $15.95. Paperbound, $6.50.

MOWER, A. GLENN, JR. *The European Community and Latin America: A Case Study in Global Role Expansion.* Pp. xii, 180. Westport, CT: Greenwood Press, 1982. $27.50.

MUNNELL, ALICIA H. *The Economics of Private Pensions.* Pp. xiii, 240. Washington, DC: Brookings Institution, 1982. $22.95. Paperbound, $8.95.

NIKITIN, VYACHESLAV. *The Ultras in the USA.* Translated by Dudley Hagen. Pp. 349. Moscow, Russia: Progress Publishers, 1982. Distributed by Imported Publications, Chicago. $7.00.

OLSON, ROBERT K. *U.S. Foreign Policy and the New International Economic Order: Negotiating Global Problems, 1974-1981.* Pp. xviii, 168. Boulder, CO: Westview Press, 1981. $22.50.

OOSTERBAAN, JOHN. *Population Dispersal: A National Imperative.* Pp. xix, 136. Lexington, MA: Lexington Books, 1980. $18.95.

OWEN, DAVID. *Face the Future.* Pp. xxi, 279. New York: Praeger, 1981. $24.95.

PATERSON, WILLIAM E. and GORDON SMITH, eds. *The West German Model: Perspectives on a Stable State.* Pp. 176. Totowa, NJ: Frank Cass & Co., 1981. $29.50. Paperbound, $12.50.

PEATTIE, LISA. *Thinking About Development.* Pp. x, 198. New York: Plenum Press, 1981. No price.

PENNOCK, J. ROLAND and JOHN W. CHAPMAN, eds. *Ethics, Economics, and the Law: Nomos XXIV.* Pp. xix,

323. New York: New York University Press, 1982. $25.00.

POLLOCK, JOHN CROTHERS. *The Politics of Crisis Reporting: Learning to be a Foreign Correspondent.* Pp. xvi, 221. New York: Praeger Publishers, 1981. No price.

POLSHIKOV, P. I. *Capital Accumulation and Economic Growth In Developing Africa.* Pp. 206. Moscow, Russia: Progress Publishers, 1982. Distributed by Imported Publications, Chicago. $5.70.

RACHAL, PATRICIA. *Federal Narcotics Enforcement: Reorganization and Reform.* Pp. xiii, 170. Boston, MA: Auburn House, 1982. $19.95.

RANSONE, COLEMAN B., Jr. *The American Governorship, Contributions in Political Science, No. 69.* Pp. xvii, 197. Westport, CT: Greenwood Press, 1982. $27.50.

REICHART, JOHN F. and STEVEN R. STURM, eds. *American Defense Policy, Fifth Edition.* Pp. xii, 860. Baltimore, MD: Johns Hopkins University Press, 1982. $35.00. Paperbound, $14.95.

REISS, DAVID and HOWARD HOFFMAN, eds. *The American Family: Dying or Developing.* Pp. xvii, 246. New York: Plenum Press, 1979. $21.95.

RITTBERGER, VOLKER, ed. *Science and Technology in a Changing International Order.* Pp. 263. Boulder, CO: Westview Press, 1982. $27.50.

RONEN, DOV. *The Quest for Self-Determination.* Pp. xiv, 144. New Haven, CT: Yale University Press, 1982. $17.50. Paperbound, $5.95.

ROSSI, INO, ed. *Structural Sociology.* Pp. xv, 363. New York: Columbia University Press, 1982. $35.00.

SCHIEVE, WILLIAM C. and PETER M. ALLEN, eds. *Self-Organization and Dissipative Structures.* Pp. xii, 361. Austin, TX: University of Texas Press, 1982. $50.00.

SCIIMANDT, JURGEN, ROSEANN SHOREY, and LILAS KINCH. *Nutrition Policy in Transition.* Pp. xxv, 289. Lexington, MA: Lexington Books, 1980. $22.95.

SEERS, DUDLEY and CONSTANTINE VAITSOS, eds. *The Second Enlargement of the EEC: The Integration of Unequal Partners.* Pp. xx, 275. New York: St. Martin's Press, 1982. $29.95.

SIMPSON, LESLEY BYRD. *The Encomienda in New Spain: The Beginning of Spanish Mexico.* Pp. xv, 263. Berkeley, CA: University of California Press, 1982. $18.50. Paperbound, $6.95.

SINHA, RADHA. *Japan's Options for the 1980s.* Pp. 269. New York: St. Martin's Press, 1982. $27.50.

SNIDERMAN, PAUL M. *A Question of Loyalty.* Pp. x, 186. Berkeley, CA: University of California Press, 1981. $18.95.

SOMJEE, A. H. *Political Capacity in Developing Societies.* Pp. xi, 124. New York: St. Martin's Press, 1982. $18.95.

SPIEGEL, STEVEN L., ed. *The Middle East and the Western Alliance.* Pp. 252. Winchester, MA: Allen & Unwin, 1982. $28.50.

SPIRO, MELFORD E. *Buddhism and Society: A Great Tradition and Its Burmese Vicissitudes.* 2nd ed. Pp. xxiv, 510. Berkeley, CA: University of California Press, 1982. No price.

SPITZ, DAVID. *The Real World of Liberalism.* Pp. ix, 232. Chicago, IL: University of Chicago Press, 1982. $20.00.

STEEDMAN, IAN et al. *The Value Controversy.* Pp. 300. London, England: Verso Editions and NLB, 1982. $19.95. Paperbound, $9.50.

STEWART, PHYLLIS L. and MURIEL G. CANTOR, eds. *Varieties of Work.* Pp. 311. Beverly Hills, CA: Sage Publications, 1982. $25.00. Paperbound, $12.50.

SULLIVAN, JOHN L., JAMES PIERESON, and GEORGE E. MARCUS. *Political Tolerance and American Democracy.* Pp. x, 278. Chicago, IL: University of Chicago Press, 1982. $25.00.

THOMPSON, LEONARD and ANDREW PRIOR. *South African Politics.* Pp. xiii, 255. New Haven, CT: Yale

University Press, 1982. $25.00. Paperbound, $5.95.

TOBIAS, MARILYN. *Old Dartmouth on Trial: The Transformation of the Academic Community in Nineteenth-Century America.* Pp. xii, 249. New York: New York University Press, 1982. $35.00.

TOBIN, JAMES. *Essays in Economics: Theory and Policy.* Pp. x, 685. Cambridge, MA: MIT Press, 1982. $45.00.

TSONGAS, PAUL. *The Road from Here: Liberalism and Realities in the 1980s.* Pp. xvi, 280. New York: Vintage Books, 1982. Paperbound, $5.95.

TUOMI, HELENA and RAIMO VAYRYNEN. *Transnational Corporations, Armaments and Development.* Pp. xv, 312. New York: St. Martin's Press, 1982. No price.

VAN HORNE, WINSTON A. and THOMAS V. TONNESEN, eds. *Ethnicity and Public Policy, Vol. 1.* Pp. xvii, 133. Milwaukee, WI: University of Wisconsin System American Ethnic Studies Coordinating Committee/Urban Corridor Consortium, 1982. $12.00. Paperbound, $5.95.

WAISMAN, CARLOS H. *Modernization and the Working Class: The Politics of Legitimacy.* Pp. xii, 244. Austin, TX: University of Texas Press, 1982. $27.00.

WELLS, ROBERT V. *Revolutions in Americans' Lives: A Demographic Perspective on the History of Americans, Their Families, and Their Society.* Pp. xvi, 311. Westport, CT: Greenwood Press, 1982. $29.95.

WHITNEY, CHARLES D. and ELLEN WARTELLA, eds. *Mass Communication Review Yearbook, Vol. 3.* Pp. 766. Beverly Hills, CA: Sage Publications, 1982. $37.50.

WILSON, DAVID L. and JOHN Y. SIMON, eds. *Ulysses S. Grant: Essays and Documents.* Pp. 145. Carbondale, IL: Southern Illinois University Press, 1982. $13.95.

YAKOVLEV, NIKOLAI, *CIA Target: The USSR.* Translated by V. Schneierson and D. Belyavsky. Pp. 279. Moscow, Russia: Progress Publishers, 1982. Distributed by Imported Publications, Chicago. $7.00.

YERGIN, DANIEL and MARTIN HILLENBRAND, eds. *Global Insecurity: A Strategy for Energy and Economic Renewal.* Pp. xiii, 427. Boston, MA: Houghton Mifflin, 1982. $15.95.

INDEX